# DISCOVER YOURSELF

# DISCOVER YOURSELF

NOURISH YOUR BODY
&
NURTURE YOUR SOUL

Andreea Raicu

JAICO PUBLISHING HOUSE

Ahmedabad Bangalore Chennai
Delhi Hyderabad Kolkata Mumbai

Published by Jaico Publishing House
A-2 Jash Chambers, 7-A Sir Phirozshah Mehta Road
Fort, Mumbai - 400 001
jaicopub@jaicobooks.com
www.jaicobooks.com



DISCOVER YOURSELF
ISBN 978-93-90166-34-3

First Jaico Impression: 2021



Page design and layout: R. Ajith Kumar, Delhi

Printed by
Trinity Academy For Corporate Training Limited, Mumbai

*To my mother,*

*who always supported my quest for the truth.*

# Contents

## Part 3 – Personal Development

# Introduction

*It's important we learn to find our inner peace, to stop and look at what is inside of us, to ask ourselves what we like, what we want, what makes us happy.*

"It's fashionable to write a book.", "Is she finally going to tell us the truth about her diet?", "Does she eat anything other than salad leaves?", "What does she mean, Discover Yourself?", "She's not as tall as they say she is", "The picture on the cover has clearly been doctored, she doesn't look like that in real life"... it amuses me to think of all the things that will be crossing your mind – not all of you, I know – before you begin reading this book, which has been something of a labour of love for me. But all of these things are typical of the questions and comments I received over the course of twenty years working in television. I'd hear them almost every day, and while early in my career some of them would really upset or baffle me, I've now not only grown immune to them, I've also come to view the people who say them with compassion. I've reached a point where I no longer pass judgment on them, because I can understand what must be going on inside those who make such comments.

I know that some will be intrigued by this book, some will seek only to criticise it, and others will probably be disappointed that it doesn't contain any revelations about my love life. Yet I'm sure most of you – those who know me best, those who are part of the andreearaicu.ro community and who provide me with inspiration each and every day – will know what the driving force is behind this book. And I'm sure you can hardly wait to read all about my experiences, about what shaped me and helped me become who I am today. So I sincerely hope that this book will inspire you and give you the courage to experiment, that it will be of use to you, because it is dedicated to you.

First of all, I'd like to ask you a question. Viewed from a personal perspective, from the hidden corners of your soul where only you have access, answer this question as frankly and honestly as you can: have you ever felt you're not beautiful enough, not intelligent enough, not slim enough, not brave enough and not strong enough? I certainly have! And I can't tell you how often I used to abandon myself to those terrible, nagging thoughts! A critical, merciless inner voice would keep on pointing out the things I wasn't proud of, and over the years this resulted in my spending too much time focusing on my fears, frustrations and anxieties, which I felt I would never be rid of. We all go through phases like these, but very few of us ever arrive at any solutions, right?! A feeling of resignation and a lack of determination place us in a corner, which we often feel incapable, entirely unwilling even, of leaving, so instead we just stay there, overwhelmed by our own powerlessness, sadness and shame…

Before I began putting my thoughts down on paper and was able to say "no more!" to the things that were harming me, my life used to be a merry-go-round of contradictory feelings: probably just like anyone else, I had my moments of disappointment and self-doubt, and I wasted precious time going down roads that led to nowhere, but I also learned some important lessons. I realised, once again, that there is nothing more precious than that moment of revelation when you realise you are your own visiting card and that you actually like yourself, that you can draw some benefit from your disappointments (obviously, only after you first get over them), because it was thanks to them that you learned how to fall, how to pick yourself up again and carry on, how to live beautifully and how to forgive yourself. And, in particular, I realised how wonderful it is to be able to laugh both with and at yourself – and without turning everything into a drama! And you know what? When people see me smiling so much, their usual reaction is to give me a funny look. Thanks to my nearly always being in a good mood, having learned to stop taking everything tragically, instead choosing to always look at the good side of things, half-seriously, half-jokingly some people have suspected me of being on medication or taking illegal substances, because they simply can't imagine being able to view the world in this way.

Admittedly, I am addicted to being balanced, to the energy that makes me feel happy the whole time, to smiles, to people who want to grow, people who choose to talk about themselves, not about others, about what they're feeling, not necessarily what they're doing. I'm only too happy to accept this weakness of mine!

I like to see people who smile a lot, who take pleasure in the smaller things, who brighten up your day just by walking past you, all of which affects your mood. This is why I like America, a country I visit whenever I get the chance. I get this wonderful feeling when I interact with warm people, people who have inherited a culture of smiling, of positive things. Did you think that, just like us, they don't have all kinds of different wants and fears? Well, I'm pretty sure they do! However, they have chosen to make their lives and daily experiences more enjoyable. Yes, I know a lot of people say Americans are superficial and that when they smile it doesn't come from the heart, it's more a robotic gesture. However, whether you believe me or not, I prefer to see people around me who choose to approach life and their problems with a smile on their faces, rather than a constant anger, sadness and bitterness. If we surround ourselves with optimistic people, some of their optimism will rub off on us, it's contagious, and we too might end up realising that nothing is as bad as it seems.

Above all, I really want you to know that the thoughts laid out in this book are reflections of myself, of my own experience; they are answers to questions I have spent a lot of my life thinking about and which have helped me to realise what it is I really want from myself. In the end, this is what's it's all about: knowing what it is you want and focusing all your energies in that direction. It's incredible how many things change when you begin to find yourself and to connect with your body: countless new paths open up to you and ambitions that often weigh us down needlessly and stop us from seeing what really matters begin to melt away. So, first and foremost, I advise you to ask yourselves what it is you really want from yourself and from life. You – not society, not your parents, grandparents or relatives, not your friends or your partner. Think about the things which bring a smile to your face, which make you feel fulfilled, which give you energy when you think about them, which allow you to breathe and motivate you when you wake up in the morning and wonder whether you should continue down the path you've set out on.

Knowing who we are is the easiest route to getting what we want, because we then begin to attract the energies that help us move in our chosen direction. Years spent living according to the ideas and wishes of those around me and above all, of society – i.e. starvation, extreme dieting and working through the night in order to show I was strong and could do anything and more than anything to prove I was perfect – were followed by years in which I no longer recognised myself, I no longer had the energy to do much at all and I was far from being happy. So I called a halt to this scramble for an imagined state of happiness. To be fair, it was life itself that decided to offer me this break after I suffered some serious health problems. It was only because of this that I realised I had forgotten to breathe and to look within me, that I had locked away a part of myself that wanted something different from life – and it was then that I decided it was vital I made a change.

This is not just another book of advice about how to lose weight or eat healthily – it's more than that. It brings together different parts of my life, experiences that helped me to get to know myself, to forgive myself for the sins of the past, to love my body and stop believing that happiness depends on my relationship with the bathroom scales. I would like you to see it as an open invitation to enter my world, and as a challenge that will lead you towards different experiences in your relationship with your bodies. *Discover Yourself* is a little bit of everything: an appeal and a source of encouragement, help and motivation for those wishing to take better care of themselves. I have already been through all the stages of this transformation and I will be there with you throughout your process, because I feel a need to share with you the experiences that brought balance into my life.

Theory is all well and fine, but putting something into practice is always hard and it's really easy to become demotivated. So you should be aware from the outset that it won't be easy to make these changes and you should view the whole endeavour as a challenge. I can tell you from experience just how priceless the feeling is, with each day that passes, you are getting to know yourself better, you're beginning to accept yourself and face your demons! I know what it's like to start from the beginning, to doubt yourself, to cry every night that you want to embark on a different path and to feel consumed by a terrible feeling of anxiety and lose yourself in the fear of loneliness. Have you ever tried doing something to address the causes of what it is that makes you feel this way? Answer this question honestly, when you're on your own, because your happiness depends on it! And if you yourself don't know what brings you peace and fulfilment, what gives you energy and joy, then there's no one else who can!

A few years ago, I gave up television and decided to embark on a different path. I had realised that life was a journey we set out on with a one-way ticket and that you have to savour every moment of it. I began asking myself whether I was happy, whether I was living in tune with my feelings and whether I had the courage to change the things I didn't like. By asking the right questions I was able to change destinations and, more importantly, to start enjoying to the full my journey towards what I wanted to become.

So, in order to find out what it is you need to change, ask yourself these three questions: "Am I happy?", "Am I living in tune with my feelings?" and "Do I have the courage to change the things I don't like?". Then try to see if there is a balance to be found between the good things and the things making you unhappy. You can do this exercise just in your head, or you can write your ideas down on a sheet of paper, on your phone, notebook or in your diary – whatever's easiest for you. What's important is that you answer honestly and that this exercise helps you come to a decision. Nothing you feel is wrong, because what you have within you is authentic.

Over the years I have amassed a lot of different experiences and information, things to do with my lifestyle, as well as many a story from my life. I hope you like them and can relate to them, that you will laugh with me, and that they will help you articulate your frustrations, leave them behind you and not to give up hope. A diet or weight loss plan only lasts a few days or weeks, but a healthy lifestyle, if it is understood correctly and its rules applied properly, is for life. Even if you're always adapting it, to reflect how the mind and the body are continually changing, it is a healthy lifestyle that will ultimately help us to be happy.

More than just a weight loss plan, a book about healthy foods and the so-called dangers in the kitchen, *Discover Yourself* is a kind of map. In fact, it was with this very idea in mind that I first began putting my thoughts down on paper. It is a map that tells us how to look after ourselves, both physically and spiritually. As you've probably guessed, I didn't just wake up one morning with the formula for balance all ready to go. No, it was something I came to over time and I'm still discovering new things about this complex process today. Details are important, so I didn't simply resort to including various bits of useful information. I first tested them out and, after experimenting with them myself, decided to pass them on to you.

I used to believe that losing weight was the solution to all my problems. That a skinny person is a beautiful, content and above all, fulfilled person. However, I would discover that losing weight is not the same thing as self-acceptance and self-love. The goal should be different, i.e. to realise that there is no such thing as perfection (or that if it exists, it is boring), that accepting and looking after your body, the way it is, is the first step on the path towards feeling good about yourself. And this state of fulfilment will be reflected in your weight, in your complexion, and in the way we relate to those around us. Over the years, I have learned that looking after myself doesn't mean just squeezing into a really tight dress and being admired for my figure, but being connected to myself. By being connected to my body and being conscious of the present, I feel more focused and in control when I move from one project to the next, when I need to function under pressure or when my schedule gets really busy. I may be up to my ears in my work, but there's still order in my mind. By being connected to myself, listening to my body and allowing my emotions to surface, I realised how and what I could eat without gaining weight and without needing to follow a specific diet; and I understood which exercises are good for me and which ones I like, but also what things truly make me feel content.

For those of you who want to know what I eat, how I exercise and what my rituals are, I will of course tell you all about them. But this doesn't mean you have to follow the same routines yourselves or that they will also be suitable for you. Maybe my experience will be a good source of inspiration for you or will help you clarify ideas you've heard about elsewhere; or maybe you'll find some of my experiences don't resonate with you. What's important is that in the end you come to know yourselves better. I will share with you the things that changed my life and I hope this will help you take better decisions in your lives; but in the end it's up to you to decide what things best meet your needs.

My destination in life is clearer than ever. If someone had asked me about this in the past, I'm sure my answer would have been different, but now I know what it is I want: I want to feel good in my own body and to feel good about myself! It's a goal I think should be obligatory for each and every one of us, but unfortunately we often lose ourselves in details and forget what truly matters. While I will discuss a number of rules that will help you lose weight and stay in shape, what I am not able to provide you with is a recipe that will help you look like me or live the same way I do. I won't be citing any scientific evidence from the fields of chemistry or biology that will require a dictionary or you will find hard to understand. Instead I will provide brief, practical, easy-to-read explanations you will be able to apply quickly and which won't take much time.

It's a long time since I've been on a diet. Instead, I have been learning to listen to my body and give it the things it needs, teaching myself how to eat by trying out dozens of different weight loss plans. Now, when my body asks for things I wouldn't normally eat, I take it as a clear sign of a lack of balance somewhere, the source of which I need to identify. *Discover Yourself* is a book intended to help you find out what things you enjoy and what works for you. It is a diary in which I have recorded the process of my transformation and which I invite you to read in order to (re)discover yourselves and to accept yourselves the way you are. All I know is that, having reached this point, I am no longer able, and nor would I want, to choose a different way of living my life. I hope we can learn together to love our bodies more, for the body is the place where we spend our entire lives. What do you think, should we get to work?

# PART 1

# HEALTH

# 1

# The body is intelligent and we must learn to listen to it

*Many years ago I realised that life is a journey and it's important we enjoy every moment of it. It's not so much the destination that matters, but how we feel along the way. You never know when it will end.*

Over the years, I've often been asked questions about my lifestyle: what I eat, how I maintain my weight, what type of exercise I do, whether I'm a vegetarian or a vegan, what my beauty secrets and favourite recipes are, etc. Run-of-the-mill questions that sound clichéd, and yet they come up again and again. When I asked myself why this was so, among other things I realised that other people's stories are a source of inspiration for us; they show us that it's possible to reach beyond our limits, that if we truly want something, the examples of others will strengthen our motivation. For all those who want to know what it means to live beautifully, who wish to go beyond their limits, who want to learn how to be in harmony with their bodies, I have gathered here all the things which over the years have helped me to find balance, both physically and spiritually. Perhaps what works for me will fit you perfectly too, perhaps it will only fit you in part, or perhaps not at all; there is no universally valid formula for happiness. But this is my experience, put down on paper, of how I came to know my body and to understand its needs. After years of trying to discover the formula that would allow me to function at my best, I now feel able to share my experiences with you. I realised that it is not only my career that has changed, but also my relationship with myself and how I have come to relate to myself.

The most valuable gift we are given – and, for that matter, were born with – is our bodies. The body has a unique intelligence all of its own and it sends us messages whenever it encounters a problem. What's more, it makes us aware of our desires and needs. Unfortunately, we're not taught to listen to and cherish our bodies. On the contrary, we're brought up to ignore the signals they send us. Some of these signals are already familiar to us. Headaches, dizziness, bloating, loss of or excessive appetite, sexual urges, etc. are all things we are more or less aware of. Even if we do nothing to mitigate or satisfy them, we at least notice them and are conscious of their existence.

But there are also messages which, for one reason or another, we pay no attention to. Indeed, we are not taught to pay attention to them, to try to accept them and to take them on board; we are brought up to overlook our emotional states. Anxiety, sadness and anger are some of the emotions we most frequently repress. I'm sure we've all experienced these emotional states directly and done our utmost to conceal them, brush them under the carpet and keep them secret, because society does not encourage them. Children provide the best examples in this respect and there's a lot we can learn from them. When they have a problem and they want something, they externalise their feelings, start to cry and ask for help. They are sincere and direct and they send us clear signals, especially in multi-decibel tones. However, as we grow up and become adults, we're taught to repress these emotions; we're inoculated with the idea that to have needs is a sign of weakness. Society has no need of such people; it needs powerful people without needs, people capable of managing on their own without asking for help and without verbalising what they really feel. As a result, we end up repressing most of these emotions out of a desire to fit in and to be valued and accepted.

While on a mindfulness course, I learnt that animals can provide some of the best examples of this. For example, a dog that likes to run around all day long (such as Efi, my mix-breed dog, a cross between a German Shorthaired Pointer and an American Staffordshire Terrier who looks like a Labrador) will take a nap right after it's finished running around the park or garden. It won't worry about whether it's too early or too late; its body has signalled to it that it is tired and it takes the appropriate action. We, on the other hand, do things differently. It even happened to me that I arrived home one evening around 8 pm feeling dead tired, but then, despite feeling really sleepy, I didn't go straight to bed, because for some reason that seemed to me to be a strange thing to do. I told myself that it wasn't normal to go to bed so early and that I should be doing something else with my time rather than wasting it on sleep. I had been conditioned to go to bed at a certain time, even though my body was telling me it was tired and needed to rest.

We are clearly not taught to listen out for these signs on one hand, while on the other hand we don't even try to discover the real cause of our problems. If we have an issue with our digestion, for example, we take pills that combat the symptoms but don't eliminate the source of the problem. We may eat something that doesn't agree with us or we overindulge and consume too many heavy meals, while what we should be doing is protecting ourselves from those things that do us harm. Similarly, when we have a headache, we quickly down a pill without considering that what we really should be doing is seeking to identify and heal the source of our discomfort. In my case, this usually means I haven't drunk enough water or eaten enough or I didn't get enough rest. If I start getting spots, this will be the result of a hormonal imbalance or a bad reaction to something I ate or a particular beauty product.

As I was saying, the body lets us know when there's a problem, but unaware of this, we choose to combat the symptoms rather than seeking out what it is that is causing us to feel unwell in the first place. When we learn to decipher what our bodies are telling us, we become healthier and begin to take much better decisions in terms of what we eat and drink and the other things in our lives. If, for example, someone offers me a fizzy drink or some processed food (this doesn't really happen anymore, as almost everyone knows I no longer consume those kinds of things), I now no longer feel tempted – and not because I want to stay slim or want to win the praise of others who lead healthy lives, but simply because I no longer feel a need to consume those things, as I know they're not good for me.

So our bodies are constantly sending us clear signals about the state of our health and we need only pay them a little attention. A few years ago, I attended a course called "From Trauma to Tantra". It wasn't a course about how to have better sex. Regrettably, I know many people think Tantra is only about what goes on in the bedroom. However, Tantra is about much more than that; namely, it is about becoming cognisant of the fact that the body is the temple of our being and that it is therefore vital we are able to sense it, to feel connected to it (so as to be able to know ourselves), to respect it and to love it unconditionally. As part of this course we performed many exercises that helped us to sense our bodies. I know it may seem strange, but we don't normally sense our bodies except when we have a problem and something hurts. Otherwise, we tend to ignore them completely. Well, with the help of these exercises, I realised for the first time that I was ashamed of my body. I could hardly believe it, but it was true: I really was ashamed of my body. It was a realisation that hit me really hard at the time.

During a meditation[1] session while on this incredible course (which I can wholeheartedly recommend), I realised just how important and precious our body is. With its help we are able to do so much. In fact, it is responsible for the most important things in our lives. We breathe, we move between one place and another, we eat, we love, we suffer, we conceive a new life and help it to grow, we experience happiness, we work, we hug, we laugh, we cry… all thanks to and with the help of our bodies. I bet you've never thought of it that way before! You simply took it as a given, without asking too many questions. That's certainly what I used to do!

We allow ourselves to become overwhelmed by everything around us and never think about our body in this way; we either completely forget about it, or the only time we notice it is when we criticise it for not being the way we want it to be. Because it's always just there, silently going about its job every day…

It's so close to us and yet we're no longer conscious of its presence. Not only do we not appreciate it, I also realise that we tend to be really brutal with our body. And I think you know what I'm referring to: I'm talking about all the harsh words we

---

[1] In Part 3 of the book I will describe this concept in more detail and will explain how meditation helped me get to know my body better.

direct at it when we look in the mirror and we don't like what we see. It was with great sadness that I realised I had been doing this myself for many years!

I've been on many different diets in my life. I used to starve myself: I'd look in the mirror and find only faults, never anything good, and I was engaged in a constant dialogue with myself, saying only really bad things to myself. I subjected my body to some terrible punishments just because I believed it to be horrible. I know this sounds incredible, but that was the reality of the situation. But why do this? Because society conditions us to seek perfection in all things, especially the way we look, and this naturally makes us strive to eliminate all our flaws and try to live up to the 90-60-90 standard. The compromises we make are far too great, we force ourselves to be slim, flawless, if only to look like the models in the magazines. Year after year I would do the same thing, which is why I'm now extremely happy that I came to realise that life is not about being perfect, but about being okay with yourself.

With tears in my eyes and a terrible sadness in my heart, I realised just how many wonderful things my body had been doing for me, despite my having mistreated it for so many years. That was the moment the penny dropped for me. It was a really powerful feeling! I began to realise how much I had been abusing my body in everything I did, how I wasn't giving it the food it needed, how I'd been treating it like it was my enemy and, more than anything, how I didn't love it just the way it was. I thought it unfair that it was giving me so much while I was not repaying it with anything; I would even punish it every time it didn't conform to the way I wanted it to be. It was an important moment in my life and one which made me change the way I thought about and behaved towards my body.

The climax of the meditation session was a real challenge for me and something I was in no way able to foresee: I had to look at myself naked in the mirror and to accept myself the way I was. Never for a second did I think this could be so hard! It was completely terrifying!

I'd never looked at myself like this before – or perhaps only for a split second and clearly it had made me feel uncomfortable. I guess you know the feeling. I had to look at myself, to look at every part of me I didn't like and felt eternally ashamed of. It was an incredible exercise and one which helped me to be gentler with my body, to accept and to love it as it is. I know this sort of confession may be entirely unexpected coming from me, but the way we perceive ourselves, i.e. our own personal reality, is often different from the reality we inhabit.

Although I was advertising lingerie at the time, which provided me with confirmation that I had a beautiful body, my opinion of the way I looked was totally different. Today, after many years of working with myself, after having achieved balance, I understand that our relationship with our bodies is like the way we treat others. If we are nice to other people, they will be nice to us. So why shouldn't this rule also apply in our relationship with our body? When we say bad things about it and focus only on the bits we don't like, when we insult it and only see its ugly parts, it closes itself off from us and denies us access to it.

What I discovered was that I have an intelligent body that was sending me signals; I learned that I need to seek out the cause of my pain, not merely to treat the symptoms; I tried and continue to do everything I can to accept it the way it is; and, most importantly, I no longer deny myself food and no longer say bad things to myself. Now I don't want you to go thinking I spend hours in front of the mirror studying my body :). It was hard but I have eventually come to understand that the secret is to stop aspiring to achieve perfection, because I have realised, once and for all, that perfection doesn't really exist. Perfection is merely a poisonous myth. Or if it does exist, it's really a terrible bore ;).

It's important we give our bodies everything they need to function properly. If we don't eat the things we need, we upset our balance: we start piling on the kilos; our bodies start retaining more water than needed and rapidly storing fat; and our immune systems become weak, giving rise to inflammatory diseases and pain. Insomnia, feeling weak, pain – these are some of the body's ways of telling us something's not right and that we need to take better care of it. In the worst case, if we don't give it what it needs or if toxins are not eliminated when they should be, sooner or later it will cave in. I'm not saying there's some universally valid formula out there, because everyone is different. It's up to each of us to discover which things work for us and which not, which things suit us and which do not. It's important to find out what's right for you, because what worked for a friend might not necessarily also work for you. I suggest you try out and then select from my lifestyle the foods, physical exercises, beauty habits and ways of relaxing that you best enjoy, because it's essential they reflect your particular needs and desires.

If you want to make a change that will make a difference, it's important to try out as many new things as possible and to identify those you not only like but which also make you feel good. Like a child exploring the world around you, try to do things differently each day; try to discover your body and learn as much as possible about yourselves. The truth is that if we are to establish a real connection with our body we need to be present in every moment of our lives and to be aware of its needs.

# 2

# Starvation and the myth of perfection

*It's only when all is peaceful and quiet around you and within you that you will discover what you really want.*

We live in a world that is obsessed with perfection and in which we are not allowed to make mistakes; above all, we live in a society in which physical appearance is our best calling card. Being slim is a prerequisite for success. I grew up with these ideas myself and, because they had become deeply rooted in my mind, I made many compromises so as to never have to deviate from what I had been taught. I was so obsessed with not putting on weight, with trying to please others, with being successful in every project I embarked on, that I forgot to live for myself. The expectations of others were transformed into a long list of no-noes: no food after seven in the evening, no sweets, no crying, no asking for help, no being a bother to others, no being seen dealing with problems, and so on and so forth. My life was full of prohibitions and I would shift rapidly from one extreme to the other, especially when it came to food. I'd starve myself because I wanted the perfect body, but then I'd end up feeling so frustrated that I'd eat everything in sight and pile back on all the kilograms I'd lost, or even gain a few more.

I know many women associate dieting with the sensation of being permanently hungry, which leaves you feeling irritable and miserable. But things don't have to be that way at all. I strongly believe that life was given to us to enjoy, and for this reason we should also enjoy what we eat. For me food is one of the pleasures of life and I have decided not to give it up :).

A healthy lifestyle should be based on balance and as few moments of hunger as possible, because when placed under stress our body enters a state of alert and burns calories slower, meaning our metabolism slows down. If we don't eat properly, whatever's on the menu, however healthy or however small the portion of food we consume, it will be stored and not burnt by the body. What's more, our ability to concentrate suffers, we end up feeling drained of energy and the risk of depression and anxiety rises. Faced with a diet low in nutrients, the body adapts to the lower number of calories and, even if we eat normally, it still has a tendency to store additional calories.

One thing I have realised over time was that everything I was denying and forbidding myself was generating an incredible amount of frustration in me. Things changed, however, once I allowed myself to break the rules. Indeed, I entered into a state of balance and became free from the pressure that existed in my mind and from the voice that would scold me every time I failed to stick to those extremely inflexible rules.

I know many women ignore the basic rules of the body and hate their figures. For many years I also fell into this category. However, as I was saying, the body responds to the way we treat it. It is said, and not without good reason, that the body we have when we grow older and come towards the end of our lives is the body we deserve, a body that reflects all the things we've put it through, both the good and the bad. Instead of starving and punishing ourselves, it is better to say kind things to ourselves and to accept our bodies the way they are. Nothing good will come of all this pressure! That doesn't mean we should relax to the point we end up eating whatever we like, whenever we want, day or night. It's important to achieve a balance that helps us to be in harmony with ourselves.

### Let's do an exercise.

Find a moment when you're at home alone. Go into a room where there's a large mirror and not much light, at least not at first. Then try taking off your clothes and looking at yourself in the mirror. I know from experience how hard this can be, but stick to it. Be alert to every thought that passes through your head, every sentence you hear spoken in your mind. You only need to look at yourself and to analyse your body as if you are getting to know someone you've only just met for the first time.

I recommend you do this exercise once a day until you truly come to know yourself. Once you feel you've got to know yourself really well, you'll start to discover parts of your body that you like. If at first you don't find anything and keep returning to what you don't like, I recommend you just stop criticising those parts. Allow them to exist without labelling them. It's okay not to like those parts, just leave them the way they are.

It's important to keep doing this exercise until you are able to look at yourself in the mirror with the light on and to love your body for what it is and for what it does for you.

This may take you a week, maybe two, maybe even a month or more. There's no fixed time limit, but what I do know is that what you're going to need to do it is a lot of patience, tenderness and love when you look at yourself.

It's important to understand that the person in the mirror is not your enemy but your best friend, so it's good to remind ourselves of that each morning! Our body is more than just a beautifully decorated shell; it is the place where we come into contact with ourselves and our thoughts. By our nature we are predisposed to fluctuations of mood, energy and productivity, something which can result in contradictory emotional states. But then this is what makes every day feel unique and an experience worth living. The next step, therefore, is to understand the mechanism by which the body functions and to cooperate with it, not oppose our various natural states. Indeed, the levels of our hormones fluctuate all the time, we have good days and not so good days, but this is not the end of the world.

When everything seems dark and pointless, the body tells us it's time to take a break and to pay more attention to it. In order to balance out the moments of exhaustion and frustration, we need to compensate with things that bring us pleasure, things we enjoy and recharge our batteries: a massage, a free weekend during which we do nothing, a walk in the park, time spent with loved ones, a good book or even a holiday.

We are extremely complex beings and there is a relationship, an interdependence, between our mind, body and spirit. If one of these elements is not functioning normally, all the others will suffer, resulting in a lack of balance. Consequently, we need to use all three in moderation – and this impulse for harmony will arise naturally from within us after we have learned to accept ourselves the way we are.

People are becoming increasingly aware of the fundamentals of a healthy lifestyle and I'm happy these things are no longer viewed as fads and labelled as impossible to put into practice, at least less so than before. If we adopt them because we know they can change our lives for the better, not just because they happen to be on trend, then the whole effort was worth it. I know it's not easy, but where there's a will there's also the energy you need to get to where you want to end up.

The cabbage soup diet? I've tried it! The alkaline, paleo, vegetarian, raw vegan and vegan diets – I've tried all of them, and many more besides. Some worked, others left me with more kilos than when I started, not to mention what I put my body through in the process. I'm naturally curious and admittedly I have experimented a lot on my own body (especially in terms of starvation) without thinking of the consequences. Long-term results are not achieved with diets lasting just a few days or weeks; they are the consequence of a healthy lifestyle (which you come to understand in time) and of healthy eating. And, yes, sometimes there's a need for the odd culinary treat – and I'm the first to say this, as I don't deny myself anything – only you shouldn't forget to make amends afterwards. But not through starvation, but healthy alternatives which detoxify and help the body get back to normal!

In today's world, information is easier than ever to come by, being only the click of the mouse away. With the help of an internet connection, anyone can find the answer to a question in less than a minute. So why don't we get to the place we want to be and why do we fail to achieve all the things we aspire to, especially when it comes to our relationship with our body? It's a paradox. We have all the tools we require at our disposal: we can find information from different studies and scientific experiments online, all around us there are success stories and sports facilities (not to mention parks in which to go jogging), we have access to books and recipes and self-knowledge, we have access to specialists in nutrition, psychology and meditation, and much more besides. And yet for various reasons – some well-founded, others less so – we fail to make use of many of these things. Excuses don't burn calories and it also doesn't help that we always put off till tomorrow those things which, on a physical and emotional level, we should be dealing with today.

As I am a very determined person who tends to not leave anything to chance, I began asking myself why things would always go wrong every time I came off a new diet. I asked myself why, with the information I had at my disposal, I was not able to be in harmony with myself and what was stopping me from having a balanced lifestyle. At that time I wouldn't have a clear goal in mind when starting on a new diet, all I knew was that I wanted to be slim. As soon as I got down to my desired weight I then had a tendency to eat too much, because, having starved myself for so long and eaten things not necessarily to my liking, I found I'd stored up a lot of frustration. So, I was never in balance with myself! Consequently, in recent years my goal has changed: I want to be balanced, I want a healthy body because I want to feel well, both physically and mentally, and emotionally.

Once you have established your reason for wanting to eat healthily, you begin to be aware of and to identify with your goal. When you truly believe in something that it is within your power to achieve, you take it to heart and no longer feel the draw of temptation. Of course temptation still exists, it never goes away; but you are now much stronger, much more motivated, and therefore no longer feel the need. Or maybe only sometimes :). That's how I felt when I said "no more!" to the starvation and when I stopped being so harsh with myself when I failed to achieve perfection. When I weighed just 50 kilograms (for a height of 1.75 m) I used to get lots of compliments, and I believed this would help me to be accepted more readily by those around me. But it wasn't really the kind of attention I wanted to receive and, at the end of the day, I didn't really feel good about myself. These weren't the things I wanted, and I had this constant feeling I could and should do more. I remember arriving home one evening feeling exhausted and starving, despite being only 18 years old at the time! Ever since the day I decided to focus more on how I feel, and listen less to what others were saying about me, I have been a happier person.

When we get rid of all the anger we aim at ourselves, we find we have even more energy. Of what use to us is a ripped, perfectly toned abdomen if we're always on the point of fainting with hunger? There is no universally valid ideal to strive for, no "right" way to look; it's not healthy to strive to achieve a look that exists only in magazines or films. Many of the public figures you see in magazines and whom we try to imitate (something I have often done myself) have an entire army of people and things behind them helping them to look perfect, i.e. makeup artists, hair stylists, professional lighting, filters and post-production. It's impossible not to look (almost) perfect!

Our hectic and chaotic lives today stop us from doing what we really want, and unfortunately the really important things – food, rest, hydration and physical exercise – are often pushed down on our list of priorities. Everything happens in fits and starts and in a disorderly fashion, but with a little will power and discipline we can make the changes that make a difference. It's good to keep a record of important activities, without which we're unable to be productive. The first items on the list should be those things that give us energy and put us in a good mood – as this will help us to keep up with a busy schedule. However busy my day is, I make sure I eat healthily, drink enough water, meditate, do some yoga and physical exercise, have a massage (at least once a week) and get enough sleep. What needed to change – something I found incredibly difficult to do – was to stop piling pressure on myself. At least less than I was used to. This has allowed me to take every day as it comes and to enjoy life more. Admittedly, I still don't always find it easy, but at least now I'm conscious of what I'm doing. So I am passing this advice on to you here and I hope you'll give it a try, at least for a few days. I guarantee you'll be amazed by the results! We're not just an image. We're made up of thoughts. Pure emotions. Beautiful experiences. We are life. So we should celebrate our relationship with our body and the wonderful things we have been given every day.

# 3

# Eating styles and recipes I've tried out over time

*Balance is the path towards a peaceful life. Never expect spectacular results overnight, don't believe in miracle recipes and don't put pressure on yourself.*

There are people who put on weight quickly and people who can eat everything – sweets, pastries, pre-cooked meals, fast food, ANYTHING – and still stay slim. And you know what? I belong to that last category and yet I've still always been obsessed with losing any excess kilos! Or, to put it better, those kilos I believed were "in excess". I used to envy skinny people, those who didn't have to make an effort, because I believed their weight was a guarantee of happiness. I never considered that they might be unhealthy or that they had complexes of their own. It took me 20 years to understand that having a healthy lifestyle was key – but maybe it's better that way. The sins of youth have their role to play and maybe back then I wasn't ready to understand and accept the way things really are.

I can remember how guilty I'd feel if I ate some pasta, French fries or a dessert, or if I ate late at night. I reprimanded myself for these transgressions until I came to realise there was nothing wrong with having cravings and that sticking to the rules only left me feeling frustrated. This doesn't mean I now eat everything – rather I make conscious choices, at clearly defined moments, and, above all, I've stopped punishing myself. I used to take drastic measures that would involve me spending three days only drinking juice or only eating salad or spending hours on end at the gym. The list is very long and, as I've already mentioned, I used to be very creative when it came to punishing myself. It wasn't just that this behaviour was of no use to me whatsoever; it was worse than that. I was torturing my body, which had gone into a kind of self-defence mode and begun storing everything I gave it to eat so as not to be left with no energy.

I can almost see you raising an eyebrow, sceptically, at the idea that I might have food cravings and that I enjoy eating. But it's true! Those who know me well, loved ones or the people I work with every day, are in no doubt about it. I've said it and I'll say it again: I like eating and I fully deserve my reputation as a "termite" among my group of friends. I like to try a bit of everything, so I don't limit myself just to what I order for myself, I also help others to finish their meals. Come to think of it, they ought to be thanking me for lending them a hand! :). Jokes aside, there really are people who think my daily diet consists of two leaves of salad, an olive and a couple of almonds, but it's not true. Or people who suspect I am still starving myself – but, again, this is not the case, my life really has changed. How then do I manage to keep in shape? Obviously, I stick to a balanced diet. I know I'm repeating myself, but balance is so important and I really want you to see it through my eyes, to feel how much my life has changed since I adopted these principles.

I feel more beautiful at the age of 40 than I did ten years ago, even with wrinkles and bags beneath my eyes. And if you suspect me of having had cosmetic surgery, I can tell you that I (no longer) believe in the power of the scalpel, nor have I injected any Botox or hyaluronic acid into my skin in an attempt to turn back the clock. At least that's how I see things at this point in my life! In fact, I'm not being entirely truthful, I have actually done something: I began to love myself more and to take care of my body, and I've learned, in time, to have a balanced lifestyle. If I really think about it, the hardest part of this process was to change my mentality and the way I react to social constraints. I wanted to demonstrate that perfection is not an attribute attainable by people, not even celebrities, and that I don't need to live up to all the standards of those around me. There's no way I could do that anyway! I'm sorry to disappoint you, but celebrities cry too, sometimes, it's not all glamour, and the manufactured image they wish to project doesn't exist.

We all wear masks in public, but, when we get home we remove them and sometimes we don't like what we see anymore. It doesn't matter that others like us, if we can't stand ourselves anymore and maybe even hate ourselves. In my desire to achieve perfection, I came to realise it was only a myth and so I no longer need to pressure myself to appear to be something I am not. I was brought up to want to be independent, to take care of myself, not to ask others for help, because that would have made me look inadequate (that is, in the opinion of my father, whose voice I can still hear in my head trying to remind me of this!). I'm convinced that many people will resonate with this way of thinking, but maybe the time is now ripe for a change, not least if you find yourself reading this book. Sometimes we need to recognise our limits and to accept them without seeing ourselves as incomplete. It is our right not to be invincible. Don't you find it liberating to know and even truly to believe that you are already the best possible version of yourself?!

"We're all different. Fortunately!" is, I believe, the slogan of a furniture store in Bucharest. To be honest, I don't recall which one, but I remember that the message made me think of just how important diversity is and how we should be cherishing the fact that we are unique, each of us special in his or her own way. Yes, we're not all tall or slim, we don't all have what are considered perfect bodies, with eye-catching features, we don't all have penetrating gazes and rich hair or eyelashes that perfectly frame our faces – not even a Procrustean bed would, I think, be able to make us look the same. But then why would we want to force ourselves to be like everyone else when we can instead become the best version of ourselves?

When I was around 30, I would always focus on things I didn't have, never appreciating what I did have. And this was also true when it came to my body. I needed to look good in photos and I'd always be finding faults. Pictures of me were constantly appearing in the press, and I always only saw the things that bothered me. Not to mention how it pained me when the photographers seemed bent on highlighting every millimetre of cellulite I had or catching me without any makeup on. I'm a lot more relaxed today and even agree to pose without makeup. It sounds so simple and seems like another theory taken from a motivational book, but it took me a long time to understand that I am still beautiful regardless of any extra kilos, the bags beneath my eyes or who knows what other things I used to have a complex about… Whatever we do, we will never be perfect in the eyes of all those around us, so we shouldn't lead our lives according to the standards imposed by others, but our own standards. And this is just as true when it comes to beauty.

"My body is my buddy" – sounds good, don't you think? The

truth is that our first partner in life is the body into which we are born. The way we behave towards it should be the same as the way we act towards our best friend. We are together for better or worse, we help each other in difficult times, we experience happiness together, as well as moments of existential crisis and hardship. With so much talk recently about the language of the body, why don't we learn to translate its needs more often? Our body speaks, it sends us signals, it tells us things and it repays us with the joy of inhabiting it with our minds and our energy. However, we need to meet certain conditions.

We are living energy, and every part of our body transmits this message. We feed on energy and our daily food is the fuel we provide to our internal organs. Beside food itself, it is emotional factors, stress, the social and professional group we belong to, and genetic inheritance that make us what we are, all define us as a living organism – a unitary whole. As soon as the harmony between these elements is disturbed, our body rebels. Pain, illness, obesity – these and other disorders take hold and sound the alarm.

We are what we eat, and our body is a cumulation of emotions, energies and vibrations. When it comes to eating habits, our bodies do not lack stimuli. Where an imbalance exists, this gives rise to addiction, an excessive appetite for sweet or savoury things, skin problems, etc., just as a lack of vitamins and minerals is reflected in various physical symptoms: decreased energy levels and excessive tiredness, asthenia (due to large deficiencies of carbohydrates, fats, vitamins and minerals), headaches, irritability, dizziness and nausea. Digestive problems can also occur, especially constipation (too little fibre results in a slowing of the intestinal transit). And extreme diets, when followed for a long time, can also be accompanied by hair loss, depression and anxiety, as well as panic attacks (due to the high expectations created and the effort required to shed excess weight), gall bladder issues and/or gout.

"Miracle diets" promising spectacular weight loss over a short period of time (one or two weeks) will result not only in a loss of fat, which is the purpose of the diet, but also dehydration, possibly also accompanied by a loss of muscle mass. Consequently, as soon as you come off this kind of diet, the kilograms will start to pile on again (as the body rehydrates itself and begins to accumulate the nutritional substances it had been deprived of). In general, for an adult, the rate of weight loss considered to be healthy and recommended by doctors is a half to one kilo per week. This might seem too slow, especially to those who want to become slim overnight, but it is more likely to allow you to maintain your weight in the long run.

Adopting a healthy lifestyle is an important step to take and will lead to a (re)connection with your body. So if you feel hungry all the time, even if you haven't been to the gym, you're not premenstrual, you're not undergoing treatment with adverse side-effects and you're not about to bring a child into the world, then try to identify what is causing you to be constantly opening that fridge door. Only then will you discover what things the body needs to function correctly and, most importantly, will you avoid eating too much of the things you don't need. For example, people always confuse dehydration with hunger, so I've got a tip for you. In order to be able to differentiate between the two, drink a glass of water whenever you feel hungry, and if, after a quarter of an hour, you feel less hungry then this means that your body is more in need of liquids than food.

Insufficient rest increases the level of ghrelin, the hormone that stimulates the appetite, and decreases the level of leptin, which is responsible for the sensation of satiation, so after staying up all night our feeling of hunger is much greater. Our need for sugar and salt is at its greatest when the number of hours of rest we get is less than five. Types of food rich in unhealthy carbohydrates, such as pastries, pretzels and cakes, which are known for creating dependency and not satisfying our hunger, rapidly increase glycaemia, only for it to fall again just as quickly, leaving us feeling drained of energy and with the sensation of an empty stomach, as if days had passed since we last put something in our mouths. It's better to replace these foods with almonds, raisins, chia seeds and pistachio nuts. I know it may seem a bit clichéd to talk about stress and its effects, but it's too important not to bring it up. Do you know another situation when we feel hungry for no reason? When we feel really stressed out. I find it hard to believe there's someone for whom this is not true in the fast-paced society we live in. We stay late and are always busy at work, we have deadlines to meet and we're always under pressure, eating at our desks to save time, and then when we finally get home we find other pressing things to do. Always rushing, trying to get as much done as possible, not to miss out on anything, we're slaves to our deadlines and things that need to be done perfectly – it's no wonder, therefore, that our body feels exhausted and hormonal imbalances appear. Adrenaline and cortisol, the stress hormones, trick the mind into producing more energy, hence the increase in appetite and the sensation of hunger, even if it's not long since we last ate something.

Ever since ancient times, eating, besides being a pleasure, has been one of our primal instincts, a source of energy for the body, as well as a means of socialising. When it becomes a source of stress, as usually happens when on a diet, the whole body suffers. So, again, we need to listen to the signals our body is sending us, to be patient and to treat ourselves with tenderness and love. Our body knows what it needs to eat and how much it needs to eat to be healthy. I've always been impatient and wanted things to happen quickly. When I'm feeling balanced, I am able to take things one step at a time and I realise that nothing in this world that lasts is created without patience. I've always enjoyed eating and I strongly believe that you need to enjoy what you eat because life is a journey in which we are always able to enjoy something. And this includes food, so it's important we discover which foods and recipes are best suited to each and every one of us.

I have – in an attempt to win the approval of others – been on many different diets, but it never seemed enough. So I went back to scratch and learned the lessons of the traveller who alone must discover the mysteries of the kitchen as well as those of our relationship with our body. Currently, I am at the station called "Live Beautifully" and I feel just great. But it wasn't always this way, so I'm going to tell you a story. In fact, it's more of a diary: how I started to go on different diets, what my most bizarre experiences were, and what things I learned along the way and I believe this will also be useful to you. It's a confession that has a little bit of everything, from drama, humour and irony to compassion, optimism and life lessons – all of which being emotional "accelerator pedals" that represent different facets of my life as someone #ObsessedWithLosingWeightAtAnyCost.

So, let's take it from the beginning. Once upon a time there was... Andreea Raicu. A young woman always concerned with looking good, determined, always competing with herself, bent on surpassing herself. Never in harmony, quickly shifting from one state, or should I say from one diet, to another :). I didn't like anything about myself. I used to believe my hips were too big, my face too bloated, my abdomen not in the least sexy and my knees horrible. I wasn't able to find anything good about myself because I was always aware of what I lacked. Whenever a new diet appeared that promised to work miracles, I was the ideal guinea pig. It was my goal to be slim, but I didn't have the wisdom to understand that this wouldn't make me happy, that I was endangering my health. It took me a long time to realise that when you're healthy you feel good in your body. Not only did I not have a clue about how to listen to my body, I was also unaware of the existence of the concept itself – and anyway I'm sure I'd only have made fun of it at the time!

I felt eternally frustrated because starving myself would yield good results for a while, only for me to put even more weight back on afterwards. My first solution in my struggle to lose weight was, therefore, to deny myself food. Not a single peanut, olive or pretzel – nothing but water or other liquids for a couple of days. Sometimes it was really hard, I saw food everywhere. You know those scenes from cartoons where Tom sees Jerry walking through the house and imagines him already in the frying pan? You get the idea :). There were also times when I no longer felt a need to eat because my body had already become accustomed to being starved. Anyway, I didn't have the energy for it and I was always unhappy because, as already mentioned, I simply love eating and have a lot of food cravings.

I remember how once when I went to Milan I started comparing myself to all the models there. I thought I was way too fat and I had this permanent complex about my body. I wasn't eating much and I wasn't drinking a lot of water either – at least not until I began to feel really ill. That's when I realised that my life was in danger and I had to make a decision. No, not to begin eating healthily, but to switch from starving myself for days on end to… a whole array of different weight loss diets. Well, at least it was something, right? :)

And, guess what, after deciding I wanted to live and to enjoy life, after having understood – finally! – that starving yourself was dangerous, I became a veritable encyclopaedia of weight loss plans. I think a lot of you will know what I'm talking about because I'm sure you too have been on all kinds of extreme diets. I can count on the fingers of one hand the number of women I know of my age who haven't tried the infamous cabbage soup diet. It was, I must admit, an efficient method, but in the long run you ended up putting more weight back on than you lost in the first place. I remember not being able to get past the fifth day of the cabbage soup diet, when I was supposed to be on it for two weeks, but then it was at least better than starvation. Like a toxic relationship you keep going back to for want of anything else and in which you lie to yourself that things will change, I also forced myself to go back onto this diet, but I never managed to see it through to the end. Now, when I see cabbage soup, I feel like I'm going to be sick.

After that I heard about another diet that promised to change your metabolism. For breakfast, I was allowed to eat half a grapefruit and a slice of toast and drink some tea. My lunch menu included grilled chicken breast and lettuce, while for supper I had… well I can't quite remember what it was. Anyway, this diet must have left me traumatised if almost two decades later, I can still more or less remember what I was supposed to eat. I soon grew sick of those foods, I hated them, and after only a few days I couldn't stand it anymore and decided to try something else.

I also tried out a diet that involved eating only rice, something which had the effect of turning my digestion on its head. You can imagine how terrible it made me feel, I was constantly uneasy and didn't feel well at all. It's funny now, but back then I would force myself to stick to these extreme diets, always giving up only to go back to them. I am quite strong-willed and don't give up easily. I remember the famous dissociated diet where every day the only thing I would eat was lettuce and some tuna. For a while I enjoyed it. But soon I began to hate this diet, too. By eating the same thing constantly you develop food intolerances. The second week always seemed the hardest and I usually gave up.

Every time a new diet appeared, I would be enthusiastic at first, but then it would start to feel like a drag and I wouldn't make it past the seven-day barrier. I realise how much I was disrespecting myself by subjecting myself to those unhealthy nutritional regimes, but I can't turn the clock back now. I've never felt a similar feeling of hate towards anyone, not even towards people who have let me down. It's incredible how little respect I had for my body and how little wisdom I possessed at the age of 18, or even at 20! I would have liked someone to have come up to me and told me where and why I was going wrong, as well as to make me see just how much I was torturing my body, although, I was so desperate to lose weight I'm not sure I would have listened. Or maybe I would have, depending on the arguments presented to me. So that's what I'm trying to do in this book: to tell you about what I went through and therefore to encourage you not to go through the same experiences as me, because – yes! – there are other ways to lose weight that don't involve harming our bodies.

On the other hand, the concept of "balance" didn't even exist 20 years ago. Today, now that I treat it better, my body gives me exactly the things I need. I'm much slimmer, I'm happy and I feel good about myself. I can't negate all the experiences I've had, because they are what brought me to where I am now. Some of my other bad experiences involved my asking various people what kind of diets they'd tried and then giving them a go myself. Or going on a diet together with friends. This seems crazy now, because everyone is different and has a different past; we all like different foods and react differently to the same stimuli. And it's important we like what we eat. Not to eat because we have to, but because we enjoy what we eat.

Nine years ago, I felt a need to fast, even if I fully expected it to make me feel devoid of energy and put on weight. Digressing for a moment, I can only laugh when I think about how stressed out I used to get during my childhood when I was expected to fast. I come from a religious family, and it went without saying that we had to observe this religious custom, at least the first and last week, and I was constantly complaining about not being allowed to eat the things I wanted and how miserable it made me feel – I was well known for this, even among the people from church! :) So as soon as I was able to decide for myself, I told myself I'd never fast ever again. And yet the time came when, as an adult, I would go on a fast of my own free will, choosing the one that takes places before Easter, which is somewhat stricter than the one in the run-up to Christmas because it only has two dispensations for fish.

I was in need of physical and spiritual cleansing, and I felt really good afterwards, incredibly good in fact! My skin felt much cleaner, I had more energy and I even lost some weight. The explanation for this was that the body was no longer being forced to work to digest heavy foods like meat and as a result I had more energy. What's more, after doing some tests, I found out something very important: namely, that my body doesn't secrete enough pepsin, an enzyme whose role it is to break down the proteins in food that come from animals, such as meat, eggs and dairy products. That's why I would always feel bloated after eating those things. The changes I made to my diet did me a lot of good: I could sleep less without feeling tired, I had more energy and my complexion was much improved.

Why did I give up meat? I had begun researching and reading up on the subject and I remember being struck by something that kept cropping up in different publications. Apparently, when animals are killed, out of fear they release a toxin that spreads throughout their bodies. This means that the fear and pain felt during slaughter is encapsulated in their meat, and we absorb these emotions, which are toxic to the human body, every time we eat meat.

The film *Food, Inc.* and other documentaries that tell the truth about the food industry, about how meat products are made and the journey they undergo before ending up on the supermarket shelf, made me think a lot about this subject. I began to delve deeper into how animals are bred, how the products we purchase at the supermarket are processed, and as a result I no longer felt like buying anything meat-related ever again. The way animals are maltreated, both in the film and in reality, had a great influence on me and I decided I didn't want to be encouraging these things and didn't want to have this cruelty on my conscience. My decision to go vegetarian was therefore taken both for aesthetic and health reasons, and, above all, because I had decided no longer to be party to the suffering of other creatures. I began to read a lot about how this would affect me, how to replace the meat in what I ate without creating an imbalance in my body and how best to choose what I put in my shopping basket. I began to read carefully what it says on the label and to try to choose quality products that provide me with the nutritional substances I need.

A year after having given up all animal products, I began to feel the need to eat something other than just vegetables, fruit, cereals and seeds. So, while still not eating meat, I decided to introduce goat's cheese and eggs to my diet. However, somehow it felt like I was undoing the cleansing of my body and I didn't feel comfortable: on one hand, I wanted to eat cheese and eggs, even if not all the time; while on the other, I knew that these foods have all kinds of unwanted effects on my body.

This was followed by further nutritional experiments: during this period I also tried out a vegan diet, and, for a while, a raw vegan diet,[2] too. I was always curious about anything new and keen to try all kinds of different regimes and diets. Perhaps my best dieting experience was at a wellness clinic in Spain, where I followed a macrobiotic diet. I felt so good on this diet that I learned to prepare my meals in keeping with its basic principles, which I will describe for you later in this chapter.

What other changes did I make? I gave up gluten, especially after reading the book *Grain Brain: The Surprising Truth about Wheat, Carbs, and Sugar - Your Brain's Silent Killers*. I found it hard to believe I'd never eat pasta or bread again, which are things I've always had a weakness for, but I decided to at least give it a try. I went to America for a month and a half, I went gluten-free, because it was much easier to find those products there, and I felt fantastic. And at a certain point, after having understood how toxic it is for our bodies, I also decided I would have to give up sugar.

As of today, I always eat three meals a day and carry some snacks around with me, usually almonds and raisins. I strongly believe that when embarking on a weight loss plan or going on a particular diet we shouldn't let ourselves be guided only by what's fashionable, but also take into consideration what our bodies need and like. It's also very important not to forget to do regular blood tests, among others, both before and after deciding to exclude certain foods from our diets and adopting a different nutritional system, such as veganism or raw veganism.

We are all different and the same nutritional model won't suit everyone, so we need to do proper research before taking

---

[2] A raw vegan diet involves eating only raw food or food cooked only at low temperatures, thus retaining its vitamins and other nutritional substances.

a decision. I remember how once when I went for some tests because I wasn't feeling well, my friend, Anda Avramescu, who is a doctor who specialises in diabetes, nutrition and metabolic disorders as well as being a nutritional consultant, told me that for some people their stores of vitamin B12 will become depleted, after not eating any meat for a number of years. This was also the case with me and I began to feel the need to eat meat again after a long period of abstinence. I didn't reprimand myself for this, rather I accepted the situation, realising I needed to be aware of how I was feeling and to give my body what it needed.

Now, ten years after having given up, I sometimes feel the need to eat some meat, although only very rarely and I always make sure to rebalance myself and to allow my body to detoxify afterwards. We shouldn't deny ourselves things and it's important to understand why we do something, otherwise frustrations and imbalances will occur. If we eat nothing for a week, because we want to lose weight, at the end of this period we will likely open the fridge door and throw out the rule book. I believe that if we feel like eating some chocolate, then we should go ahead and allow ourselves to enjoy a couple of pieces. At the office, for lack of anything else to eat, I ended up consuming some products made with white flour, which I'd normally steer clear of. I was hungry and so was forced to compromise in order to help my body and avoid feeling ill. I also felt a certain craving, so I ate a bit of cake, thus satisfying my craving and stopping me from feeling frustrated or faint with hunger :-). After that I would always be sure to bring healthy foods with me and not to be tempted by things that aren't good for me. In fact, this is quite easy to do, but it requires us to stay focused on the basic principles: our relationship with our body and how we can learn to cherish it. Now, even if nothing is off limits, I no longer feel the need to eat unhealthy things and am far less tempted than I used to be. I believe we should be allowed to treat ourselves every now and then, not to keep on starving ourselves.

I love cooking at home, it relaxes me and at the same time I know exactly what I'm eating – and here I'm referring to the provenance and quality of the ingredients I use – and anyway the things I like to eat are hard to find at a restaurant. We don't have to spend hours and hours in the kitchen in order to eat good food, which is something I also said in the recipe book I published. I want everything I eat to be clean, such as organic eggs, bio vegetables and wild (i.e. not farmed) fish. They're more expensive, I know, but it's an investment for our bodies. I prefer to refuse something than to do myself harm; we need to give our bodies the best, especially in terms of our time and care.

As soon as I became balanced, everything in my life changed – for the better! I came to know my body and this helped me realise what I wanted to see on my plate. However, in order to be balanced, it's not enough just to eat the right things; it's also vital to be your body's best friend. It's not just what and how much we eat that matters, but how we talk to ourselves and how we relate to our bodies when we look in the mirror.

I know there are many books about how to achieve a balance between mind, body and soul, and that there are many seemingly contradictory theories out there. Discovering what's good for you is hard, but not impossible. The rules of balance function in a different way for each of us and I can't say that what suits me will also be valid for others. My goal is much simpler but still very important: I believe it is essential to honour our bodies and ourselves, to love ourselves and to stop judging ourselves so much. When we make this our priority, we discover an extraordinary force within us, a force that helps us overcome the obstacles we raised in the past and to forget the times we felt unhappy, unwanted, sad, afraid, anxious, depressed, etc. Of course, it's a difficult process, but if we establish a connection with our bodies we will find the necessary resources within us to overcome our problems and disappointments, without sacrificing our health and happiness.

Have you ever taken the time to note down how you feel after eating certain foods? I have and it made me realise just how much the food I eat affects me. I adore eating avocados, for example, they always make me feel good, especially when eaten in the morning, for breakfast, and then there's chia seeds and goji berries, which also fill me with energy. I can't say the same about products containing a lot of sugar or fried foods. I start to feel restless and lose concentration, and, what's more, my body immediately warns me it's not happy with what I've been eating and I begin to feel bloated. The conclusion to be drawn from this is that the relationship between our mind and body depends in part on how we feed ourselves: the cleaner and healthier the products we consume, the greater the connection between the two, thus giving rise to harmony and balance.

In what follows, I will go into detail about some of the healthy eating habits I have experimented with. From my experience, I can tell you that once we change the way we eat and once we become more conscious of each moment and grow accustomed to setting aside at least ten minutes each day for meditation, then we will begin to gain confidence and develop the courage to leave behind all the things stopping us from achieving our goals, even those that have to do with our physical appearance. The truth is this: everyone has a body. Only one, which belongs only to him or her. It is up to every one of us to become conscious of this and to build for ourselves both the present and the future. The first step is to develop a relationship with our bodies and to speak kindly to it, then to learn to eat healthily and to exercise in order to maintain our muscle tone, and then to test out different experiences meant to help us accept ourselves and be happy.

## The alkaline diet

The alkaline diet is not a new idea: it has been used since ancient times, having roots in the Ayurveda[3] system. It has been gaining popularity for some time now and has been widely promoted by international stars. The idea behind it is that when there exists a balance between levels of alkaline and acid, our bodies will similarly be in a state of equilibrium and all our internal processes will occur exactly the way they are meant to.

I really like this comparison because it shows once again how important it is to pay attention to how we relate to our own bodies. Our bodies are like chemical laboratories and they possess intelligence, not least on account of their ability to regulate the pH level of every organ. Why is the level of pH important? Because it indicates the degree of acidity or alkalinity of a given solution and therefore also of the substances found in the human body. A reading of 0 means our pH is acid, while 14 is an alkaline pH, with 7 indicating a neutral value. Inside the human body, the level of pH varies depending on the organ, which is quite normal because the body ingeniously regulates the activity of all its internal components. That is, as long as it is healthy and getting all the things it needs! For example, blood has a pH of between 7.35 and 7.45, which makes it is slightly alkaline.

I found it really interesting to read that scientists are able to say how food reacts inside the body by incinerating[4] food

---

[3] The oldest Indian healing system, which is based on the idea of re-establishing equilibrium in the body by means of diet, physical exercise and the detoxification of the body such that the mind, body and spirit are in harmony.

[4] The food is actually burned.

and analysing the mineral content of the resulting ashes. If the mineral content is highly alkaline, then the food will have an alkaline effect on the body, and vice versa. In other words, the way the body reacts to certain foods determines which foods are alkaline and which are acid. Of course, there are some exceptions that confirm the rule. For example, lemons and honey are acidic by nature, but they have an alkalising effect on the body when digested. Similarly, milk is alkaline outside of the body, but acidic when digested.

This lifestyle – for it is more than just a diet – is not maintained only for a limited time and it does not promise the rapid loss of a given number of kilos in a given space of time. Its rules are meant to be respected permanently, because they lead to weight loss and prevent the accumulation of excess kilos. Perhaps most importantly, they play an essential role in maintaining health.

Unfortunately, unhealthy foods and our hectic lifestyles have a negative effect on our pH values, so we need to choose natural products containing many vitamins and minerals which can help re-establish a balance. The ideal situation is for us to have as alkaline a pH as possible, something that mainly depends on diet. Robert Young, the microbiologist and nutritionist from the US who laid the foundations for the alkaline diet, believes fat is created by the body in order to shield it from the acidity of our vital organs. Consequently, the more effort we make to lower the level of acidity in our bodies, the slimmer we become and the more our fatty deposits will decline. The best foods with an alkaline effect are vegetables, essential oils, alkaline water and mineral salts, all of which are easy to digest and help lower acidity, meaning vitamins and minerals will be more readily absorbed into the body.

**Foods can be acidic, alkaline or neutral**

| Acidic | Neutral | Alkaline |
|---|---|---|
| meat | natural fats | fruit |
| milk | starch | vegetables |
| eggs | sugars | |
| cereals | | |
| alcohol | | |

If we don't eat any alkaline foods and are not in balance, then acidic foods, such as meat, processed foods, white flour, cereals, beans, dairy products, fish, coffee and fizzy drinks, will leave residues in the body that upset our digestion, overwork our internal organs and impede their functioning. What's more, our body will take the nutritional substances it needs from our organs, bones and tissue, which results in a compromising of the immune system and the appearance of various ailments: digestive disorders, irregular sleep, headaches, muscle and joint pain, infections and colds, allergies, lack of energy, rheumatoid arthritis, osteoporosis, diabetes, lupus, tuberculosis, high blood pressure, high cholesterol, heart disease, cancer, eczema, acne, gallstones, hernias, anxiety and behavioural disorders, insomnia, irritableness, palpitations and many others.

> The alkaline diet involves eating as much salads, seeds, oleaginous fruits and raw vegetables as possible

Acidic foods are not entirely forbidden, but they should account for no more than 30% of your diet, while coffee, sugar, cow's milk and gluten are to be consumed only in limited quantities. By adhering to the rules of an alkaline diet, I was able to pay more attention to what I eat and to focus more on eating fruit and raw or steamed vegetables, as well as to cut out sugar. This is not to say that I stick to the rules all the time. As I was telling you, in order to avoid feeling frustrated I no longer deny my body anything. However, alkaline foods help me feel much better and to have the body I want. That being said, if you have gastritis or colitis, it's possible you will experience some unpleasantness from eating raw foods, so it's best first to ask the opinion of a specialist doctor.

Water is very important to an alkaline diet, but not just any kind of water, you need to choose liquids with a higher pH. There are devices available to filter and ionise water, but you can also raise the pH of water simply by adding the juice of half a squeezed lemon to one litre of water. If you don't like the taste of lemon then you can try some alkaline drops from your local pharmacy instead.

This diet is not without its critics. The founder of the alkaline diet, Robert Young, lost a lot of credibility after being arrested for fraud and practicing alternative medicine without a licence. It has been widely said that the alkaline lifestyle is based on a lie and that the body is capable of regulating its pH on its own, regardless of what we eat. All the same, no one can deny that a diet based on raw foods helps prevent the appearance of kidney stones and lowers urine acidity. Eating alkaline foods also aids the slow release of glucose into the bloodstream (unlike processed foods, which contain only simple sugars) and keeps blood sugar levels within normal parameters, therefore lowering the risk of diabetes. Why shouldn't we eat acidic foods in large quantities? Because they block the arteries and lead to heart attacks, you will feel far more stressed and devoid of energy, and the body will struggle to rebalance the pH of the blood and thus release "borrowed" alkaline minerals into the body, i.e. calcium, phosphorus and magnesium. If we don't provide it with these substances by eating alkaline foods, it will "draw" minerals from the bones, teeth and organs, leading to a weakening of the immune system and an unexplainable state of exhaustion.

**Note**

**Water retains its alkalinity if kept in a glass bottle as opposed to a plastic recipient.**

**Tip**

**Drink a large glass of alkaline water in the morning, a quarter of an hour before breakfast, and it will improve your digestion.**

**Acid-alkaline food chart**

| ALKALINE FRUITS ↓ | ACIDIC FRUITS ↓ |
|---|---|
| raisins, dates, figs, pineapple, apples, apricots, peaches, cherries, avocado, grapes, ripe bananas, strawberries, grapefruit, mango, cantaloupe and watermelon, nectarines, olives, papaya, pears, pomegranates, quinces, kiwis; lemons and limes, while acidic, have an alkalising effect | sugared, glazed fruit, dried fruit preserved in sulphur dioxide or sugar, green bananas, plums, blueberries, oranges, mandarins |
| ALKALINE VEGETABLES AND PULSES ↓ | ACIDIC VEGETABLES AND PULSES ↓ |
| mushrooms, broccoli, cauliflower, red and white cabbage, onion, garlic, leek, lettuce, beetroot, carrots, potatoes, spinach, artichoke, cucumber, endives, parsley, parsnip, red and yellow peppers, pumpkins, radishes, turnips, aubergines, chickpeas, beans, pulses | chilli pepper, tomatoes, asparagus, rhubarb, soya, peas, lentils (with the exception of sprouted lentils), green peppers |

| ALKALINE CEREALS ↓ | ACIDIC CEREALS ↓ |
|---|---|
| Fresh cereals, such as green barley | patisserie products, white bread, wholemeal or Graham bread, starch, pastry, popcorn, maize flour, pasta, semolina, rice (white, brown, basmati), oat flour or flakes, barley, rye, wheat |

| ALKALINE DAIRY PRODUCTS ↓ | ACIDIC DAIRY PRODUCTS ↓ |
|---|---|
| kefir, buttermilk, fresh milk (cow or goat), plain unpasteurised yoghurt or sour milk | parmesan, fermented cheese, hard cheese, cottage cheese, ice cream, sweet yoghurt or fruit yoghurt, boiled milk, powdered milk, fermented cream |

| ALKALINE COOKED FOOD ↓ | ACIDIC COOKED FOOD ↓ |
|---|---|
| boiled and baked vegetables; vegetable stew, but without tomatoes or tomato purée; vegetable or root vegetable soups | boiled tomatoes, tomato purée or paste; meat broths; soups with added vegetable stock cubes; cooked spinach, canned food |

| ALKALINE SWEET FOODS ↓ | ACIDIC SWEET FOODS ↓ |
|---|---|
| sugarcane juice, dock leaf extract, brown rice syrup; honey is acidic but has an alkalising effect | cakes, biscuits, wafers, chocolate, artificial sweeteners (saccharine, aspartame, sorbitol), fructose, lactose |

| ALKALINE ANIMAL PRODUCTS ↓ | ACIDIC ANIMAL PRODUCTS ↓ |
|---|---|
| None | cold meats, all types of mammal meat, fish, gelatine, animal fats, roe, eggs |

| ALKALINE BEVERAGES ↓ | ACIDIC BEVERAGES ↓ |
|---|---|
| root vegetable juice; still and spring water are considered neutral, although in reality they have a slightly acid pH (between 6 and 7) | all alcoholic drinks, artificial soft drinks, cola-type drinks, coffee, cocoa, fizzy drinks, tea |

| MISCELLANEOUS – ALKALINE ↓ | MISCELLANEOUS – ACIDIC ↓ |
|---|---|
| almost all condiments made from alfalfa; algae, ginger, amalaki, sea salt | mayonnaise, refined salt, sauces, ketchup, tomato paste, mustard (paste), curry, artificial food additives: flavourings, colourants, glutamate, preservatives |
| **ALKALINE OLEAGINOUS PRODUCTS ↓** | **ACIDIC OLEAGINOUS PRODUCTS ↓** |
| cold pressed sunflower or olive oil; fish oil; primrose oil; almonds, pumpkin and sesame seeds, chestnuts, raw sunflower seeds, fresh coconut | refined sunflower or olive oil, oleaginous fruits and roasted or fried seeds, walnuts, pistachios, peanuts, cashew nuts |
| **ACTIVITIES AND EMOTIONAL STATES THAT ALKALISE THE BODY ↓** | **ACTIVITIES AND EMOTIONAL STATES THAT CAUSE ACIDOSIS ↓** |
| sleep, relaxation, sauna, physical exercise, meditation, breathing exercises, joy, happiness, calm | smoking, artificial flavour enhancers and perfumes, lack of sleep, synthetic drugs, overwork, sadness, anger, stress, hate, outrage |

## The macrobiotic diet

As already mentioned, before figuring out that it wasn't the beauty of the body but its well-being that should have been my main focus, I had become something of a specialist in weight loss diets. Why? Because I am incredibly curious and as soon as I hear about something new I want to try it. For a long time I lacked confidence in myself and was asking too much of my body without giving it much in return; because I'm stubborn; because I wasn't eating to be healthy, but to satisfy my cravings, only to end up regretting it later and punishing myself. Because I quickly grow bored and always need to find new ways to motivate myself and make me go beyond my limits. I hadn't consulted a nutritionist who might explain to me the medical implications of starving myself and extreme weight loss diets. I was naïve and believed in perfection. Moreover, I was lying to myself that I had a body that could take everything I could throw at it.

Some diets and weight loss programmes left their mark on me, while from others I retained invaluable information that helped to me find balance. This confirms to me once again that nothing in life happens by chance, not even my obsession with discovering the most efficient weight loss diet. I made choices – which some people may consider mistakes – that changed my life and helped me to understand that what I needed to do was not to go on yet another diet, but to adopt a healthy lifestyle. As soon as I understood that it wasn't necessary to starve myself to get rid of my cellulite, that it wasn't necessary to deny myself culinary pleasures in order to have a flat abdomen, I was able to become my own best friend and I am happier for it. I am now no longer chasing rainbows but things that really do produce results, and I savour every beautiful experience that comes my way.

**Important!**

**Don't go looking up information about diets on the internet – consult a specialist instead. Read specialist studies and books!**

The first step I took on this autodidactic journey in pursuit of a healthy lifestyle was very important: I began to do some research. Just like in the plot of a novel or a film, I had reached the point where I had begun to realise I was heading down a blind alley and I needed to change something. So I armed myself with some patience – a LOT of patience :) – and I began reading about the needs of the body, about healthy food combinations, about our relationship with our bodies, etc. I know your first instinct is always to look stuff up on the internet, but I feel a warning is in order here. In order to do things properly, especially when it comes to weight loss and healthy living, we need to use multiple sources. When using Google it's very difficult to filter information, to work out what applies to us and what doesn't; and it's even harder to judge the quality of the source providing us with information. That said, we have so many other options: nutritional specialists, studies, magazines and specialist books, people who have tried different diets and know exactly what they're talking about.

When people visit me at home they're constantly surprised at how many books about personal development, nutrition and food there are to be found on my book shelf, my bedside table, my coffee tables, my sofas and on my bed. And, no, they're not there just for decorative purposes or to impress, indeed that's not something I'm in the habit of doing anyway, and anyone who picks them up will see that parts of them are underlined and highlighted, that they're full of post-it notes and that I've extracted the information I deemed most interesting and useful. I keep them at the key points around the house, so I'm always tempted to look at them, to remind myself of certain things, to keep my mind active.

When you travel by car or public transport, what do you listen to on your headphones? For example, I put on all kinds of audiobooks or YouTube videos about things that interest me. A lot of these things are free and it's down to us to discover them and make use of them. I'll give you a few examples at the end of the book of the sources I use, which I really hope will also be of use to you. They help me keep up-to-date with the latest developments, and I can do this in my free time. That way it's simple: I combine utility with pleasure!

Coming back to the diet I want to tell you about, it was during my stay at the wellness centre in Spain I mentioned in the introduction to this chapter that I learned about the macrobiotic diet. What convinced me to go on this diet were its founding principles and the fact that it helped me bring order to my life. Developed in Japan, the macrobiotic diet,[5] like the alkaline diet, is more a lifestyle than merely a diet because it combines eating with a particular approach towards food and towards the world. When chasing after the perfect diet we tend to overlook what's essential. We think more about the form and less about the heart of the problem. This marathon of different weight loss regimes is in fact a race to achieve self-knowledge, but one without any particular direction. Because it's not exterior beauty that should be the supreme aim of a diet, but well-being, a balance between the external and internal.

I have noticed how, due to lack of time, people are always eating on the go, in front of the computer or television, or while on the phone. This is mechanical eating! The mind is not exclusively concentrated on eating and dysfunction sets in automatically: we don't feel full, our food doesn't agree with us, the sensation of hunger returns quickly, etc. The macrobiotic diet eliminates these adverse effects because here to eat means only… to eat. To concentrate on what is on your plate, to enjoy every last bit, to savour all kinds of food. You are therefore not only feeding your body but your mind too! Before finding my balance, I used to be really chaotic, both in my thoughts and at

---

[5] The word "macrobiotic" comes from Greek and means "beautiful life" or "long life".

home, in my work environment, in my diet and in many other areas of my life besides.

After discovering the macrobiotic diet I felt I not only no longer had any problems with my digestion and that the fatty deposits on my abdomen had reduced, I also learned how important it is to cook at home, because only then can I guarantee that the meals I eat are cooked properly and the ingredients carefully chosen. However, the benefits of this diet, which is more of a lifestyle, don't stop there. I learned how important it is to have an orderly home, to eat in a relaxed way, in an atmosphere that makes you feel good, e.g. with candles, ambient music, etc., to be conscious of every aroma that stimulates your taste buds and to enjoy every portion of food you consume. Somehow I don't think it's an exaggeration to say that adhering to the rules of a macrobiotic diet will change your life, not just your eating habits, helping you to feel good about yourself and the place where you live.

This diet is similar to that of a vegetarian – i.e. based on vegetables, fruit, seeds, wholegrain cereals, sprouts, etc. – but fortunately lean fish is also allowed! In the macrobiotic diet, all food and drinks consumed must be as natural as possible, i.e. not industrially processed using various chemical synthetic substances or artificially treated. If you nonetheless wish to cook your food, then you should either steam or bake it. Chew slowly, don't combine too many different things, and don't drink liquids during your meal. Alcohol, coffee, sugars, black tea, white flour, preservatives and emulsifiers are all excluded. Everything works according to a standard food pyramid, as follows (see box).

**Red meat**

**Eggs and meat from free-range poultry**

**Dairy products**

**Sweets**

**Seeds and oleaginous fruits**[8]

**Fish,**
especially with white meat[7]

**Seasonal fruit**[6]

**Vegetable oils**[4]
Including sea salt, miso[5], soya sauce, etc.

**Condiments**

**Lentils, chickpeas, beans, tofu** **Sea food**[3]

Should account for 5-10% of daily food consumption

**Cooked and raw vegetables**

Should account for 30% of daily food consumption[1] **Fermented foods**[2]

**Cereals**

These form the basis of a macrobiotic diet and should account for 50-60% of daily food consumption: brown and wild rice, barley, millet, wholegrain whcat

---

1 Preferably green vegetables, with the exception of spinach, which has yang properties and should be consumed only occasionally. It is best to choose locally grown vegetables, depending on the season, but we should always take into account the yin and yang properties of certain vegetables.

2 Tempeh (a mixture of soya and other wholegrain cereals, such as millet, wheat and rice, which is fermented and pressed into batons) is recommended, as are pickles, which are an important source of probiotics in winter.

3 Sea food (shrimps, crayfish, oysters, lobster, crab, scampi, mussels, cuttlefish, octopus) is rich in minerals and vitamins and thus has excellent health properties and should be included in your diet.
4 Sesame oil and corn oil are best, as well as sea salt, brown rice vinegar, tamari, tahini and brown rice syrup.
5 Miso, a traditional Japanese soup made from miso, a salty and buttery fermented soya paste, various types of algae and vegetables, is a permanent feature of the macrobiotic diet.
6 Fruit is perfect as a starter or dessert, but is not recommended more than three times a week. Tropical fruits, such as bananas and pineapple, are to be avoided.
7 The macrobiotic diet allows for the consumption of fish three times a week. Naturally, vegans and vegetarians need not follow this rule.
8 Walnuts, almonds, cashew nuts, pecan nuts, macadamia nuts, Brazil nuts and pistachio nuts.

The macrobiotic[6] diet was made popular again by Nyoichi Sakurazawa, also known in America as George Ohsawa, a doctor in the Japanese military who devised a nutritional and medical theory based on the traditional oriental diet. He suffered from many illnesses and studied both western and oriental medicine in order to come up with a programme that would help him get rid of his illnesses.

I'm happy to tell you that in this lifestyle the focus is also placed on balance. This time, the harmony generated by Yin and Yang (forces whose interaction underlies all the phenomena of the universe) takes centre stage. In his works, George Ohsawa draws attention to the connections existing between eating and the way we act, feel and think, as well as those that lead to the

[6] The word macrobiotic is formed of "macro", meaning large, and "bios", meaning life – that is, the art of a great life. Therefore, it is not only a diet but a lifestyle that includes a spiritual dimension and teaches us how to view the entirety of existence, as well as to consider life's joys and hardships as gifts that help us to grow.

appearance of illness. His entire thinking is based on the idea that our purpose in life is to consciously place ourselves in harmony with the laws of nature and the universe.

> *"Eating is the foundation of health and happiness; wise men consider it a true art of living."*
>
> — George Ohsawa

Through its energy, food influences and shapes our lives both physically and emotionally. The first effect food has, as you can imagine, is on the physical body, but it also influences our thoughts, the way we view the world and our relationships with other people. What's important is that we choose foods that are rich in nutritional substances and which have both Yin and Yang properties. If we have a macrobiotic lifestyle it doesn't mean we'll never again eat chocolate or enjoy guilty pleasures. It's important to remember that moderation is the key to avoiding illness and living beautifully.

Someone who eats a lot of hot food (Yang) will clearly behave differently than someone who prefers sweet things (Yin), just as someone who prefers processed foods (Yin) is different from someone who likes sunflower seeds (Yang). Someone with a sufficiently well balanced Yin and Yang will be better able to resist the harmful influences, tensions and frustrations that everyday life throws at them. In order to protect ourselves from illness and to find peace, we should consume Yang foods like cereals, apples and walnuts on a daily basis.

George Ohsawa proposes a series of ten macrobiotic diets designed to achieve a balance between Yin and Yang. The Yang foods are introduced gradually, allowing for the elimination of different health issues. Diet number seven is considered to have the most purifying effect and should be respected without deviation for ten consecutive days, with possible repeats after breaks of three to five days. If what we are looking for is detoxification and maintaining our health as best as possible, then this diet should be undertaken a few times a year. The best times are usually around the changing of the seasons or during the Christian fasts, i.e. in the run-up to Christmas or during Lent.

Four such courses a year are generally sufficient for a relatively balanced person not suffering from any serious illnesses and following a lacto-vegetarian diet. During the entire period of nutritional and spiritual detoxification, the only things eaten are wheat, rice, millet and buckwheat – preferably prepared in different ways (e.g. boiling, grinding, baking and frying) in any combination or quantity – together with water and a small amount of salt.

When I first heard about this diet, I was sceptical about the consumption of cereals. I didn't know if this would be good for me and I had the feeling I'd only end up putting on some extra kilos. And yet I lost weight, I got rid of my water retention and I no longer felt bloated. But the most interesting thing is that I no longer needed to starve myself to obtain these results and was instead eating only what I required. I even felt full after eating only small portions. The rules of the macrobiotic diet are to be applied at all times, in particular to your lifestyle and the way you eat, and especially during a 10-day course of detoxification. At first I found it very difficult to follow the macrobiotic diet, but after three days, during which I had cravings for fruit and vegetables, it became much easier. For the first few days I suffered digestive problems, which was a sign there were a lot of impurities in my body and I was in need of detoxification, but then I was amazed by the results after that. I had come to realise that we unfortunately often eat for reasons that have nothing to do with feeding ourselves, i.e. in order to satisfy certain cravings or in order to cope with busy and stressful periods.

### *Wheat*

Contains many vitamins – A, B complex, D, E and K – and minerals – calcium, magnesium, potassium, silicon, iron, zinc, manganese, cobalt, copper.

#### *Therapeutic use*

If you suffer from heart, dermatological, digestive or liver diseases, various endocrine disorders or neurological or renal conditions, then try to include this food in your daily diet. This cereal is also effective in cases of anaemia, arteriosclerosis, asthenia, colitis and chronic constipation.

### *Wholegrain rice*

I don't know what you think of this food, but it used to be one of my favourites. That is, until I went on that rice-based diet that caused me more problems than it helped me lose weight. There are many different types of rice on sale in the shops: plain white rice, long grain rice, wholegrain rice, etc. The latter type is also the healthiest, based on the principle that the last shall be first… on your plate. Wholegrain rice contains vitamins A and B, which are normally lost through milling, as well as calcium, phosphorus, iron, potassium, magnesium and manganese.

#### *Therapeutic use*

There are many therapeutic uses, not least because wholegrain rice is filling and helps us to eat less. In terms of its health benefits, it's recommended in the case of high blood pressure, heart disease and renal insufficiency.

### *Millet*

If what you're thinking is the millet used in bird feed then you're mistaken. There's also a second type of millet, which is much more... domestic :) and is rich in minerals: phosphorus, magnesium, iron, potassium, zinc, as well as plenty of vitamin A.

#### *Therapeutic use*

While reading a book about the macrobiotic diet I came across what for me was a new word, namely that millet has "diaphoretic"[7] properties. While I took note of this term, I forgot the name of the book... but then at least I didn't come away empty handed :). Millet helps the body when it is weak and helps boost your powers of concentration. It is effective in cases of digestive, pulmonary and renal disorders, in convalescence, asthenia, diarrhoea, abdominal pains, mental exhaustion and different forms of visual impairment.

### *Buckwheat*

Of all the cereals I have mentioned so far, buckwheat has the greatest Yang property. It contains protein, vitamin P, calcium mineral salts, phosphorus, magnesium, potassium, iron and zinc.

---

[7] It stimulates the elimination of toxins through perspiration, thereby aiding the detoxification process.

*Therapeutic use*

Buckwheat is energising and nutritious, it has tonic properties and offers vascular protection. It is recommended for those with digestive problems. Given its high protein content, it is ideal as part of a macrobiotic diet. It helps prevent sclerosis and is effective in cases of heart disease.

While following a macrobiotic diet it's best to use unrefined sea salt. Of course, where this is not available, coarse salt can also be used. Where possible, it's recommended to use fresh water, taken from a spring, but as this is difficult to come by in the city, still mineral water is recommended in place of any other type of liquid.

### *List of foods with a preponderance of Yang*

CEREALS:

1. Rice, millet, wheat
2. Buckwheat

VEGETABLES:

1. Lentils, white cabbage, dandelions, lettuce, endives, savoy cabbage, leeks, radishes, turnips, onions, parsley, soya
2. Pumpkin, carrots, burdock

SEEDS:

1. Sesame, sunflower, pumpkin

FISH:

1. Salmon, crayfish, shrimps, lobster, herring, sardines
2. Roe

MEAT:

1. Pigeon, partridge, turkey
2. Eggs
3. Pheasant

DAIRY PRODUCTS:

1. Roquefort cheese, goat cheese

FRUIT:

1. Wild strawberries, blackberries, chestnuts, apples, walnuts, sunflower seeds

LIQUIDS:

1. Chamomile tea, rosemary tea, natural Japanese tea (Bancha), malt, chicory, Oshawa coffee, dandelion coffee
2. Dragon tea
3. Ginseng

CONDIMENTS:

1 Cinnamon, dill, basil, thyme, rosemary, wild thyme, onion
2. Parsley, sage, horseradish, saffron, wild chicory
3. Gentian, unrefined sea salt

The numbers in the above list indicate the intensity of the accumulation of Yang energy in the corresponding foods, as follows:

1 – moderate level of Yang energy
2 – high level of Yang
3 – extreme Yang

It may at first be hard to get hold of foods that have undergone as little processing as possible, as required in the macrobiotic diet, but there are a number of websites where you can order fruit and vegetables that have received the least amount of chemical "enhancement". I'm an avid user of online shops that sell bio products or products that are as close to their natural state as possible. It's much easier for me to do my shopping online because I don't have the time to be running from one place to the next in search of all the things I need to buy. That said, I must admit to being a great fan of going to the market.

Do you know how I make sure I'm able to choose the healthiest fruit and vegetables whenever I go to the market? You might laugh, but this is a really useful trick. I tell the vendors and those working the stalls that I'm allergic to food that has been injected or doesn't come from local farmers – something which also happens to be true. I sometimes also say that if they sell me those kinds of products then I'll end up in hospital. I'm then often presented with a different basket from which to select the products I want and am told not to choose anything from those on display; not because they're not healthy, because they might just be a little dusty. It's strange not to be able to buy quality products without resorting to this kind of trickery, which I admit is nothing to be proud of. But, as I told you, my body comes first and I'm determined, as best I can, to give it the royal treatment.

I decided to write this book because so many people were asking me how I was able to change and what my secrets were, as well as how I came to realise that healthy eating is not a goal in itself but a means by which we can lead a good, balanced life. It's very important we each choose the eating style that best suits us. It shouldn't be our goal to have as few kilos as possible! Our goal should be our good health. Similarly, it's not sufficient just to eat our food in a given way. We also need physical exercise, sleep and hydration. Each of these has a role to play because our body is a complex piece of "machinery". It won't work properly if we only satisfy one of its various needs! Even a car needs more than just petrol to run smoothly!

Like every eating style, the macrobiotic diet can have side-effects, especially if its rules are not respected or the person in question is predisposed to certain health conditions. That's why I do regular tests, so I know whether to exclude or include various foods in my diet, and I always ask my nutritionist about the consequences of my choices. Following the macrobiotic diet has been linked to a number of cases of iron deficiency, as well as deficiencies in vitamins A, B12, C and D, carotene and calcium, as well as anaemia. There have also been reports of renal disorders, especially kidney stones, because it recommends consuming cereals with only a small quantity of water.

As you can imagine, in the limited space available to me here, there's no way I can cover everything about the diets and healthy eating styles I have tried over the years. I can only provide some general conclusions and basic information, but if you really want to try them for yourselves, you'll need to consult many different sources and, most importantly, to first seek the advice of a nutritional specialist, who is the only person able to tell you whether the macrobiotic diet is a wise choice for you.

**Information**

**Although there is no scientific proof, those who promote the macrobiotic diet claim it can help reduce the symptoms of serious diseases, such as cancer and AIDS.**

**Good to know!**

**Yang foods are best for the body when consumed as part of a macrobiotic diet, because they have a purifying energy and boost the body's resistance to infection.**

**Remember!**

**The macrobiotic lifestyle is not just about losing weight, it is also about...**

**... being friendly**
**... respecting all living creatures**
**... being aware of the environment and protecting it**
**... laughing a lot**
**... meditating and searching for meaning in our lives**
**... enjoying eating and being grateful for every meal**
**... avoiding extreme diets and taking care of our bodies**
**... chewing our food thoroughly**
**... reducing portion sizes and choosing variety**
**... being generous**
**... being responsible and owning up when we make mistakes**
**... listening to our intuition, especially the signals sent by our bodies**
**... living in as simple and orderly a way as possible**
**... using as many things made from natural materials as possible**

## The ketogenic diet

The first time I heard the word "ketogenic" I thought it very funny and it brought to mind two things: Ketonal (you've probably heard of this drug used to ease pain) and kerosene, with my idea being that we need to eat certain substances that will burn off, both metaphorically and literally, any excess kilos we have. Well, let me tell you it has nothing to do with either – but at least I was right about one thing: it is a weight loss diet, and after doing some more research I discovered it was growing in popularity all over the world, and so I too became interested.

Unlike high protein diets, the ketogenic diet favours fats, to which special attention is paid during the weight loss process. In brief, in order to achieve our desired weight, we need to reduce the quantity of carbohydrates in our diet and to increase the quantity of fat-rich foods we consume. The body produces small energy molecules called ketones. These are formed when we don't eat sugar, when we drastically reduce our carbohydrate intake and when we don't consume enough protein. Ketosis, the process whereby the body produces ketones, helps reduce the level of insulin, which can prevent the appearance of certain types of cancer or slow down their development (cancerous cells feed on sugar), and raises the metabolic rate. The good news is that the body, when starved of carbohydrates, begins to burn its fatty deposits in order to have energy. Ketones are an inefficient fuel for the body because they contain very few calories for their mass, and as a result the body burns lots of fats but without producing a lot of calories.

One of the main advantages of this diet is that it forces the body to use body fat to produce energy. A low-carbohydrate diet not only makes us burn fat, it also helps us maintain our body shape because we are no longer creating such large stores of fat. Instead of burning glucose and storing fat, we burn the latter. But for this to happen we need to limit the amount of carbohydrates in our food. According to some studies, a low level of carbohydrates protects nerve cells (with this diet also being used to treat epilepsy and to prevent Alzheimer's and Parkinson's disease) and ameliorates acne. The increased amount of fat stops the body from producing excess cholesterol and helps normalise cholesterol levels.

In the ketogenic diet your calorie intake should be 5% carbohydrates, 20% protein and (the largest amount) 75% various forms of fat. You can lose quite a lot of weight this way, even up to three or four kilograms in the first week in the form of water and glycogen. However, the stores of fat we are aiming to reduce begin to disappear only after seven to eight days on the diet.

If you're tempted to try the ketogenic diet, you should know from the outset that you will need to eliminate all forms of sugar from what you eat, even those considered healthy sugars, so that means no brown sugar, no corn syrup, no honey. But the hardest part, for me at least, is that you also need to reduce your consumption of fruit, because fruit contains fructose and sucrose. Forest fruits have the lowest carbohydrate content, so you can still enjoy a few from time to time. The list of foods to avoid also includes wheat flour, pasta, potatoes, jam, canned soup, beans, peanuts, lentils, milk, polenta and fizzy drinks. The ketosis that occurs as a result of following a ketogenic diet has the benefit of regulating glycaemia, reducing the sensation of hunger, raising our powers of concentration, increasing the rate at which we burn fat and reducing cellulitis.

The ketogenic diet comprises two stages, or phases, as they are also called in the specialist literature. During the attack phase you need to eat four meals a day, not three, as we are accustomed to doing, and the calorific content of these meals should be 1,500 calories for women and 2,000 calories for men. This phase lasts for 14 days and, as the name suggests, it is a time when the body is most active and burns the most fat. During the next stage you are allowed to add 500 calories a day to your diet; this is a phase of maintenance and it will be harder to lose weight, but we have set our sights on a given weight and we stick to our goal.

There are a number of different theories about the ketogenic diet. Some say the second phase should not last for more than two weeks, while others recommend the long-term use of this kind of diet as a way to achieve a healthy lifestyle. I also read that there are in fact four different phases, and that you should avoid making a quick transition from a normal diet to the ketogenic diet without allowing for a period of adaptation. If the rules of the ketogenic diet are not carefully respected, or if we skip certain phases or have certain deficiencies when we decide to take up this kind of diet, then this can lead to migraines, nausea and extreme tiredness, among other health problems, due to the reduction in carbohydrate intake. Those who consume a lot of protein while on the ketogenic diet not only won't lose any weight, they may also end up with some extra kilos, so you need to be careful what you eat. Sometimes when on the ketogenic diet you will need to take vitamin and mineral supplements, as well as to eat foods with a high fibre content, because your digestion may also be affected.

Although ketosis occurs when we consume fat, and it's best to opt for healthy fats, such as those found in coconuts, salmon, tuna, cod, mackerel, sea food, walnuts and oleaginous seeds – e.g. hemp, flax, sesame, forest nuts, pumpkin and chia seeds. As a good source of fats it is also recommended you consume cocoa butter, avocados, olives, as well as vegetable oils from sprouted wheat, flax, hemp, grape seeds and coconut. The list of permissible foods containing carbohydrates includes green beans, cucumber, tomatoes, spinach, cabbage and onions.

**Important!**

**A ketogenic diet should contain 65% fat, 30% protein and only 5% carbohydrates, with the latter coming predominantly from vegetables.**

**Tip**

**If you've been on the ketogenic diet for a month and you feel fine and your blood tests are all okay too, then studies show that for one day a week you can eat even more carbohydrates provided you also drastically reduce the amount of fat you consume on that day.**

## The vegan lifestyle

Every important decision in life, especially when it comes to changing our diet, should be taken only after we've first done some reading and have sought the advice of a doctor. I strongly believe that adopting a new diet or changing your lifestyle should not be a sudden process, because the body needs to adapt gradually to the new type of food. It's only normal that everything will be turned upside down when after years of eating meat and lots of animal derived foods we suddenly decide to go vegan overnight. Through their aromas and taste traditional foods remind us of childhood, and so we find it difficult to adapt to a new regimen and will quickly give up if we don't do things in stages and are too harsh on our bodies. The first steps are the most important and your reason for making this change will make all the difference. Being vegan doesn't mean merely eliminating meat and eating foods that help us to lose weight and to be healthy; it also means showing our love for animals and refusing any meal that contains products that come from animals: milk and milk derivatives, eggs, honey, etc. The main difference between vegans and vegetarians is that the former are more extreme, they eliminate all products of animal origin, they are usually campaigners for animal rights, and they even avoid wearing clothes made using leather, wool or silk. I must admit that I found it hard to make this change.

Proponents of this lifestyle say there are plenty of replacements for traditional dishes containing meat, milk and eggs, and we are indeed able to enjoy many delicious meals containing none of these things – for example, while fasting – without feeling like we're making a sacrifice, that we're starving ourselves or we're on a permanent diet. If we pay attention to it, our body will gradually grow accustomed to new textures and colours, and what we eat should be tasty and as varied as possible so as to make up for the lack of animal products. Meat-free foods do not mean only rice, potatoes, vegetable spreads and beans – that is, the typical things we eat while fasting (some of which, especially if we eat a lot of them, will make us fatter rather than slimmer); it also includes a wide range of fruit, vegetables and cereals, which we need to have the patience to discover.

No one can deny that a diet rich in fruit, vegetables and plant-based foods is a good place to start when it comes to adopting a healthy lifestyle. A vegan diet helps to prevent heart disease and diabetes and is recommended as a means to get rid of gallstones and kidney stones and to combat osteoporosis. Of course, opinion is divided when it comes to the vegan diet. Some nutritionists view it as a healthy lifestyle choice that not only prolongs your life, but also helps you avoid many health problems provided you have a balanced diet. Others claim that it requires you to take food supplements, because the vegan diet cannot provide all the substances the body requires and deficiencies can occur as a result that will lead to an imbalance. Others still believe that a vegan diet places strain on the body, which is accustomed to consuming animal origin foods and that depriving it of dairy products and meat endangers our health in the long term. Being a vegan does not automatically mean you will be healthy. For example, many people who give up traditional, meat-based food and other animal origin products will start to feel more tired and hungry and develop protein and iron deficiencies.

The most popular components of a vegan diet are fruit, vegetables, high-starch foods,[8] salad greens, nuts and seeds. This might seem like a short list, but there are so many different types of vegetable and fruit on this earth compared with animal origin products, and it's up to each of us not to limit ourselves to a monotonous menu and to diversify our vegan diets. Anyone looking to go vegan should be prepared to seek out new tastes and combinations, to dare to experiment with what they eat and to check the list of ingredients in the products they buy. For example, whey, rennet and lactose, which are found in many commercial foods, all derive from milk, so they have no place in a vegan diet.

If the principles underpinning this diet are in keeping with your beliefs and you believe they will be useful to you not only in terms of your health, but also as part of a lifestyle, then remember that you will need to plan your meals well in order to ensure you don't lose out on essential nutritional substances or don't end up eating processed vegan foods.

Above all, it's very important to choose products representing all colours of the rainbow in order to make sure we consume all the substances our body needs in order to have energy.

---

[8] Wheat, maize, pasta, beans, rice, lentils and potatoes.

The vegan diet is low in protein, so it is a good idea to prepare your main meals using a number of protein-rich ingredients, such as lentils, quinoa, tempeh, beans, chickpeas and tofu. Recently, I read that in order to function optimally the human body needs 60-70 grams of protein a day for women, and 80-90 grams a day for men.

**Sources of protein in the vegan diet**

| | |
|---|---|
| **Vegetables** | Avocado, broccoli, spinach, cabbage, sweet potatoes, fennel, carrots |
| **Fruit** | Apricots, guava, figs, passion fruit |
| **Pulses** | lentils, soybeans, peas, chickpeas, haricot beans, Fava beans, kidney beans |
| **Nuts and seeds** | Cashew nuts, Brazil nuts, pecan nuts, peanuts, pumpkin seeds, sunflower seeds, flax seeds, pistachios, chia, almonds, sesame seeds |
| **Cereals** | granola, bran, quinoa, millet, brown rice, couscous, sprouted wheat, wholegrain wheat pasta, wild rice, maize |
| **Food Supplements** | spirulina, whey protein, yeast |

I recommend you spice up your vegan meals with some yeast extract, which is not just a tasty supplement, but also a useful source of vitamin B12. As a general rule, you need to consume a spoonful of flax seeds and chia seeds, or two spoons of vegetable oil every day. Plants are a good source of iron, but it's important to enjoy them together with foods rich in vitamin C, which helps with absorption. For example, you can combine lentils, which are rich in iron, with various citric foods or pepper. Vegetables are an excellent source of vitamins (A, C and K), zinc, which keeps the immune system healthy, and potassium.

Omega-3 fatty acids are found in flax seeds, nuts, canola oil and soya, while vitamin D is found in soya and almond milk and fresh orange juice. Some mushrooms which have been exposed to

UV light are also good sources of vitamin D.[9] Vitamin B complex can be obtained by eating wholegrain cereals, such as brown rice and quinoa. Vitamin B12 helps transform food into energy in our bodies, and in the absence of any animal products it can be obtained from cereals and specially made bars. The best thing to do is to seek the advice of a nutritionist, who will be able to give you recommendations based on your medical history.

The vegan diet is low in fat, especially omega-3 fatty acids, which play an important role in brain function, as well as in maintaining the health of the cardiovascular system. If we don't consume enough fat-rich foods, our powers of concentration will fall and our memory will suffer, meaning that the cognitive capacity of the brain will be affected, especially focalisation and clarity. Negative effects will also be felt on the skin. While omega-3 fatty acids are found in abundance in fatty fish, such as salmon, the problem is that, as mentioned earlier, this food is not allowed as part of the vegan diet. However, there are some vegetable-based products that can supply the body with good fats, even if in much smaller quantities.

**Did you know?**

**On average, a vegan weighs 15% less than someone who eats meat.**

[9] According to a study conducted by the Boston University School of Medicine in the US, when exposed to ultraviolet light mushrooms begin to produce large amounts of vitamins. In order to benefit from these properties, mushrooms should be removed from their packaging and exposed to the sun for half an hour before eating.

| Sources of fat in the vegan diet |
|---|
| flax seeds, hemp seeds, pumpkin seeds, sesame seeds and sunflower seeds |
| soya |
| walnuts, almonds, cashews, pistachios |
| olive oil, coconut oil and coconut milk, flax seed and rapeseed oil |
| chia |
| fortified wholegrain cereals and wholegrain bars |
| peanut butter, almond butter |
| avocados, olives |

## The raw vegan diet

I learned a lot about my body from this diet, but I found it really challenging to stick to it. As I love cooking and savouring the smell of food, being on this kind of diet was really hard, especially in winter, when I didn't realise it was also important to provide my body with hot food. Anything *raw* is in fashion nowadays, although the raw vegan diet also has plenty of detractors, many of whom have no knowledge of the principles underlying it. It's also known as the raw food diet, as 60-75% of your food intake should be made up of fresh, whole, unrefined foods in their natural state, such as fruit, vegetables and seeds, with the remaining 25-40% comprising food cooked in the oven, steamed, or cooked in clay pots at temperatures no greater than 40 degrees C.[10] The theory behind this diet is simple: there are no essential nutritional substances in cooked food, nor in food that comes from animals, that aren't also to be found in fruit, vegetables, nuts and seeds in a more easily digestible form. Indeed, there are many essential nutritional substances that can only be found in plants.

[10] Some nutritional specialists claim that cooking at temperatures of over 42 degrees C leads to a loss of the nutritional properties of the food.

As I was saying, I wouldn't recommend this diet in winter, especially after Anda, my nutritionist, spent years trying to convince me that the raw vegan diet is not suitable during the colder months. Why? Because I need to eat warm foods in order for my body to be able to cope with the lower temperatures – although this doesn't mean it wouldn't work in your case. It may sound like a cliché, and I know I keep repeating myself, but speaking to a nutritionist is absolutely essential, so don't put your health at risk. In the raw vegan diet, the nutritional substances and enzymes in food are destroyed if they are cooked at high temperatures, so it's best to choose raw foods instead.

The ingredients in raw vegan recipes are chopped, squeezed, mashed or dried, and, in order to prepare them, blenders, mixers and dehydrators are used. Most people who go on a raw vegan diet are already vegans, i.e. they don't eat any products originating from animals. There are also some vegetarians who eat cheese made from unpasteurised milk but don't cook the food they eat.

According to proponents of raw veganism, the immune system reacts to the introduction of cooked foods to the bloodstream in the same way it does to foreign pathogens, such as bacteria, viruses and fungi. Cooking food alters the proteins, fats and carbohydrates it contains, with the other nutritional substances also being altered or destroyed during the heating process and for the most part resulting in only empty calories. A regular diet of cooked food may lead to dangerous growth of the pancreas. Boiling beans causes fermentation, which produces gases, alcohol and acetic acid. Cooking meat creates an excess of uric acid and ammonia in the body, both of which are toxic. While boiled pasta and rice prepared with no condiments may be insipid, the latter distract our taste buds and stop us from truly savouring the flavours of our food. The same is true of sauces like mustard, ketchup and mayonnaise. Dehydrated food is not a whole food, it has had the water removed from it, so it can never be as good as fresh food, even if the water is replaced. Some nutrients are inevitably destroyed during the process of dehydration and rehydration.

The best vitamins, minerals, antioxidants, phytonutrients, enzymes, coenzymes, fibre, water, protein, carbohydrates and fats come from fruit and vegetables. These are complete nutritional packages and provide our bodies with all the things they need to function correctly. The best way to start a raw vegan diet is to increase the quantity of raw foods we eat, while simultaneously reducing the quantity of cooked foods in our diets. Some foods that are never missing from a raw vegan diet include coconut oil, almonds, almond milk and flour, nuts, goji, hemp, pumpkin and flax seeds, hemp protein powder, chia, spirulina, quinoa milk, rice milk or coconut milk, cocoa butter, coconut, honey, dates and carob.

At first, most people fail to eat enough raw foods in order to obtain the number of calories they need on a daily basis. You need to eat a greater quantity of fruit and vegetables to obtain the same quantity of calories you got prior to going on this diet from cooked foods, because fruit and vegetables are less calorically dense. On the other hand, they contain a considerable amount of water and fibre, as well as other nutritional substances the body requires. Fruit is rich in calories, while vegetables and other plants are not. Consequently, it's best if the largest component of a raw vegan diet, especially in the first stage, is made up of fruit and salads, in order to ensure the necessary mineral intake and a balanced diet. The percentage of raw food consumed depends on each individual and it's not a case of "this is how it should be", but rather "this is what makes me feel best". It's important to understand that food does not cure us; our body is the only thing that can provide a cure. Food, whether boiled or raw, provides the materials the body needs to function.

A raw vegan diet will lead to a decrease in "bad" cholesterol and triglycerides, an increase in the level of vitamin A and beta-carotene, and may have a weight loss effect, especially as raw food, not subjected to heating, is low in calories and fats but rich in fibre. Raw foods are a good source of vitamins, minerals, fibre and phytochemicals, being present in greater quantities than in cooked food. What's more, a diet consisting predominantly of raw food will strengthen the body against infections, ameliorate diabetes, revitalise the body and soothe discomfort caused by arthritis, improve memory function and blood quality, and help prevent heart disease.

What's the ideal percentage of raw food in this diet? It's hard to say and opinion is divided, but many recommend you follow the "80/10/10" rule, i.e. 80% carbohydrates (fruit and vegetables), 10% fats (avocado, coconut oil) and 10% protein (nuts and seeds).

On the other hand, some studies show that, regardless of how many healthy foods are consumed, a raw vegan diet may lead to deficiencies in vitamin B12, protein, calcium and iron, which can result in osteoporosis and a reduction in bone density, anaemia, fatigue, digestive disorders and skin problems, changes in blood pressure, as well as other unpleasant symptoms, especially at the start, during the period of adaptation, when the body is getting used to the new diet. What else should we know? Well, some specialists say that cooking destroys the bacteria found in raw foods and thus lowers the risk of illness, but also that some foods are better eaten cooked than raw, as in the case of tomatoes, carrots and spinach.

| Sources of fat in the raw vegan diet |
| --- |
| flax, hemp, pumpkin, sesame and sunflower seeds |
| soya |
| walnuts, almonds, cashew nuts, pistachios |
| olive oil, coconut oil, flaxseed and rapeseed oil |
| chia |
| peanut butter, almond butter, avocados |
| olives |

**Tip**

**Try using soya milk in your dressings. It goes really well with the raw vegan diet and is a great source of iron.**

**Important!**

**Raw bars, sweets and savouries bought from shops may contain large quantities of "bad" fats and sugar, so read the labels carefully.**

## The vegetarian lifestyle

Giving up meat seemed a really difficult, if not impossible decision for someone like me who has a lot of cravings. At first, I thought there wouldn't be that many alternatives to meat, but I soon discovered a multitude of different delicious and healthy foods. I can remember how it was at the beginning: everyone was telling me I was crazy and that this kind of diet would be bad for me, as the body would not be used to not getting its weekly ration of meat; my mother was worried about me, and my whole family and friends were already in a panic about my getting ill. Despite all this, I didn't doubt my decision for one moment. And when I saw just how many alternative recipes there were, and especially just how good I was feeling, I decided to see how long I could stick at it and what the results would be.

Recently, I've been cooking at home almost every day. I find this relaxes me and helps me put my thoughts in order, as well as keep tabs on what I'm eating. The other day I even found myself craving a salad and I burst out laughing at the thought of someone in the past telling me that one day I would be craving a salad, a lowly salad – I'd probably have refused to believe them. My body is much happier with this lifestyle: my skin is more beautiful than when I used to eat animal products, I have more energy and – God willing! :) – I have less cellulite. I simply feel that my body is cleaner and healthier than when – admittedly not very often – I eat food that comes from an animal.

As I mentioned in earlier chapters, it is not my intention to convince you to become vegetarians or vegans or to go on a macrobiotic diet. It's possible that what's good for me is not good for you too. But what I do want to do is to describe to you how I came to achieve balance and to encourage you to find your own balance, if you haven't done so already.

Above all, you need to feel you want to give up eating animal products, not impose it on yourself, as otherwise you'll almost certainly end up succumbing to temptation. It's not a decision you take overnight – the transition from a normal diet to a vegetarian diet should take place gradually, so you don't feel you're harming yourself and don't feel hungry the whole time. Do you want to have a more balanced diet, a healthier lifestyle and be more concerned for animal welfare? If so, then a vegetarian diet is the right path to follow. If, however, your only concern is how many kilos you can shed and how you're going to achieve this, then the diet best suited to you is not necessarily one involving the elimination of animal origin products, but a series of rules you will need to follow.

**Types of vegetarians**

| | |
|---|---|
| **Lacto vegetarians:** | consume plants and vegetables, milk and other dairy products, but not eggs. |
| **Ovo vegetarians:** | consume plants and vegetables and eggs, but not milk and other dairy products. |
| **Lacto-ovo vegetarians:** | consume plants and vegetables and both eggs and dairy products. |
| **Vegans:** | consume no animal origin products, not even honey. |
| **Raw vegans:** | vegetarians who predominantly consume raw foods but also very small amounts of foods cooked at temperatures below 40 degrees C. |
| **Fruitarians:** | prefer to eat only fruit in combination with oleaginous seeds and chestnuts. |
| **Semi-vegetarians:** | consume plants and vegetables and sometimes fish or white meat. |
| **Flexitarians:** | consume predominantly vegetarian food (90%), but without entirely excluding animal origin foods. This is the category I belong to :). |

A vegetarian diet is really a lifestyle based on healthy eating principles that we should take into account when setting out on this path to be able to enjoy a balanced life. In my opinion, these rules are a matter of common sense and should be respected if we want to be healthy, whether we choose to eat meat or not. Balance and moderation are vital concepts for vegetarians. A change of lifestyle can occur as a result of various factors, from moral and ethical factors relating to the treatment of animals, to religious, health, aesthetic and environmental factors. In my case, switching to a vegetarian diet helped me to discover a multitude of different foods which I found I enjoyed more than meat. It's good to be able to enjoy the food we eat as part of a vegetarian diet, not merely to eat it because we are forcing ourselves to.

Meat should be eliminated gradually, starting with chicken and fish, then, one week later, pork, and, after a further seven days, beef; it is only during the final phase that sea food and other products of animal origin are also eliminated. During this period you should eat as much fruit and vegetables as possible, since these are sources of energy, fibre, vitamins, minerals and antioxidants, as well as carbohydrate-rich foods, such as wholegrain cereals, wholegrain pasta, brown rice, quinoa and sweet potatoes (apart from being healthy, these also make for excellent side dishes to accompany many other vegetarian recipes). It's also important we include vegetables of all colours in what we eat, so to ensure we receive the necessary amount of minerals and vitamins.

Animal protein, which the body is deprived of when we stop eating meat, should gradually be replaced with vegetable protein, e.g. from pulses, nuts, seeds, wholegrain cereals and red lentils. We shouldn't forget to also consume at least two litres of liquids a day and to take a bottle of water with us wherever we go. At home it would be good to invest in a special filter to purify water. Liquids have an important role to play when we switch from one diet to another in that they help us overcome any cravings we might develop.

Dried beans, especially black and red beans, also represent a good replacement for meat because they are rich in fibre and low in fat. Mushrooms also make the list of foods with a texture and consistency similar to cooked meat. Besides, they also have another quality: they are rich in protein and make you feel full for longer.

**Information**

**Brown rice syrup and stevia rebaudiana syrup can be used as substitutes for sugar and honey.**

When we adopt a diet such as this a lot of pressure may be placed on us by the people around us. This is something I have experienced myself, and it can be quite a challenge explaining your decision to others, so have some easy-to-understand explanations on hand and don't be afraid to express your opinion. You will be called different things, from demanding and fussy to pretentious and ungrateful, by those who serve you dishes containing meat, but you know best why you took this decision and they don't have access to your experiences, needs and desires. And, anyway, at the end of the day you don't have to explain yourself.

I should warn you of something. Many vegetarians complain that they end up putting on weight after giving up meat, so you need to be aware of why this is happening. It's possible, for example, that you're eating too much sugar, you have a protein deficiency or you're not drinking enough liquids. Don't replace meat with cheese! A diet based primarily on milk and dairy can be bad for us, as not only is it likely to cause us to put on weight, it will also raise our level of "bad" cholesterol and leave us more predisposed to cardiovascular disease.

To conclude, I would like to share another piece of advice which I've already given via my blog but which is very important: trust your taste buds! The more you limit yourselves to thinking that nothing tastes good without meat and that you're never really going to feel full, the more opportunities you will miss to discover foods that are both healthy and incredibly tasty! I'm telling you this as someone who not only likes to eat but who is also very demanding when it comes to how something tastes. Eating should be a pleasure, not just a necessity, and the best person to provide you with this pleasure is you!

### *The benefits of the vegetarian diet*

- boosts your immune system
- prevents heart disease
- helps maintain weight
- increases longevity
- regulates digestion
- encourages the burning of fat and the elimination of toxins

**Important!**

**A meat-free diet can lead to deficiencies in terms of vitamins (D and B12), minerals (zinc, iron and potassium) and essential fatty acids normally found in fish.**

## The paleo diet

As the name suggests, this diet involves eating the most natural, non-processed and healthiest foods that were available to humans during the Palaeolithic. Again, this is a lifestyle, not a weight loss programme, a means of connecting with our bodies and with nature. This diet goes by a few different names: the Caveman Diet or the Stone Age Diet, which makes me think of the Flintstones cartoons and films :). Jokes aside, this diet has many followers all over the world. There is no individual responsible for inventing this diet, as it is as old as the world itself, but the person who rediscovered and popularised its benefits in our times is Dr Loren Cordain. He believes that the ancient foods – especially fruit and vegetables grown naturally, without fertiliser or other additives that can modify their structure – which our ancestors used to feed themselves are able to reset our metabolism and make us more resistant to modern-day diseases.

The basic idea is to introduce as much variety as possible into our cooking, making use of all the things nature provides us with, such as seasonal vegetables (baked, steamed or grilled), fruits, green leaves, fish and sea food, eggs, seeds and "good" fats. Where possible, it's recommended we spend as much time in nature as possible, that we enjoy eating outdoors and that we find time for things that bring us into harmony with the outside world, as well as with our thoughts and emotions.

Not everyone will be able to fully adopt this diet, especially as it requires us to eliminate the use of oil in our cooking, such as sunflower, soybean and rapeseed oil, as these polyunsaturated fatty acids are thought to be the cause of many health conditions like heart disease, diabetes, arthritis, osteoporosis and cancer. What can we replace them with? Well, according to firm believers in this lifestyle, we should use extra virgin olive oil, coconut oil, avocado oil, oil extracted from oleaginous fruits (with the exception of peanuts) and fish oil.

The Palaeolithic diet encourages the elimination from our diet of two of the four food groups, i.e. cereals (especially bread) and dairy products, because, among other things, these cause bloating and irritable bowel syndrome. It belongs to the group of low-carb diets. In order to avoid feeling frustrated, we should allow ourselves two or three meals a week in which we eat things we're not normally allowed, especially at first, but it's recommended to eat only small quantities of any "forbidden" foods, so as to avoid a sudden transition. In summary, the things we're not allowed on a paleo diet include milk, cereals, pulses, potatoes, salt, and processed foods in general.

There are no restrictions in terms of the number of calories consumed, but it's important that the source of our food is as natural as possible. For example, meat, if we still eat it, should come from an animal that has been fed on grass, not cereals, because the latter affects the quality of the end product. The same rule applies to fish, so it's best to choose wild fish over farmed fish. In order to achieve balance, it's essential always to maintain the same proportions of food on our plates: 60% vegetables, 15% fruit, 20% meat and 5% eggs, vegetable oils and nuts.

When researching a diet, I look at the benefits it provides as well as any criticism. With the paleo diet, you will lose a lot of kilos, especially during the first six months, and your state of health will improve if you adhere to the basic rules. However, this kind of diet, if it's not balanced, can lead to malnutrition, gallstones and digestive disorders. There are no studies showing that eliminating cereals and pulses is actually beneficial, so we need to be extra careful not to end up going on yet another diet, losing lots of weight and then returning to our normal eating habits and duly putting more weight back on than we lost in the first place. And there's one more thing to be aware of. In order to have a diet like those who lived during the Palaeolithic we ought really to have access to the same environment as back then, to the same activities and other things that formed part of a healthy lifestyle during that period. So, what the paleo diet is criticised for is that it does not take into account the way humans have evolved in the meantime. On the other hand, it does no harm to be more aware of the types of food we eat and, especially, to eat heavier foods in the morning and those easier to digest in the evenings. You should weigh up the advantages and disadvantages and always try to have a balanced lifestyle.

**Important!**

**In the paleo diet you are not allowed to eat packaged and processed foods, as these contain additives, preservatives, salt and sugar, which have a negative effect on your weight and, more importantly, promote a lack of balance in your body.**

## The flexitarian diet

I have noticed how the vegetarian diet is very often viewed with suspicion. One question I'm often asked is this: "Come on, how delicious can a meal of only vegetables really be?!" Well, I want you to know something: I am very happy with what I eat and I really don't deny myself anything, because I have decided to always allow myself the things I like! And, although it may not seem like it, I really enjoy cooking and eating in general! There's an enormous variety of meat-free recipes out there, we only need the courage to try them. There's no need to stick religiously to certain recipes, you can improvise something instead as dictated by your imaginations and taste buds. It's like when we are standing there in front of our wardrobes packed with different clothes and we complain – like the true fashion victims we are – that we've got nothing to wear. If we allow ourselves to be creative and show a little courage then we'll end up making some really great food – although we still need to be careful how we combine different foodstuffs and what quantities we eat, as otherwise our clothes won't fit us anymore :). And it's very important we do our research and test out as many different combinations as possible. Our food tastes best when we start to learn and experiment, I can tell you this from my own experience! Still, if you feel you're missing lots of things and placing too much stress on your body by following a vegetarian diet, then there's another option to consider: it's called flexitarianism[11] or, as I prefer to call it, a part-time vegetarian diet.

Created by the nutritionist and dietician Dawn Jackson Blatner, the flexitarian diet is not a clearly defined, strict or calorie-restrictive eating plan. Instead it encourages the consumption of plant-based foods while reducing the consumption of meat as much as possible, especially red meat, which has a lot of fat and has an adverse effect on weight and health. According to proponents of the flexitarian diet, there is a direct link between salt and the chemical substances found in processed meats and cardiovascular disease and cancer, so these should be excluded as far as possible from any meal. The idea is to concentrate more on protein derived from vegetable sources rather than from animal products, and not just because it is healthier, but because in doing so we will feel fuller for longer and no longer be tempted to eat large quantities.

If you want, you can look at it as being a healthy lifestyle that also helps you shed any excess kilos. It's a diet we are able to control ourselves, depending on our needs and wishes, but which also contains as many products as possible that are primarily intended to help us to be healthy and only then to achieve our desired figure. If you'd like to try such a personalised programme, then it's important you discuss it first with a nutritionist, who will help you design your meals and set clear, realistic goals that will motivate you to lose any excess weight in a natural and stress-free way. The semi-vegetarian diet is also effective in terms of preventing diseases related to poor nutrition, such as diabetes, cardiovascular diseases and excess weight.

---

[11] A portmanteau of two words: flexible and vegetarian.

The flexitarian diet is suitable for people who don't want to commit fully to a vegetarian or vegan lifestyle. It allows us to adapt what we eat to suit our lifestyles, social lives and health conditions. I like to call it the "compromise and personal choice" diet. What foods are best? Broccoli, spinach, lettuce, carrots, sweet potatoes, pumpkin, dried beans, lentils, soya, onion, mushrooms, tomatoes, peas, potatoes, maize, eggs and fish. The first thing we have to do is to reduce our consumption of meat by half and to replace it with vegetable protein: tofu, lentils, chickpeas, peas, oleaginous vegetables and fruit. Similarly, it's best to introduce some variety to our diets in the form of wholegrain cereals (brown rice, oats, buckwheat, rye, quinoa, amaranth and millet) eaten together with a variety of different dairy products (i.e. skimmed milk, yoghurt, fermented milk or kefir). You are allowed to eat homemade sweets containing honey, agave syrup, maple syrup and agave nectar, as well as to use condiments and aromatic herbs that give flavour to your food, e.g. dill, parsley, basil, mint, garlic and ginger.

There are many arguments for and against the flexitarian diet: it is less risky than the vegetarian diet in that there is no increased risk of vitamin and mineral deficiency as the occasional consumption of meat and animal-origin products is permitted. It is also less frustrating than other weight loss plans and the health benefits are worth taking note of. On the other hand, being a personalised plan, there is a risk you will lose motivation, so it's good to have a few clear goals in mind to guide you. It is very important to choose healthy sources of food and to test as many fruit- and vegetable-based recipes as possible, which will help you reach your desired weight and prevent the onset of certain diseases. I try as best I can to follow the basic rules of the flexitarian diet and I declare myself happy with the results. Indeed, this is how I managed to achieve balance and to maintain my figure without starving myself or ending up feeling frustrated with what I was eating.

**Information**

**If you're finding it hard deciding how big your portions should be, then remember that the flexitarian diet is basically a 3-4-5 type of diet: breakfast should contain an average of 500 calories, lunch 400 calories and supper around 300 calories. Add to this a couple of snacks, at 150 calories each, and we arrive at a total of 1,500 calories.**

# 4

# Essential superfoods for a healthy lifestyle

*Why torture your body and risk harming it just to be a certain size, when you can choose your own size of healthy food instead?*

The first piece of advice I give to those who ask me whether they should become vegetarian or vegan is to make their decision based on how they feel and what their needs are, not what happens to be in fashion at that moment. For this reason I tell everyone to look for substitutes for animal products, so they will continue to get the necessary nutritional substances and that no imbalance is created in their bodies. Our bodies need to be in a state of perfect balance if we are to be healthy, feel good and be full of energy. It took me some time to learn all these things; I did some research, I read up on it, I consulted nutritionists and I found out why this balance is important and what I needed to do to obtain, and, more importantly, maintain it. In terms of my own lifestyle, the type of foods I consume are very important, because they need to serve as substitutes for animal derived products alongside any food supplements.

Not only do superfoods give us energy, like all other foods, they are also a rich source of the substances that help boost our physical and intellectual performance, they can heal certain illnesses and are a real treasure trove in the kitchen. They contain high concentrations of vitamins, minerals, enzymes, amino acids and antioxidants. Unlike ordinary healthy foods, which are normally known to have two or three nutritional properties, superfoods each have a minimum of ten. Every day I try to consume at least one type of food rich in such special properties, and so superfoods are always on my shopping list. I don't force myself to eat them; I have selected the ones I find the tastiest and have tested various absolutely delicious recipes using them. I'm now going to tell you what my favourite superfoods are, and while you can use my list as inspiration, I encourage you to discover for yourselves other superfoods that help you to live a balanced life.

## Vegetables

### *Broccoli*

This is one of my favourite vegetables. I'm a big fan of Chinese broccoli, which is a source of vitamins A, C and K, as well as folic acid, fibre, potassium and manganese. Besides its anti-cancer properties, a small portion of broccoli provides you with the entire amount of vitamin C required by an adult each day.

### *Sprouts*

These contain more nutritional substances than mature plants, in particular protein, but also vitamin A, vitamin B complex, vitamin C complex and vitamin E complex. They reduce acidity in the body, which is responsible for the appearance of diseases, and are ideal in vegetarian or vegan diets.

### *Wheatgrass*

I eat this mainly when I'm feeling low on energy. A shot of wheatgrass juice provides me with the perfect solution when I'm feeling really tired, especially as it is rich in chlorophyll, vitamin K, vitamin C, folic acid, iron, calcium and protein. Chlorophyll molecules are similar to those found in our blood and aid cell regeneration.

### *Okra*

I love it! I even have some in the fridge right now – my kitchen is never without some okra. I know not everyone eats this, but I've been eating it since I was little and I just adore it, especially when eaten young. It is also an important source of vitamins A, B6, C and K, folic acid, magnesium, copper, potassium, as well as antioxidants. And the good news is that it doesn't lose its properties through cooking.

### *Algae*

These absorb minerals from the seas and oceans, making them both healthy and tasty. There are different types of algae, with *dulse*, *nori* and *wakame* among the best known and also being considered superfoods and the food of the future. They contain few calories and are rich in vitamin B complex, as well as potassium, iron, omega-3 fatty acids, magnesium, chrome and fibre. You can substitute algae for lettuce, but you can also use them in soup or other delicious recipes.

## Pulses

### *Chickpeas*

Just thinking about hummus and falafel makes me hungry. This superfood is rich in vitamins B6 and K, folic acid, fibre, protein, manganese, magnesium, iron, copper, zinc, selenium and potassium.

### *Lentils*

This is one of the most important sources of vegetable protein, thus making it ideal for a vegetarian diet. A single portion of lentils provides over 40% of our daily iron requirements. I like to eat lentil soup, as well as sautéed red lentils.

## Fruit

### *Lemons and limes*

I love drinking tea, especially in winter, and to put some lemon in it. I have a recipe for tea that I always enjoy making and drink with great gusto. It contains ginger, lemon, turmeric powder and pepper. It warms my body and helps me cope with the cold. What's more, lemon is rich in vitamin C and fibre and can be used as a dressing for salads or in refreshing lemonade in summer. Green lemons or limes are also rich in vitamin C and fibre. Lime juice combined with olive oil and some spices is perfect in any fresh salad.

### *Dates*

These are perfect as snacks, especially as they are a substitute for sugar, which I eat only very rarely. They are a delicious ingredient in muffins, biscuits, cakes and brownies. They contain potassium, copper, manganese, fibre, vitamin B6 and calcium. They retain their nutritional properties when cooked.

### *Noni*

Apart from having a bitter taste and a powerful smell, noni reduces the risk of liver lesions, soothes pain and reduces inflammation. It is a good source of vitamin C, zinc and antioxidants. Noni juice is delicious and beneficial to health.

### *Avocados*

This fruit staves off hunger better than any other and is my favourite choice of food when I don't have time for a proper breakfast. I put it in the blender and make a quick smoothie with whatever I find in the fridge. I also love guacamole, which I eat on endive leaves, and salads containing avocados. Avocados abound in vitamins and minerals, folic acid, fibre, magnesium, potassium, iron and zinc. Avocados are one of the best sources of healthy fats, containing around 70% monosaturated fats. They give you a rapid feeling of satiety and help prevent heart disease and eye and skin infections.

### *Goji*

This is the fruit with the highest concentration of antioxidants. It strengthens the immune system, boosts the body's energy levels and helps maintain good health. Add some dried goji berries to cereal based foods, oven cooked dishes and other recipes. A fistful of goji berries (10-30 grams) provides the required daily dose of vitamins.

### *Forest fruits*

These, whether fresh or frozen, are never absent from my kitchen. I enjoy them in desserts as well as all kinds of other delicious recipes. They are full of antioxidants, vitamins A, B and E, copper, selenium, zinc, iron and many other elements. They stimulate the immune system, prevent infection and give us energy.

### *Pomegranates*

Pomegranates are an important source of folic acid, potassium manganese and vitamins B6 and E. Their juice is rich in antioxidants and nutritional substances. I consume them as they are, fresh, but also in cooking, when making sauces or other oven dishes. 100 grams of their fruit contains only 83 calories, so pomegranates are excellent for when you want to lose weight. What's more, they don't contain any cholesterol or saturated fats.

### *Bananas*

I eat bananas instead of snacks or use them in various breakfast dishes as they are very filling. They improve digestion, help the body combat depressive states, and protect us against insomnia and sudden mood swings.

## Nuts, seeds and oils

### *Sunflower seeds*

I eat almonds and hydrated sunflower seeds for breakfast or instead of snacks. The latter are rich in vitamins B6 and E, potassium, phosphorus, copper, magnesium and iron. They reduce cholesterol and prevent heart disease. I like to eat them as they are but also as part of various vegetable-based recipes, oven-cooked dishes and salads.

### *Flax seeds*

These are delicious in smoothies, but also as substitutes for fat in oven-cooked dishes. They contain fibre, protein, calcium, potassium, iron, zinc and selenium. The omega-3 fatty acids they contain reduces the level of "bad" cholesterol. They can be eaten by diabetics because they regulate the level of blood sugar.

### *Chia seeds*

I add these to all kinds of food, from smoothies to salads and even vegan desserts. They contain 60% omega-3 fatty acids and therefore are able to reduce inflammation and improve digestion. They are filling, gluten-free and can be used as a replacement for eggs in mayonnaise.

### *Olive oil*

When cooking I only use coconut or cold-pressed olive oil. The latter protects against heart disease and aids weight loss. It is a good source of vitamins E and K, as well as of good fats. I really like the way it tastes in salads.

### *Coconut oil*

This is a particularly nutritious food and an obligatory component of any vegetarian or vegan diet. I like the way it's resistant to high temperatures and doesn't easily oxidise. I use it to make cakes, nutritional bars, energy drinks, salads and other delicious foods. Used in shakes, it increases the body's absorption of vitamins and proteins.

### *Almonds*

Take a look inside my car or my bag and you'll be sure to find some almonds. I always make sure I have some of these superfoods with me. Apart from the fact that I love the way they taste, almonds are perfect for eating between meals, especially because they're rich in vitamin E, fibre, protein, phosphorus, copper, magnesium, calcium, potassium, iron and zinc. Almond flour is also a good substitute for wheat flour.

## Herbs and spices

### *Ginger*

I always keep some ginger in my fridge. I use it in various recipes, such as vegetable stews, as well as all kinds of detoxifying teas. It's a remedy against colds, helps burn fat, stimulates the immune system and acts as an energiser for the body.

### *Turmeric*

I use this condiment a lot in the kitchen. It has anti-inflammatory and anti-cancer properties. It contains protein, fibre, vitamins C, E and K, as well as antioxidants. It's a good ingredient to use in sauces, on fish or vegetables, in smoothies or in various teas.

## Cereals

### *Quinoa*

What I like a lot about quinoa is that it helps me to feel full quicker, so I no longer feel the need to eat something sweet afterwards. It is one of the best sources of vegetable protein and contains all the amino acids the body needs. I simply love quinoa pudding in its various different combinations!

## Animal products

### *Wild salmon*

I like to eat this raw, as part of a fresh green salad, as well as smoked. It provides the body with vitamins B6, B12 and E, selenium, phosphorus, vitamin C, potassium and magnesium. It is an excellent source of omega-3 fatty acids, which help prevent heart disease.

## Natural supplements

### *Eggs*

I always choose organic eggs, which only come from free-range chickens fed on healthy food. They are an excellent source of protein as well as being one of the few natural sources of vitamin D. It's best to eat them boiled (never fried) for breakfast or lunch.

### *Spirulina*

This originates from a blueish-green type of algae and contains all three compounds required by the body (chlorophyll, enzymes and vitamins, especially vitamin B complex) as well as calcium, chrome, iron, copper, magnesium, phosphorus, zinc, and potassium. Almost 60% of the weight of dried spirulina is protein, which is more than is found in any other plant source. It helps maintain the balance between acid and alkaline in the body, which stops minerals being eliminated from the body too quickly and contributes to fat burning. It can be combined with water, fresh fruit juices, smoothies, yoghurt and soups.

### *Maca powder*

This has energising properties and contains vitamins, especially from the B group, i.e. B1, B2 and B12 (which give us energy), vitamins E and C, amino acids and minerals (calcium, iron, magnesium, zinc and phosphorus). I always add this natural supplement to smoothies, juices, protein drinks, tea, soup and healthy desserts.

### *Baobab powder*

This has a sour taste and yellowish colour, but also a set of complex aromas – an interesting combination of caramel, pear, vanilla and bitter citruses. I use it in tea, smoothies and sugar-free lemonade. It helps me to have more energy, regulates digestion and boosts iron absorption.

### *Coconut water*

This is a sweet drink with a gentle nutty taste that also contains many vitamins, minerals, sugars and enzymes. A natural energiser, coconut water should not be mistaken for coconut milk, which is rich in calories. Nutritional specialists recommend it as part of weight loss diets because it regulates digestion and speeds up fat burning.

# 5

# Things you'll always find in my kitchen

*"Efficiency is the foundation for survival."*

– JOHN C. MAXWELL

Has it ever felt like you're living inside a pressure cooker? That before long you'll explode because you have so many things to do? If the answer is yes, then, join the club! We want to do so much, however, paradoxically, there's never any time left to do anything! I've often asked myself how someone who lives on autopilot (as I do sometimes, too) can live a healthy life. What must they do in order to feed themselves correctly and not end up in a state of exhaustion? (Because that's precisely where we'll end up if we keep up this pace.) We need resources, nutritious substances, vitamins, minerals and protein. As well as no longer operating at full speed, while also trying to organise my life in a way that would allow me to eliminate any excesses and stop abusing my body, I have discovered foods and devices that help me to eat as healthfully as possible. So, apart from furniture, stories and all kinds of amusing memories, my kitchen is packed with all manner of different products that help me stay in shape.

Did I already tell you I'm a big fan of smoothies? Well, as these can be made quickly and consumed just as quickly, I've developed a real passion for them. I think I must have tested out everything there is when it comes to smoothies, not just unusual combinations of ingredients, but also different machines meant to make it easier to make them: juicers, blenders, mixers, nutrient extractors, etc. High speed, low speed, extraction systems based on centrifuges, squeezing and dicing, I've tried them all! I invested a lot in this, even foregoing other pleasures in the process, but I'm happy I did it. I should also tell you that my kitchen is a paradise for those interested in healthy lifestyles, as there's nothing it doesn't contain – there's food supplements and superfoods of every possible kinds. There's a couple of different places where some of my friends always check, especially after I come back from abroad, as they know that's where I keep all my "goodies".

## Things NEVER missing from my kitchen

- **Food supplements:** fish oil, DHA, coenzyme Q10, Ginkgo biloba, marine collagen, spirulina, brewer's nutritional yeast flakes (which contain vitamin B12 and can be used instead of parmesan), magnesium and vitamins A, B, C, D and E
- **Seeds:** sunflower, almonds, pumpkin, hemp, pistachio, sesame, chia
- **Nuts and oils:** walnuts, almonds, coconut oil, extra virgin olive oil, almond oil
- **Plant milk:** quinoa, almond, rice, coconut
- **Sugar substitutes:** brown rice syrup, stevia rebaudiana
- **Fruit:** avocados, bananas, apples (I regularly make baked apples, especially in winter, I just love them!), frozen fruit, pomegranates, raisins, citruses, mangos, pineapple, forest

fruits, plums, apricots. Wherever possible, I opt for seasonal fruits

- **Vegetables:** broccoli, various types of mushroom, chickpeas, garlic, endives,[12] sweet potatoes, asparagus,[13] aubergines, peppers, tomatoes, pumpkins,[14] cucumbers
- **Pulses:** peas,[15] beans
- **Cereals:** gluten-free bread, quinoa, gluten-free wholemeal pasta
- **Condiments and spices:** coriander, cardamom, pepper, turmeric, Himalayan salt, curry, ginger, cinnamon, pepper
- Green tea
- **Herbs:** rosemary, parsley, basil, oregano
- Protein bars
- **Animal origin products:** eggs, fish, goats cheese, honey and sea food

---

[12] I've been eating these since I was a child and I adore them. I eat them in salads with a dressing of olive oil, apple cider vinegar and salt.

[13] I like to cook asparagus in the oven together with other vegetables or with tamari and garlic in a pan.

[14] I like pumpkins in every form: in soup, in a pie, in the oven or diced for use in different dishes.

[15] Peas are one of my favourite vegetables. Every time I'd visit my friends in Iaşi they'd ask what I'd like to eat. And my answer was always peas, so much so that they even gave me the nickname of Bonduelle :). Peas with dill is simply delicious!

# 6

## The best food supplements

*Stop for a moment and ask yourself if you really need the thing you're about to buy.*

As I write these lines, it feels as if different episodes of my life are passing before my eyes, which is a wonderful but also unsettling experience. It's like getting to know myself all over again or like talking to a friend with whom just opening up in this way is helping me to see myself clearly, to accept myself, to forgive myself, to love myself. When you put parts of your life down on paper it feels liberating, but it's also funny. It's complicated and beautiful, not least because it relates directly to the way I tested out different diets and nutritional regimes. A common denominator during my journey through different weight loss diets, even where these were healthy diets, is that I felt drained of energy. This is somehow to be expected. Besides eliminating various foods from our diets, we are also living in a world that seems to be running on fast-forward. We try to do everything and to please everyone, but then there's almost nothing left for us.

The time and energy we devote to ourselves is very important, especially if we want to make changes to our lifestyles and diet. In order to have more energy, it's good to add food supplements to our diets; these will give us the boost we need. After realising their importance, my life really changed for the better. I understood that a lack of nutritional substances needs to be balanced out with the aid of supplements and certain foods rich in vitamins and minerals known as superfoods. The way I was brought up, i.e. to take some medicine when I wasn't feeling well, even if I was only feeling tired, is not good for our health. Food supplements, on the other hand, are a much better choice. I also learned that when I take supplements I need to be patient, because the effects are not felt immediately, as they are with pills, but they are substantial and occur naturally.

When I discovered food supplements there were only very few options available here in Romania, so I could hardly wait to travel abroad. In America they already had shelves full of bio products containing only these kinds of ingredients, there were food supplements for every need. I was always impatient to buy everything there was and to create my own little stockpile. I remember how, besides cosmetic products, my luggage would always contain lots of food supplements. I can't imagine what the people checking my bags at the airport must have thought when they saw so many supplements. Fortunately, there were many different kinds of supplements in there, so they would have had no reason to suspect me of smuggling! I'm only joking, it was never that bad, but I guess you get the idea. The temptation, given I only rarely got to travel across the pond, was to build up a stockpile, which was why I bought so much. The real mistake was that I had a tendency to consume them all at once. But I soon realised that taking so many together is like giving a computer ten different commands to execute at the same time. The result is that it will freeze. I realised that you need to differentiate between normal and essential supplements and, above all, I learned that these products should be taken in certain combinations.

However, perhaps most important of all, I had tests done to find out what things my body was lacking and this told me which supplements I really needed to take. It was Cristina Bogdan, a general practitioner who has specialised in acupuncture and homeopathy and a dear friend of mine, who told me it wasn't good to take the same supplements as those around me or to try out everything that was new on the market. She also told me there was no point taking a fistful of supplements every morning and that I should instead focus strictly on products designed specifically to provide my body with what it needs.

I have to be honest and to tell you that I have a whole drawer full of supplements at home. When friends come over and open this drawer, they become concerned and ask me: "My God, what's all this? Are you sick?" Well, these are the supplements I have acquired over time but which I don't use all at the same time. I take them for a while, followed by a break, then take some others, etc. That said, there are some supplements I almost always have at home and which help me to cope with busy days and stressful moments. My advice is to ask your doctor whether these things will be of any help to you, and not to take them just to follow my example. As I've already made clear, everyone's body is different and what works for me might have no effect on you. Or, perhaps worse, it could even be bad for you.

## Coenzyme Q10

This regulates the chemical reactions that take place when we digest food as well as its transformation into energy. It is present in every human cell and as a source of energy it promotes the proper functioning of the immune system, slows the ageing process and helps with skin regeneration. It's very important that there's no drop in the level of Q10 in our bodies, and to prevent this from happening I take supplements containing this substance of such importance to the body every day – first in the morning and again in the evening after meals.

## Omega-3 and omega-6 fatty acids

Every cell in our bodies contains omega-3, omega-6 and omega-9 fatty acids, and because the first two of these cannot be synthesised by our bodies we either need to eat foods that contain them or to take food supplements. In order to receive the necessary amount of omega-3 fatty acids, we need to consume walnut oil, mackerel, herring, salmon or sardines, while when it comes to omega-6 our diets should include grapeseed oil, sunflower oil, walnut oil and rapeseed oil. Unlike omega-3 and omega-6, omega-9 fatty acids are produced by the body, but it is still beneficial to consume them via food, e.g. from sunflower oil, olive oil, avocado oil, almond oil, Macadamia oil, pistachio oil and Pecan oil.

Care should be taken when it comes to omega-6 because if consumed in large quantities it can be harmful to the body and makes it liable to various kinds of inflammation. In fact, in order for there to be a balance in our bodies, our diets should contain one part omega-3 essential fatty acids to two or maximum four parts omega-6 fatty acids. Otherwise, there will be an increased risk of high cholesterol, depression, heart disease, diabetes and obesity.

Of the omega-3 type fatty acids, DHA is the most abundant in the human brain and is to be found especially in saltwater fish. The level of DHA depends on age, being at its greatest in our younger years and falling as we grow older. Supplements containing fish oil reduce the amount of lipids in the blood, such as cholesterol and triglycerides, helping us maintain a healthy balance between so-called good and bad cholesterol. They also boost the immune system, destroy free radicals and transform bad fat cells into good fat cells, which burn calories and therefore help prevent weight gain and obesity. I always have some DHA supplements at home and I take them frequently, especially at stressful times.

**Remember!**

**A healthy balance of omega-3 and omega-6 essential fatty acids can be maintained with the help of food supplements containing fish oil.**

**Important!**

**Hemp oil has a good balance of omega 3 and omega 6 because it contains one part omega-3 fatty acids to two parts omega-6 fatty acids.**

## Turmeric extract

Supplements containing turmeric extract eliminate stress and anxiety, energise us, help us to be more full of life and protect the brain from ageing. Curcumin, a bioactive compound found in turmeric, is responsible, in a good way, for all of these beneficial effects, but it also helps a lot in the prevention and treatment of abnormal states involving inflammation inside the body. What's more, it reduces bad cholesterol, thus preventing the blood from clotting and blocking the arteries. Turmeric extract improves memory function and the ability to concentrate by increasing blood flow to the brain, and for this reason daily consumption is recommended.

## Vitamin A

A lot has been written about how vitamin A is good for the skin in that it regenerates tissues and therefore delays ageing of the skin and the appearance of wrinkles. But its benefits don't stop there. It has an antioxidant effect and helps the body combat the effects of free radicals, meaning it stimulates the immune system, thus protecting us from bacterial, viral and fungal infections. Vitamin A deficiency leads to a difficulty in distinguishing between light and dark and increases the risk of infertility and various types of skin disease, which is why we need to consume vitamin A, whether from food or food supplements. Vitamin A is found in foods like sweet potatoes, carrots, apricots, cantaloupes, fish, eggs, tropical fruit and lettuce.

**Important!**

**The daily dose of vitamin A should not exceed 700 micrograms for a woman and 900 micrograms for a man.**

## Vitamin B complex

Vitamin B complex is essential for health, especially as it eliminates feelings of tiredness, regulates the metabolism and contributes to tissue repair. Thiamine (vitamin B1), niacin (vitamin B3) and vitamin B6 regulate appetite, so they are recommended in the case of weight loss programmes, as well as vegetarian and vegan diets. On the recommendation of Cristina Bogdan, who, as already mentioned, advises me in these matters, I always keep some B12 supplements at home, because this vitamin is not found in large quantities except in animal products, i.e. chicken, pork, beef, liver, kidney, sea food, tuna, salmon, eggs, milk and cheese. And as I don't eat a lot of those things, there's an increased risk of certain health issues, such as anaemia. Besides B12 supplements, you can also add to your fresh fruit juice and smoothies a certain substance containing large quantities of vitamin B12, namely inactive yeast. Similarly, you should also eat unpasteurised miso and tempeh, as these also contain vitamin B12.

### *Symptoms of vitamin B12 deficiency*

- chest pain, palpitations, dizziness, constipation
- excessive tiredness without exerting any effort which places a strain on the body
- lack of appetite
- sudden weight loss
- pale complexion

**Information**

**The daily amount of vitamin B12 required is 2.4 micrograms for both men and women.**

**Did you know?**

**Sauerkraut is one of the few foods that does not come from an animal but which does contain vitamin B12.**

## Vitamin C

Vitamin C boosts the level of serotonin, which, while known as the happiness hormone, also has a powerful antioxidant effect. Especially during the season of colds and flu, vitamin C boosts the body's natural defences against all kinds of infections, helps clear the respiratory tract and ameliorates the symptoms of asthma. What's more, vitamin C supplements improve blood circulation and help regulate blood pressure. I also use it externally to care for my skin and stimulate the production of collagen, especially as vitamin C helps me get rid of dark spots.[16]

**Information**

**The recommended daily dose of vitamin C for adults is 75-90 milligrams.**

**Tip**

**Vitamin C supplements improve the body's ability to absorb other vitamins and minerals from food, which can speed up our metabolism.**

## Vitamin D

Animal products contain large quantities of vitamin D, so vegetarians risk developing a deficiency if they don't take supplements. As I've already mentioned, I only very rarely eat meat and animal-derived products, so I need to supplement

[16] I will look at this subject in more detail in the second part of the book, where I describe my beauty routine.

this vitamin. Those who are 100% vegetarian can take vitamin D12 supplements, as these are derived from vegetables. Other sources of vitamin D include mushrooms, tofu, as well as simple exposure to the sun when it's really hot, although not during peak sunlight hours, when we might burn. A low level of vitamin D is associated with low levels of leptin, a hormone that suppresses appetite, which would explain why many vegetarians complain of always feeling hungry and end up putting on weight after giving up animal products. Vitamin D also helps the body to absorb minerals, to boost the body's resistance to infection, to increase muscle mass and to regulate the amount of hormones in cases of sterility, heart disease and depression.

### Vitamin E

While this is normally found in walnuts, almonds, avocados and various vegetable, the greatest quantities are still obtained from animal products. This vitamin plays an essential role in maintaining the normal functioning of our metabolism: if the body develops a deficiency of tocopherol (as this vitamin is also called), this will lead to an increased appetite for unhealthy fats. Vitamin E deficiency also causes tiredness, eye diseases, dark spots, heart disease, lack of concentration and many other problems. Vitamin E supplements are particularly recommended for those with skin problems, as well as those who intend to become parents.

# 7

# Tips for when we eat out and our choices are limited

*Eating should be a pleasure, not just a necessity!*

I've always encouraged those around me to enjoy their food. Even those who are always on a diet or have given up certain foods and are trying to avoid temptation. It's a shame not to take advantage when we go out and to enjoy, if only every now and then, a different kind of meal containing things we're not good at making at home or wouldn't normally cook ourselves. I like discovering new flavours, especially different combinations of exotic foods. As I already told you, I'm a very curious person and really like experimenting with food. When it comes to eating at a restaurant, it's important not to panic when we see there's nothing on the menu we can eat as part of our diet. When this happens, my solution is to opt for the lesser evil and try to strike a compromise. After all, the whole idea is to go out and have a good time. No matter how delicious I might find quinoa, I can't always stay home and eat it all by myself.

Of course, the first thing we can do in these situations is to try to convince our friends to choose restaurants where the menu contains things we like and that are allowed on our diets. When eventually – as is the case with my friends :) – they grow bored of going to the same two or three places I tend to go to, then I have a few tricks up my sleeve. I try bringing them to newly opened restaurants; a number of new restaurants serving vegetarian and raw food have begun to spring up in Bucharest, which increases the chances of my finding something I might want to eat there. But in the end, it's still sometimes necessary to compromise and to go to places where they serve things that are not normally on my list. But it's not the end of the world! Naturally, not everywhere I go do I find gluten-free pasta, wild fish or other favourites. Even so, as best I can, I refrain from ordering fatty foods, which always make me feel sick afterwards, and instead I look for alternatives: vegetables, preferably boiled or pan-fried, sea food or rice, if it's a lunch and not a dinner, or light soups. There are some places where they cook right in front of you, and so I always ask them if they can prepare something I choose or if I can change the recipe here and there… in all the essential parts :). If you're prepared to discuss and to ask politely, a solution will always be found. So I ask how the dish I intend to order is prepared, whether I can change something about it (for example, grilled instead of fried fish), what side dish it comes with and whether this can be changed for vegetables, how big the portions are, if they can be reduced, and so on and so forth.

If I go out to eat in a large group of friends, then I ask the people sitting to the left and right of me what they're having, because I tend to get a lot of cravings – my friends will know what I mean :-); and if I think I'm going to crave what they've ordered, then I ask them to let me try it, so I don't feel frustrated, and that way I avoid ordering a whole portion for myself. Generally speaking, starters come in smaller portions and you will also find some healthy options: sea-food, guacamole, bruschetta, etc. Add in a salad, preferably with lots of lemon juice, which aids digestion, and a soup, and you're in for a culinary treat.

If you've gone ahead and ordered a heavier meal, be aware that restaurants tend to serve pretty large portions (two to three times more than we need). My advice is not to eat everything on your plate. You could also share a single portion with someone else at the table, take any leftovers home with you, or simply leave them there! It's important we eat until we're full, not until we physically can't eat anymore. According to nutritionists, the recommended portion size is as much as fits into a fist. And if you still find yourself eating unhealthy foods, then make sure to drink some water, not fizzy drinks or alcohol, during your meal. And afterwards, try to skip dessert or, if you really want some, eat only very little, enough not to leave you feeling frustrated.

In recent years I've all but stopped eating after 8 pm because 80% of the food we eat after this time is deposited in the form of fat. On the other hand, 80% of the food we eat in the morning is burnt, which is why I always recommend eating a large breakfast. After 8 pm, our digestion gradually slows down, allowing the processes of detoxification, processing and assimilation of what we've eaten during the day to take place. Our stomach needs a break of 12-14 hours between our evening meal and breakfast in order to recover and rest. I don't know about you, but I always wake up with swollen hands if I have a late meal and, what's more, my digestion slows down and it takes me some time to re-establish a balance.

**Good to know!**

**It's good to leave the table feeling slightly hungry. This feeling will soon disappear as the stomach starts to do its job and begins digesting what you've just eaten.**

## Foods to avoid, wherever possible, in the evening

- fried food
- chicken, beef and pork
- sauces – mayonnaise, garlic sauce and ketchup are high in calories (if you can't stop yourself then it's best to ask for a natural tomato sauce)
- white bread
- fizzy drinks
- lemonade sweetened with sugar
- sweets[17]

If you choose to eat at a restaurant with an international menu, then your chances of finding something lighter and just as tasty to eat as local food will be greater. My favourite places are Japanese restaurants, because I always find something to eat there: sushi, mushrooms, vegetables, soup or fish. My second favourite kind of restaurant is Lebanese, followed by French. Every now and then I eat at an Indian restaurant, but their dishes are very well cooked and I'm not used to eating processed foods.

---

[17] I have included here only those things I find to be really bad for me, but the full list is much longer. It is also not recommended to eat fruit (which I love) in the evening. The sugars contained in fruit affect our digestion, raise glycaemia and lead to weight gain. We shouldn't eat fruit for at least three hours before going to sleep.

Another type of cuisine I really like, but which I try to steer clear of, is Thai food. They use a lot of sugar in their recipes, which maybe explains why Thai food is so tasty!

# 8

# My guilty pleasures

*If you deny yourself things, you'll only end up frustrated and will forget to enjoy your food.*

Even I, the person encouraging you to eat healthily, to cook at home, check the ingredients in the products you use, do physical exercise and drink lots of liquids, I, the person who has achieved balance and is shouting from the rooftops that you should love your body, yes, even I have a confession to make and many sins to own up to :-). Like anyone else, I have my weaknesses, especially when it comes to what I eat. And I want you to know what they are, so you don't go away thinking I'm pretending to be perfect and preaching things that can't be put into practice. Yes, I like eating, I've already said that, but what I didn't tell you is that I also like eating things that are not particularly healthy. It's important every now and then to eat things that bring us pleasure, even if it's a guilty pleasure, so we don't end up feeling frustrated. What should we do when we crave some chocolate or pretzels? The secret is to eat in moderation and at two-three hours intervals from our main meals of the day, so as not to interfere with the proteins or lipids in our calorie-rich meals.

Over the years, many nutritionists have advised me not to give up entirely those things I most like to eat, because, apart from the fact that it would leave me feeling frustrated, it would also mean that my chosen lifestyle would end up becoming a chore, which is not what we want. When you feel frustrated, then rather than, say, eating a square of chocolate whenever you feel the urge, you end up eating the entire bar! This is why I don't believe in diets where you're supposed to give up the things you like the most overnight, even if they are unhealthy. Everything has to be taken slowly. Step by step. Not even Rome was built in a day!

Normally, my diet doesn't contain any sugar, gluten, meat, pre-cooked meals, cold meats, processed foods or fried food; however, if I feel the need every now and then to eat some French fries or ice cream, then I see no problem in doing just that. And the really interesting thing is I don't seem to put any weight on. Why? Because in satisfying my need for a given food when I feel a craving for it, I tend to eat only small amounts, just enough to satisfy my cravings. If I didn't allow myself these guilty pleasures, then for sure at some point I would begin to disregard my diet and eat more than I'm supposed to. And if I do choose to eat something that doesn't comply with my dietary rules, then it should at least be something really worthwhile, something that really hits the spot… or my stomach :).

So what foods give me this amazing feeling of satisfaction? I'll start with éclairs. Truth be told, I simply adore éclairs with instant coffee topping, those especially delicious sweets we used to have during communism, back when I was little. I like the classic, mini éclairs with instant coffee topping, the simple ones, not the ones you get today – all super-sophisticated, elaborate and reinvented. When I was a child, my mother wouldn't give me cakes from the confectioner's shop, but, because she used to travel abroad, she'd bring me back sweets you couldn't find here at that time.

Another one of my guilty pleasures is candy floss, even if, after having given up sugar, I can no longer eat a whole one. The urge to eat it is the same, I feel like burying my face in it and smiling, as it brings back lots of nice memories. On one hand, its taste takes me back to my childhood, a time very dear to my heart; on the other hand, its smell gives me the feeling of being spoilt. As you can see, it's more emotional than it is a food craving.

If I go to the cinema, I just have to eat popcorn. To be totally honest, I normally end up finishing it before the film even begins. I prefer mine to be simple, just with salt, and a little bit better done where possible. Another of the cravings I like to indulge every year is to eat cozonac, a kind of Romanian stollen. On the morning of Christmas day, I get up and, wherever I am, I simply have to drink a cup of milk (even though I don't normally drink milk) and to eat a slice of cozonac. I think it's from childhood that I have the habit of dunking cozonac in milk. Again it's an emotional thing, like with the candy floss.

French fries with grated cheese on top – wow, how delicious! Obviously, this is something I also have since childhood and it reminds me of how I'm a true Cancer. Many of my guilty pleasures stem from the past and I always tend to relate things back to my childhood experiences. I've said it before and I'll say it again throughout the course of this journey in the form of a book: life was given to us to be enjoyed, and clearly this also means we should be allowed to eat everything that brings us pleasure. My advice to you? Take things slowly. Study your body and your needs. Don't rush to obtain results that are impossible to achieve in a short span of time. Discover what kind of diet is best for you and have the patience to achieve what you desire.

# 9

# We all make mistakes. It's what we do afterwards that counts!

*"Yesterday has gone, tomorrow doesn't yet exist. It's today, it's the present, that counts."*

– MARC LEVY

The first example that springs to mind is a dinner at a restaurant with friends or when I'm invited to a party. If there's no vegetarian dish on the menu, I can't simply drink water with lemon all night. Apart from the fact that it would make the others feel uncomfortable if I just sat there with an empty plate in front of me, I have to eat something and so sometimes I give in to my cravings. I've learnt not to feel guilty when I do this and I stray from the rules. There are times when we all need to treat ourselves. Has it ever happened to you that while you're studying the menu in search of something healthy to order, the waiter turns up with some bread fresh out of the oven and some butter? Well, it has happened to me and I simply couldn't resist! By the way, I forgot to include this on my list of guilty pleasures and I must admit it is a temptation I am quite incapable of resisting! In the past, after eating something like this, the guilt would always kick in, but thankfully this is no longer the case today. It's not like I eat these kinds of things every day, so I just try to enjoy my food and to take things as they come. Life is so much better around people who enjoy their food and feel good, so for at least one evening every few weeks I try to relinquish control and to be at ease with my decision.

If it turns into a late night, and the odd glass of wine, fatty food and an equally calorific dessert come into play, then the next day I always make sure to get enough rest. The first thing I do when I get up in the morning is to drink lots of water, as much as three large glasses. I want to focus on the present, not the past, as the thought that I've been bad can become an obsession, and this may lead to anxiety and other dark thoughts. When the body becomes dehydrated, it's hard for it to overcome tiredness, our circulation and brain activity is affected as a result.

I don't eat any animal products for breakfast, just some small quantities of light foods and liquids meals, like a protein shake or a smoothie. While on the subject of shakes, I always make them myself. I use plant milk – made from almonds, quinoa or rice – and then add some banana, chia seeds, protein powder and basically whatever fruit I have at home – e.g. blueberries, raspberries or blackberries – as well as some cocoa powder. The basic ingredients are plant milk, protein powder and bananas. I also make sure I do some extra physical exercises: I run on the treadmill at home, at the gym or in the park (especially if the weather's good), or I do some yoga, dance, or go to a functional gym or Pilates class. For a minimum of one hour!

Contrary to expectations, eating sweets is not helpful after having failed to stick to our diet and having had a late night. Nor is drinking coffee. In terms of the former, the sugar they contain gives us a quick energy rush, only to leave us feeling even more tired afterwards, while after a coffee the caffeine remains in our blood stream for a long time and stops us falling asleep when our body is telling us it's tired. To be honest, I don't drink coffee anyway; as it happens, I prefer tea. Apart from diet, the body also needs to relax in order to recover. Warm water lowers body temperature, which makes me feel sleepy, so whenever I "sin" in this way I've gotten into the habit of taking a hot bath at the end of the day and talking to myself; it's a great way to find out how I'm feeling and what my body needs. At the crazy pace at which we lead our lives today, this is something we forget to do and so we lose contact with ourselves and our needs.

# 10

# Why I cook at home

*Everything I've done outside of my comfort zone has changed my life.*

Apart from the stories in the press about my love life (of which some are true, some are not), about what I eat or what I choose to wear, I've often found myself amused by headlines referring to the fact that I like to cook: "Andreea Raicu takes up cooking: is she about to get hitched?" – so the only reason a woman starts taking an interest in the kitchen and thinking about what she eats is for the sake of a man? :). Or "Andreea Raicu swaps haute couture for the kitchen apron" – well, not exactly, as it's still a branded apron, even if it is my own brand :). Beyond these more or less innocent jokes, it's true, I really do like cooking and being in the kitchen, and the main reason is that I want to be able to control the food I eat. I'm very careful about what ingredients I use in my meals – in fact, this was the first change I made when I decided to start eating healthily, and I always read the labels carefully. It might seem hard at first, but as soon as you make a habit of it you will begin to make better choices, of this I'm convinced.

***Information to look for on food packaging:***

- Calories per 100 ml/100 g (energy value).
- How much protein is there in 100 ml/100 g?
- How many carbohydrates are there in 100 ml/100 g?
- How many grams of lipids are there in 100 ml/100 g?
- How many grams of saturated fats are there?
- How much fibre does it contain?
- How much sodium does it contain?

As a general rule, we should opt for low calorie foods with less than 20 g of fats, less than 6 g of sugar and at most 300 mg of sodium per 100 ml/g. The amount of fibre we consume every day should not exceed 40 g and the amount of carbohydrates 300 g. It's also recommended that our meals don't contain more than 2 g of protein per kilogram of body weight in 24 hours. The shorter the list of ingredients in a product, the lower the risk of our eating artificial additives and other substances that do the body more harm than good.

**Information**

**If we want to maintain our weight, we should aim to consume no more than 60 g of fat every day.**

I don't want to be a hypocrite and to tell you that I cook huge quantities of food each day. There are days when I only go into the kitchen to get something and then there are days when I spend many hours relaxing in the kitchen creating all kinds of delicious dishes. I'm a busy woman with very little spare time, which is why I like to combine utility with pleasure. When I cook, I try to make tasty things in record time. I like to be extremely orderly and organised in the kitchen, which I feel makes me more efficient when cooking.

For me cooking at home is also a pleasure; it helps me to structure my thoughts and to relax. It's also an excellent opportunity to invite friends and loved ones over for a meal, and, while I'm preparing the meal, to chat about our lives and enjoy ourselves. This way, cooking is no longer an obligation but a pleasurable activity that gives me energy and brings me closer to those around me. I often don't even tell my guests what they're about to eat. Many people are extremely conservative and will reject something without even tasting it, without even trying. They are afraid of anything new when it comes to food – and I can understand them, I also went through this phase. I enjoy seeing them eating what I've made for them and even really enjoying it. Only afterwards, when they ask me for the recipe, do I tell them that I used ingredients that are less well-known or that they would have expected to be bland simply because they're the kind of things used by people who don't eat meat.

There are also those very long days packed with meetings and events I have to attend when I don't have the time to order something in or to eat out or when there are no vegetarian options on the menu. In order to be sure I don't go hungry or I won't be tempted to eat anything unhealthy, I make something the evening before and leave home the next day armed with my lunch box. I know it sounds strange and maybe hard to believe, but this really is what I do :-). My lunch box contains fruit and vegetables as well as meals I prepare myself or I buy from raw vegan or vegetarian restaurants.

One more thing: if you're vegetarian or vegan or you want to eat raw food, it's not easy finding a restaurant where you can eat more than just salad. But at home you can make delicious food without any meat or animal products and not feel frustrated at having little to choose from the menu. And if by now I haven't convinced you to eat as much fruit and vegetables as possible, then let me tell you that I only recently read an article in *The American Journal of Public Health* that said that by eating more fruit and vegetables our quality of life satisfaction rises at a rate analogous to going from being unemployed to finding a job. Makes you think, doesn't it?

# 11

# How I ended up not even knowing my weight

*I know I truly love my body when I no longer waste time weighing myself.*

I imagine the first thing that springs to mind when I say this is that I maybe don't own any bathroom scales and that's why I don't know my weight. Actually, come to think of it, there's a grain of truth in that, even if that's not necessarily the message I want to convey. Each and every time I've had one of these weight measuring devices at home, it just so happened that either it broke (and not because I weighed a hundred kilos or because I dropped it or damaged it in some way) or I left it in some corner of the house to gather dust. At some point, the longest surviving bathroom scales I had in my possession ran out of batteries. After asking someone to change the batteries for me, I stepped on the scales again, and got a surprise. So I gave up weighing myself then and there. Just like that!

More recently, I decided I no longer needed bathroom scales, as I'm very aware of my body and I always know when I've put on weight or lost some weight in a very short space of time. At first sight there doesn't appear to be much chemistry between me and my bathroom scales, but the truth is that my life has changed ever since I began teaching myself to love my body, ever since I began to see my emotions as allies on my road to happiness, ever since I stopped searching for a diet that would help me lose weight and I learned to guide myself according to MY needs.

The more aware I am of the messages my body is sending me and the more I pay attention to them, the better choices I make in terms of what I eat, the more energy I have and the better I feel in my own skin. Of course, there are days when I hardly feel like getting out of bed in the morning and days when I wake up really early and am able to enjoy the sunrise, when I go for a run in the park and fill myself with so much positive energy. While these fluctuations are normal, one thing I know for sure: I find it hard to be balanced without doing any physical exercise. If I spend hour after hour in the same position and I haven't even moved a few steps, this is reflected not only in the fact that my back starts to hurt, but also in my mood: I feel restless, I find it hard to concentrate and to see the positive side of things. So there is yet more proof that I know what I need to do in order to avoid standing on the scales and feeling depressed.

Apart from choosing to eat healthily, I try not to stay in the same position for too long and make it a priority to do some kind of physical exercise on a daily basis, something I recommend you do, too. You don't have to pay anything to go for a run in the park and it's a shame not to enjoy the beautiful surroundings, whatever the season may be. It's harder in winter, of course, but then the sense of satisfaction you get is greater. On the other hand, if you don't like jogging, try doing some training at the gym or dance, anything that gives you energy, balances you and helps you shed those excess kilos. But try not to push yourself too hard, you should build up gradually, so it doesn't feel like a chore. If you don't get any pleasure from what you're doing, you'll feel frustrated and will give up on everything you set out to do. We need to move the way our bodies want us to move, the way that feels best to them, only this way will we be in good shape. I believe our bodies are genetically programmed to be active, we only need to discover what is best suited to them.

And before I forget, I also choose to wear clothes that make me feel good. This strengthens my relationships with my body and lowers the risk of succumbing to bad habits like overeating. You'll be familiar with some of my clothes already if you've had an opportunity to see my collection of dresses, t-shirts and hoodies. The way we dress says a lot about how much we love and accept ourselves: I still think about the clothes I wear, but I no longer place as much pressure on myself as I did in the past. I don't always have to look sexy and for everything to be absolutely spot on when I go out in public. There are days when my body feels it wants something more relaxed, so I put some casual clothes on instead, but then that doesn't mean I can't be chic without heels or I won't look good. There are lots of factors involved: casual clothes are always in fashion, especially when worn in combination with a few cool accessories, like sunglasses, bags, different kinds of jewellery with inspirational messages on them; though above all it's your attitude that counts.

I don't know whether you noticed, but I always wear themed pendants and bracelets inscribed with quotations from meditations and the values I wish to promote. I believe it's important to keep these things close and to remind ourselves of them, especially in a world in which it is so easy to lose ourselves. But I don't want to touch on that subject here, as there's something very important I want to tell you instead: choose clothes you like but which are also your size. I've often met women who force themselves to lose weight in order to fit into an XS or an S, but their bodies are just not built that way. This doesn't mean they don't already look good or aren't slim enough, but they feel ugly because the model of perfection promoted by society is based precisely around these clothing sizes. It's bad to think in this way, it won't help you become balanced and to accept your body the way it is. I have clothes of different sizes in my wardrobe, so when I put on a kilo or two, say when I'm very tired or at Easter or Christmas, my body feels accepted, loved and able to return to the weight at which it feels most comfortable when it's ready to do so. Beauty and self-respect do not depend on the number shown on your bathroom scales. I know I truly love my body when I no longer waste time weighing myself.

> *My body feels good enough not to see food as its only source of satisfaction.*

What if, when we take a look at ourselves in the mirror, rather than focusing on our flaws, we choose to admire the colour of our eyes, our beautiful smiles or any of our other qualities? I believe this is more useful than standing on the bathroom scales and worrying about our weight.

# 12

# Habits that make my life more beautiful

## The benefits of being active and why I exercise regularly

*To have a balanced life and a healthy lifestyle, it's not enough just to have a conscious diet. Exercising is extremely important and should not be absent from our lives.*

While in the previous chapter I told you about how I tried every possible diet until I realised that the secret to a harmonious body is, in fact, balance and not a restrictive diet, here I will describe for you my "love affair" with sports. Yes, I love exercising, but it's also true to say that sports and I have had a complicated relationship over the years, with many ups and downs. Today physical exercise has become a way of life for me, and I don't do it necessarily for reasons of appearance, i.e. to shed those extra kilos and to have the body I want, but primarily because I want to feel good. For me physical exercise means health, energy. It helps me maintain my balance, and this feeling of well-being can be read on my face even after only half an hour's running in the park or yoga!

During my childhood my parents wanted me to be active and encouraged me to try all kinds of sports, e.g. swimming, tennis and athletics, but first came that wonderful thing that is ballet, an activity I still believe graces those who do it with a special elegance. I did gymnastics – both artistic and rhythmic – for many years, followed by handball at school. At a certain point, when school began to get more serious, I can remember my mother and father making me choose what it was I wanted to be good at, and my options were either school or... school :-). So I chose school, but I never gave up sports, notwithstanding a few brief "timeouts".

I remember how when I was in high school, because I wanted to make my life easier I chose sports as one of my baccalaureate subjects. This wasn't necessarily the wisest choice. I was good at long jump and sprinting, but my endurance was really poor, so I had to work at it almost every day. I remember running the same distance I'd have to do for the exam, i.e. almost a kilometre, and how horrible it felt. This makes me laugh now, as it's a very short distance that wouldn't take me very long today, but back then it felt like a real challenge. For a long, long time afterwards, I was left with the idea that I was not very good at running, that I wasn't made for jogging – that is, until someone told me that there was no such thing and that as long as I had no health problems that would stop me from doing it, all I needed to do was learn to breathe correctly and to practice, so I could build up my endurance. In fact, the problem wasn't that I didn't have the right physical qualities to run long distances, not even the occasional cigarette was to blame, as I had thought, but the fact that I didn't know how to run and breathe correctly, not to mention my mental block. After a number of training sessions, I realised that it wasn't as hard as it looks, not to mention how good I felt after I'd finished. To run correctly you need to know how to breathe properly as well as to be prepared to leave your comfort zone. Naturally, you shouldn't take things to the extreme and run until you literally can't move your body anymore; it's best to increase your distance and speed gradually. If today we do a five-minute run, then tomorrow we should try and hold out for six minutes, and so on. Beyond the physical challenge, it's also a battle with our own minds and the limits we place on ourselves. However, I'm sorry to have to tell you this, but excuses don't burn calories and nor do they help us grow. So we need to overcome the barriers we have set for ourselves and to smash our own records. Not only in sports, but in every field of life!

I think it's important to mention that what I used to find hardest about running was doing it alone, so I would always look for a partner. Everything was going really well until the person I usually went jogging with changed jobs and with it their jogging schedule. Left without a partner, I gave up my morning run as I didn't want to run alone. I missed running, but I didn't make the effort to overcome this mental barrier. That is, until one day, when I told myself this: my life needn't depend on someone else! It's not normal to no longer be able to do something I like and need to do just because there's no longer any one there to "hold my hand". And so, that morning I got up and went to the park without any expectations, being on my own for the first time, and guess what? I managed to finish my usual lap of Herăstrău Lake and I was extremely proud of myself!! It was the first time I'd run six kilometres on my own. And, at the end of this distance, not only did I feel good, I was also extremely happy, it all just felt so great. After that I began to go running on my own and paradoxically I now no longer enjoy running with anyone else because it's my time, a time I spend with myself during which I stop, meditate, take in the surrounding nature, breathe the clean air, think over all the things on my to-do list and listen to music and motivational books on various gadgets – it's my way of recharging my batteries with positive energy on a daily basis.

To all those always looking for an excuse not to do physical exercise, believe me I know just how it is. It's not easy, at least not at first, to go to the gym or the park, to be disciplined, to abandon your comfort zone; you go through a lot of difficult things and different phases, I know, I've been there, but it's really worth it. If we could have all the things we want just with a snap of the fingers, especially when it comes to our health, then everyone would do it.

Coming back to sports and my experience of it, I'm also reminded of the time I spent presenting 'Big Brother'. I was working long hours, late into the night, and with it being a daily show I was on air every evening, so I was constantly on my toes. If, for example, I only got to sleep around three in the morning because the programme didn't end till around one, and then someone called me at seven the next day, I'd still always pick up, never admitting to having been woken up by the call; I felt I constantly had to prove I was strong, that my stamina was unbending and I was always ready to work… Today I'd no longer do things this way, but back then I had to learn my lessons at the expense of my health.

Coming back to what I was saying, during that time I found it helpful to exercise every day; but I didn't go to any particular classes, I would just run a bit on the treadmill or do my own training sessions involving different exercises. The exhaustion eventually crept up on me, but I just kept on doing my exercises, even though my body was sending me all kinds of signals that it was overtired. On one hand, physical exercise was the solution that allowed me to get rid of my negative energy and to have the body I wanted; on the other hand, going to the gym had begun to feel like a chore. You must know the feeling.

So, there were times when I'd go to the gym[18] and would keep working out until I got home exhausted, not to mention the post-workout muscle pain. In time, I discovered that when we do something we don't like, it becomes impossible for us to enjoy the results. I learned this the hard way. I can even remember doing such an intense workout one day that I couldn't even climb the steps to my house afterwards. My legs were killing me, I could hardly move anymore, and all because the day before I had overdone it by forcing myself to exercise until I dropped. At the time, I had a trainer who wanted me to push my limits without taking into account the way it made me feel.

So, yes, I must admit that in the past I used to exercise without any guidance or only with unsuitable personal trainers; I wasn't aware of the risk I was exposing myself to. I would read, sometimes too little and only superficially, about the efficacy of certain exercises, I'd ask what other people were doing, I'd find out what was in fashion in terms of physical exercise and workouts, and I'd come up with my own plan to follow. Instead of seeing my body as my best friend, I was treating it like an enemy, and this was because, despite the endless hours I would spend working out, it wasn't responding how I wanted it to. So, instead of exercising for pleasure – which would have been the normal thing to do – I was doing it out of frustration, ambition and anger, and with an unrelenting persistence, often choosing to train with someone who would push me to breaking point. I believed this was the only way to get results… I now realise how wrong I was, but back then I was very stubborn.

---

[18] It's very important to draw a distinction between feeling tired and being lazy. Unfortunately, many people confuse the two when it comes to doing physical exercise.

There are still moments when I ask myself how I could have treated my body with so little care. Although at first sight I appeared to be looking after it by working it so hard in the gym, the sad truth was that I wasn't listening to the very clear messages it was sending me. What were these messages? Well, without a doubt the most important alarm signal was the pain. It was from Luminița Nicolescu, the personal trainer I've been working with for years, that I learned the following nugget of information: it's a good thing when our muscles ache, it's a sign they've been shaken out of their routine and put to work; but if they're still hurting more than two days afterwards, it means they've been made to do the wrong type of work and our health will suffer as a result.

After I gave up exercising without any proper guidance or only with inappropriate personal trainers, I looked for something that better suited me and I could resonate with, which is how I got to know Luminița Nicolescu, with whom I tried out many different types of physical training. From Tae Bo[19] (see the DVD I put out together with Luminița Nicolescu) to Pilates and all manner of different fitness exercises, there was nothing I wouldn't try – and I soon came to the conclusion that in order to have a beautiful and healthy body we require a large amount of information. What I really want you to remember is that only the intelligent use of physical exercise, tailored specifically to us, will have the effects we long for. Besides this we need to know the following: what foods are healthy (a subject I looked at in the previous chapter), how often we should be going to the gym or doing physical exercise (outdoors or at home), how much liquids should we be consuming, how much time we need to

[19] A combination of aerobics, ballet, karate, boxing, dance, hip hop and weight training which it is said will help you burn 800 calories in an hour. It's also a good form of self-defence, but only insofar as this is desired. By the way, when I was little I used to watch Bruce Lee films and I wanted to learn martial arts :).

spend resting and what complementary therapies will help us to have a healthy body.

Our bodies are designed to move, not to be sedentary. Many health issues, including type 2 diabetes, obesity and heart disease, appear in people who don't do enough physical exercise and spend a lot of time without getting up from their chairs, sofas, desks, armchairs, etc. Fortunately, I don't belong to this category. I only rarely sit still, in fact only when I'm feeling ill or am very tired am I not active. I like to be active, but not restless and stressed out for no reason, and I like to put my body to work, even when I'm in meetings or on a flight. I move my arms about, I stand up, I move my head and my feet, I tense my stomach muscles and do breathing exercises, always changing position. They're things I'm no longer aware of doing, I do them because I've taught myself to do them and I feel the need to be active.

It's important to find a sport we like and which also meets our needs, otherwise we won't be motivated to do it. I've heard many people say they don't like any kind of physical exercise, but I don't think this can be true. There are so many different options, it's just not possible that there's no kind of physical exercise we can enjoy. Don't like gym classes? Try a bit of tennis, volleyball, dance, gymnastics, handball, running in the park, fast walking, climbing up and down stairs... there's something for every budget. What's important is to just start somewhere and you'll soon find yourself getting a taste for it. As I was saying, you should first do physical exercise for yourselves, in order to be healthy, and only then because you want to lose weight and tone your body – otherwise, as soon as you achieve your desired shape, you risk losing motivation. Even just walking is very important. But unfortunately we forget to do this, being so dependent on cars and other means of transportation.

I recently felt the need to stop subjecting my body to such

intense training sessions. Instead I do yoga, Pilates and cardio, and I like going for a run or a swim, too. These are the physical activities I practice regularly, the aim being no longer to torture my body with the kind of harsh training sessions I used to put it through in the past. I try to exercise four to five times a week, but I freely admit to not always managing this. I used to be very strict on myself and even if I was insufficiently rested or felt really tired I would still get up at 7.30 without fail and head to the gym. I later learned that sleep takes priority. If I feel tired and don't make it to yoga class or go for a run in the park, then I do a 15-20 minute workout at home instead, usually on the treadmill.

As I was telling you before, many years ago I decided to make an exercise DVD with Luminița Nicolescu. We first looked at the different options available to us (given how she does so many different forms of exercise there was a lot to choose from), with the idea being to choose something I liked and would be able to show improvement at. After many discussions I came to the conclusion that I wanted to learn more about Tae Bo and yoga. I really enjoyed doing Tae Bo, so next up was to see what yoga was like. The only things I'd heard about yoga were pretty strange, but being open minded, I said I'd give it a go anyway. My first reaction? You'll laugh but I actually found it to be really boring, excruciatingly so; I couldn't understand why everything had to be so slow and why I was expected to just stand there doing nothing. I kept feeling the need to move, I couldn't stop fidgeting, and as a result I soon gave up this activity. I simply found it extremely boring. This being a really busy time for me, I was finding myself unable to relax. I hadn't learned to listen to myself, to be patient with my body. Long story short, I thought it was all a load of nonsense. So in the end we decided to make the DVD just about Tae Bo.

So how come I now love yoga so much and I practice it whenever I get the chance? The change came after my experience in India, where I learned to meditate. Normally you start with yoga and then move on to meditation. This is because yoga helps you to establish a connection with your body, to create a relationship between body and mind, and only then do you go on to explore the realms of meditation. With me it was the other way around: first came meditation, and then came yoga. And I began to really enjoy it, because in our busy lives it can help us relax and find balance. Today, the time I spend doing yoga is a time dedicated to myself. Of course, it doesn't always turn out the way you want it to, and I can remember reading somewhere that every experience is unique and special, but also that it won't always give you the results you're looking for. It may work the first, second and even third time, but the fourth time you try it you might find you don't get what you wanted out of it, because one yoga session will never be the same as another, given how we ourselves are never always the same; we are always changing and experiencing different moods, and what happens to us on the inside is always reflected on the outside.

There are people who only teach yoga and people who also experience what they teach. I usually do yoga in places where you find the second category of teacher, those who don't consider what they do to be a job but get involved themselves and live by what they teach. So take care when choosing your teachers because not everyone is suited to what you're looking for.

I know this might seem a little off topic, but I can't help asking you a question. Did you know that swimming and meditation make a good team? Swimming makes me feel fantastically relaxed and helps me be aware of my body (maybe this is because my zodiac is a water sign!) :). As for yoga, well, there is no need to explain.[20] What I haven't told you yet, and you perhaps didn't know, is that both activities have a common denominator: breathing.

## Let's do an exercise

Did you have a bad day, do you need to make a difficult decision or deal with a difficult situation? If the answer's yes then I recommend a type of breathing-based meditation, which is very easy to do and you can do it while swimming or doing yoga. Before entering the pool/beginning a yoga session, think of the thing that is bothering you at that moment and then set yourself a goal. Don't make judgements and don't ask yourself why you have to go through this. Just name the obstacle and then begin swimming gently/performing a few of the easier yoga poses, while concentrating only on your breathing. Do a few lengths of the pool/a few relaxing poses, breathing in and out normally, then begin to visualise the problem you have in mind and to which you are trying to find a solution. With each movement imagine you are taking steps towards conquering your fears. Do as many lengths of the pool as you like/as many yoga poses you need to be able to concentrate, but remember to transform each gesture into a symbolic step forward. You'll get a much clearer picture of how things stand and what the solutions to your problems are.

**Did you know?**

**Doing just two minutes of physical exercise an hour can prevent disease and help you to live longer.**

[20] In part three of this book I will describe in more detail how I came to discover meditation and why I meditate every day.

We all admire public figures and stars who somehow manage to look better and better as they get older, as if they have discovered the philosopher's stone and the source of eternal youth. For me the secret of those who haven't resorted to the scalpel can be summed up in a single word: "balance". That is, a harmonious coming together of mind, body and soul. Diet, exercise, hydration and rest are the basic elements that will provide us with a healthy and beautiful body.

How many of us haven't started the week on a diet only to give it up a couple of days later? How many attempts to go to the gym or for a run in the park haven't ended with us doing something different from what we set out to do? How often haven't we promised to drink more water and to set aside a time for ourselves, a time for relaxation, even a massage or meditation, only never to get around to it? Maybe it's time we began, especially as, however simplistic it might sound, life is short and time forgives no one. It's better to try things out that bring us pleasure and then gradually introduce them to our lives than for us to have to resort to them only when it's (much) too late.

I want to come back to an important idea which I can't emphasise enough, namely that there is no perfect recipe when it comes to diet and exercise. In terms of physical exercise, while personal trainers recommend we do a variety of different exercises and cardio accompanied by sustained muscle toning and muscle building sessions, they also want us to have fun doing them. The secret to success is that exercise should be seen as a pleasurable activity, and certainly not a chore. It is the path – not the destination! – towards a balanced life, while our happiness resides in the choices we make. My advice to you? Start right away by setting a sporting objective that's not impossible to achieve; do your chosen form of physical exercise for a pre-established period of time, e.g. half a year – that is, long enough for you to start seeing the desired results, but short enough not to lose motivation.

In what follows, I will describe some of my favourite yoga postures – not to be confused with physical exercises! – which are called asanas. I hope you like them and that they help you to relax and to get to know your body better. However, I should first warn you of a few things. Yoga is not a sport, it is a true path of self-knowledge. When we take up running, for example, as I said earlier, we should begin gently and then increase the time and distance we run gradually, and the improvements will come right away. However, this is not true of meditation and yoga, as I've already explained. Your journey in yoga is not a linear progression, which can at times feel frustrating. It's important we try to concentrate intensely and to free ourselves of all thoughts and expectations. In fact, all we need to do is to relax and then the things we aspire to will come naturally. I know this from my own experience.

Right now, as I consign my thoughts to my laptop and enjoy a delicious smoothie, I realise that I enjoy doing yoga just as much as I enjoy meditating. For me yoga is really a kind of escape hatch from everyday life. Like you, I have good days and bad days, and when all my meetings, photo shoots and who knows what new projects I'm working on begin to pile up, not to mention the many things always on my mind, I start to feel tired and the need to cut myself off from all that's going on around me and rebalance myself. So that's when I run off to yoga! I adore doing yoga in the evening, especially after a day in which I built up a lot of negative energy. But I also never turn down a bit of yoga on my days off, usually combining it with a massage. You might be wondering just how yoga is able to relax me so much. Well, it just does!

During a yoga session, I am able to detach myself from all the things that are bothering and worrying me and I end up not thinking about anything... only the asanas and my breathing, the present moment! After a session is over I sometimes feel pain in muscles I didn't even know existed! But there's no need to worry, it all depends on the intensity you choose to work at. And a massage afterwards relaxes the entire body, especially that one where hot volcanic stones are placed on your neck, spinal cord, legs and joints, which is simply divine!

Why is yoga good for us? Here are a few reasons:

- it gives the body energy and stimulates blood flow
- it revitalises our metabolism
- it brings us back to the present and reduces stress while also helping us to rest better
- it strengthens the joints and prevents and ameliorates various conditions caused by ageing
- it reduces back pain and helps us maintain better posture
- it boosts stamina and our ability to concentrate
- it helps strengthen the immune system and therefore reduces symptoms caused by colds and the flu
- it reduces anxiety and depression

In a world that places such importance on our physical appearance, it comes as no surprise that from as early as adolescence we are witnessing an increasing number of cases of eating and personality disorders. There are already foreign clinics where yoga has been introduced as a form of therapy used in the treatment of these conditions. The connection we are able to establish with our bodies during a yoga class is special, because it allows us to become much more aware of our emotions. When viewed in the cold light of day, 90% of people's weight problems have to do with overeating, while 90% of our time is spent "feeding on our emotions", with the remaining 10% spent being actually hungry. Yoga is therefore not a dedicated weight-loss technique – it does more than this in the sense that it helps unblock our energies on an emotional level, the results of which are visible on all levels, even in our physical appearance.

Yoga calms our restless minds while helping us to stretch our stiff muscles, become conscious of our breathing and the present moment and to relax.

## The Sun Salutation

The sun salutation in 12 easy steps. Instructions for practice at home.

1. Begin the sun salutation from a standing position. Bring your hands towards your chest into a prayer position and close your eyes and concentrate on your breathing. Gently press your hands together and relax your shoulders.
2. Inhale and exhale between three and five times. On your final inhalation, lift both arms simultaneously above your head. Stretch as much as you can and make sure you look towards the tips of your fingers.
3. Exhale and lower your torso in front of you without bending your back until you touch the floor with the palms of your hands. Keep your legs straight and don't bend your knees. If you are unable to touch the floor with the palms of your hands, don't force yourself and touch the floor with the tips of your fingers instead.
4. Inhale and move your right foot backwards in one smooth motion, while bringing your left knee forwards in a lunge. Place your hands on the floor on either side of your body with your shoulders as far back as possible. Find your balance and hold this position for one minute.
5. Move your left leg backwards so that it is next to your right leg and then raise your hips and legs up off the floor,

supporting your weight with your toes and hands. Ensure your elbows are fully extended.

6. Gradually lower your knees, chest and chin towards the floor while keeping your buttocks in the air.
7. Inhale, stretch your legs backwards and lift your torso and shoulders, pushing your hands down into the floor and forwards. Raise your head.
8. Bring your torso and shoulders back into a vertical position then raise your pelvis and straighten your knees. Keep your head between your arms and perform the Downward Facing Dog pose.[21] Hold this position for five inhalations/exhalations. Upon your final exhalation, lower your knees to the floor.
9. Inhale and bring your right leg forwards. Bend your right knee and move your left leg backwards. Place your hands on the floor on either side of your body. Try to find your balance and hold this position for one minute.
10. Come out of this position by placing your hands on the floor and bringing your left leg forward. Then slowly stand up, straightening your knees while keeping your hands on the floor and your face touching your knees.
11. Inhale and bring your hands together above your head in the Half Moon pose.
12. Exhale and bring your hands down to your chest and back into the original prayer position. Raise your chin from your chest.

[21] A description is provided later in the book.

**Tip**

**If you want your body to feel reinvigorated during the first part of the day then it's a good idea to practice the Sun Salutation technique in the morning.**

**Did you know?**

**"Namaste" is the most commonly used greeting in yoga. It translates literally as "the divine within me bows down before the divine within you". It is a gesture that symbolically sends spirituality out into the universe in the hope of receiving the same positivity in return. "Namaste" is also used to thank your yoga teacher. To perform the greeting, hold your hands together next to the heart chakra as if in prayer. Then move your hands towards the middle of your face while offering thanks for your yoga class.**

It's best to begin doing yoga with an instructor, who will help you to understand the positions better and therefore to avoid injury!

## The Tree Pose or Vrksasana

This is one of the basic yoga poses but don't be fooled by the fact that it appears to be easy to perform. I assure you, especially if it's been a long time since you last did any physical exercise, that it can be really tough on your body. Stand up straight, with your hips apart, and gradually move your weight onto your right leg while at the same time bending your left leg at the knee and placing the sole of your foot onto your inner thigh, above the knee. Bring your hands together and hold them at chest height before raising them above your head. Hold this position for at least 15 seconds, then repeat using the other leg. If you're finding it difficult, then try to imagine that, like a tree, you have roots in the ground and a trunk that is reaching up to the sky in search of the sun.

### The Warrior 1 Pose

Starting from an upright position, spread your legs apart as far as it still feels comfortable, then bend one leg until it is at 90 degrees to the floor while transferring your weight onto it. With your hands facing each other, lift your arms above your head. You should be facing in the same direction as the bent leg.

### The Warrior 2 Pose

Starting from an upright position, spread your legs until your feet are further apart than your hips while still feeling comfortable. Raise your arms to shoulder height. Rotate your right foot 90 degrees and point your toes outwards, using your left leg to support your weight. Bend your right knee forwards. Look straight ahead over your outstretched arm.

### The Warrior 3 Pose

Starting from an upright position, lean forwards with your right foot slightly behind you so that you are able to touch the floor with your hands. If you don't feel comfortable leaning so low, use a table or a chair to reduce the distance. Transfer your weight to your left leg, bend your knee and extend your right leg backwards. Once you find your balance, take your hands off the floor and either extend them out in front of your head or bring them together on your chest and face forward. Inhale and exhale five times, then repeat with the other leg.

### Setu Bandha Sarvangasana or the Bridge Pose

You probably remember doing the bridge in your childhood or adolescence. Some people still do it as adults, though many are no longer capable. This yoga position involves one half of the classic bridge we remember from our childhoods, only that now our arms are touching the floor throughout. First, lie down on the floor with your arms stretched out on either side of your body. With your knees bent, push with your legs until your pelvis lifts up from the floor. Then place your arms beneath your buttocks and clasp your hands together. Raise your body again, supporting yourself with your arms such that the lower part of the body is raised up and you are resting on your shoulders and arms, which are stretched out beneath your body. Your hips should be parallel to the floor and your chest raised towards your chin.

### The Upward Facing Dog Pose

Lie on your stomach and make sure your hands are beneath your shoulders and your legs are in line with your hips. Push your hips against the floor, then raise the upper part of your body using your arms. Your legs should be parallel to the floor and you should be supporting yourself only by your fingers. You should only use your arms to maintain balance and your chest and abdomen should not touch the floor.

### The Downward Facing Dog Pose

While on your hands and knees, with the latter spread to the width of your shoulders, raise your pelvis while keeping your arms and legs straight. Bend your knees one at a time as if walking without lifting your fingers or toes from the floor and hold this position.

### The Pigeon Pose

From a sitting position, bring forwards and bend your right leg with your knee facing outwards and your foot next to your abdomen. Extend your left leg behind you, then push down on your hands, lowering your body until you can touch the floor with your pelvis.

---

## I hydrate therefore I exist

*Every day you should be better than you were the day before.*

First, I have a confession to make. Another one :). And it's not something I'm proud of. Before becoming more interested in how to have a healthy life and to listen to my body, I didn't really drink much water. In fact, I was never really all that thirsty. I'm sure lots of you can relate to this. I even felt that drinking water in the morning, on an empty stomach, was making me feel sick. However, in time I came to realise that it was just a matter of habit, and I haven't had this sensation again since starting to drink water all the time.

If you only rarely drink water, then you won't normally feel thirsty and won't make an effort to change this situation – maybe only if you develop a health issue, have problems with your skin or want to lose weight. So, when it comes to the list of things I'm not proud of then you ought to know that I used to be a regular consumer of fizzy drinks and I would indulge myself, despite knowing it wasn't at all healthy and wasn't doing me any good. Back then, there weren't even that many warnings, not like those you get today, on every television channel, telling us how much water we should be drinking, that staying hydrated is essential for our health and that we should be consuming lots of fruit and vegetables, which contain a lot of water, on a daily basis. But then, come to think of it, I'm not sure this would have had much effect on me back then anyway, because I placed way too much confidence in the resilience of my body and, being too stubborn by far, I believed it would go on for ever. What I also didn't know back then was that when you begin to feel thirsty it means the body has already been dehydrated for some time and is now sending us desperate messages to tell us we need to replenish our reserves.

When I started reading up on this subject, the first thing I realised was that I would need to reduce or even entirely eliminate fizzy drinks from my diet. In this I was, as usual, thinking about my physical appearance, not necessarily my health, because I had read somewhere that acidic juices, which also contain large amounts of sugar, predispose us to develop cellulite or aggravate an existing cellulite problem.

I also remember an article I read on the internet many years ago about a woman who, on the advice of her doctors, drank three litres of liquids a day for a month, something which convinced me to pay more attention to my own hydration. I can't quite remember what her name was, but she was a British woman aged around 40. She gave an interview for the *Daily Mail* in which she described just how good she felt after consuming this large amount of water over the space of a month: her headaches were gone, her skin had regained its elasticity, the dark rings under her eyes and her wrinkles had faded, her stomach had become flatter, her cellulite had receded and she had lost some weight to boot, all despite not changing any other part of her diet. And the pictures spoke for themselves: she looked ten years younger than before undergoing this experiment.

What else convinced me to pay more attention to my water intake? There was a particular experience that had a powerful effect on me. I remember when my grandmother was very ill and in intensive care, and I was sitting in the hallway, worried to bits, waiting to find out how she was and if there was anything I could do to help. I'm sure there's no one who hasn't been in this situation; you don't feel like drinking or eating anything, you expend all your energy thinking about your loved one. The doctor, who subsequently became a good friend of mine, came over to me and told me I needed to start drinking water. I was taken aback, as I didn't understand why she would want to say this to me. Of course, I told her that the last thing on my mind at that moment was to drink some water. She said it was extremely important that I stay hydrated and I promised I'd do as she said, but then I got distracted and forgot about it. In fact, just as I told her, I really didn't think it was important whether I drank any water, I didn't feel the need. When I met her again the next day, she told me – she didn't ask! – that she could tell that I hadn't drunk any water. I asked her how she could know this and she said you could see it in my face. And it's true, my skin looks worse when I don't hydrate myself properly, something I unfortunately only became aware of later!!! She then said something that I would never forget. She asked me: "Do you know the difference between a grape and a raisin?" "Well," I said, "I think it's that they taste different." "Water," she said, adding that "grapes contain water, raisins don't. So which one do you want to be?" She really shocked me with this analogy, which had a powerful effect on me. And now every time I forget to drink water, I think of what she said to me, something I myself now tell other people to encourage them to drink more water.

There's still a lot of room for improvement when it comes to my hydration routine, and I must admit that on really busy days I still need to remind myself to drink water. I find it helpful to use an app on my phone that notifies me whenever I need to do this. I'm sure we all have difficult moments, when we're really worried about something and are no longer aware of this particular need of the body. In winter, I try to consume around two litres a day, while in summer I increase this amount, especially when I do physical exercise and sweat a lot. And when I eat more than usual, I also make sure to drink a lot of water the next day. What else do I try to do? Once a week or once a fortnight, especially after eating meals containing food that is hard to digest, I try to drink only water during the day and I feel fantastic as a result, not to mention that my skin looks like I've just had cosmetic surgery. If I were forced to choose between consuming only water or food for a day, I know I'd definitely choose the former.

## The benefits of hydration

- It helps the kidneys to filter blood and prevents renal and urine infections
- It aids cell formation
- It helps maintain a constant body temperature
- It regulates the blood sugar level and digestion
- It helps prevent heart disease and cancer

- It stimulates your metabolism and plays an important role in eliminating toxins
- It alleviates headaches and reduces fatigue
- It keeps skin looking young and reduces cellulite and wrinkles

How can I tell I haven't drunk enough water? There are four signs: urine colour, skin texture, lack of energy and – in more extreme cases – headaches. Previously, when I had a migraine, I would take a pill to ease the pain, even if I wasn't eliminating the actual cause of my discomfort. What was really happening was that my body was telling me that I hadn't been hydrating myself properly and that I needed to rebalance the level of fluids in my body. Now, when I have a busy day and can feel a headache coming on, I immediately drink some water and feel much better for it. If my urine is light in colour, pale yellow or almost colourless, it means that I have drunk enough liquids; however, if it's dark in colour, i.e. dark orange, and smells strongly, then the body is dehydrated. Other signs of dehydration include dry skin, chapped lips that are beginning to peel, fatigue and an inability to concentrate.

According to the nutritionist doctor Anda Avramescu, in order to stay hydrated every day we should be consuming 35 ml of liquids per kilogram of body weight, and more in the case of physical activity, exposure to high temperatures and excessive perspiration. This includes water as well as other liquids, e.g. natural juices, soup, milk and fresh fruit juice.

I never drink cold liquids because I know the effect they have on my body. My throat starts to hurt immediately and inflammation occurs, because, as I was saying, our bodies are intelligent and send us messages whenever we give it something that's not good for it. But that's not the only cause. The main reason is that the body needs to use more energy than normal to heat the water, something which has knock-on effects for its other functions. Our digestion, in particular, slows down, especially after eating heavy foods and then drinking water straight from the fridge. So I choose to drink water at a temperature that is hot enough for me not to notice it. In fact, I prefer it warm rather than cold. Every night, before I go to bed, I make sure there's a glass of water on my bedside table, while in the morning the first thing I do is to rehydrate myself. Similarly, I always have a bottle of water with me in my car. If I've eaten a lot or my meal contained acidic foods (which I told you about in the section on the alkaline diet), then I drink some water with a bit of lime in it, which has an alkalising effect, or if I don't have any lime, a bit of lemon will do instead. Water makes my skin look beautiful, it gives me energy, it revives me and it makes me feel good about myself. If I've eaten a lot the previous evening, or my meal contained things I normally try to avoid and the next morning I wake up feeling bloated, with an uncomfortable feeling in my stomach, then I make sure to drink quite a lot more water than usual.

If we're not used to drinking water, then when we hydrate ourselves the body has a tendency to store every last drop of liquid it is given. However, once the body becomes used to receiving sufficient liquids, it no longer panics and everything happens normally, meaning there's no more water retention. Many people say they don't like drinking lots of water because it means more frequent trips to the toilet. Well, so be it, it's only natural!

I have an ongoing disagreement with my friends, who don't believe me when I tell them I can differentiate between different types of water from how it tastes. Well, believe me, you can tell the taste of water provided you're in touch with yourself and are truly conscious of what you do and feel. I guess I've just defined the concept of mindfulness, something I will expand on in Chapter Three, i.e. to be conscious of what is going on, to become the lead actor in our lives, the one who takes the decisions, not just an onlooker. With the aid of meditation, you can make the brain "stop" thinking and "rest", the consequence of which is that you will come to understand yourself better; you will learn to assess yourself objectively and to enjoy more what you eat and drink; and, perhaps most importantly, you will be able to understand your emotions and what they are founded on. This is how I came to realise which water I like the taste of and what is good for my body. It's like when you're walking down the street and you glance around at different things: naturally, you can't both observe certain details while also being aware of everything that's going on around you. It's the same with food and water. As soon as you become aware of your body and begin to pay attention to details, you start seeing things you'd otherwise have overlooked.

**Information**

**According to the American Medical Association, women need to consume eight cups of liquid each day in order to be correctly hydrated. The exact amount varies, depending on age, weight, amount of physical exercise, season and diet. Remember, the best source of liquids for the body is non-sparkling water, not energy drinks, lemonade, cold tea, coffee, alcohol or sparkling water.**

At home I have a portable reverse osmosis water filtration system, which is an efficient device for filtering water that also alkalises it. Osmosis filters remove any impurities and add to water the minerals your body requires. It was Cristina Bogdan, the doctor friend I mentioned in the previous chapter, who told me that water with a neutral or alkaline pH (a neutral pH is 7, with anything above that being alkaline) should form a part of any healthy lifestyle. But it's not recommended always to drink the same type of water, even alkaline water, because even when using an osmosis filter, we can't always know what the concentration of minerals in the liquid will be compared with what our body needs. In the long term, if we drink the same type of water, problems may occur, including on a cellular level. However, if we drink a certain type of water at home but a different kind of water from a glass bottle when we go out, then this is ideal, because we are varying the type of water we consume and our body does not risk being deprived of the substances it requires.

I have been visited many times at home by Rupda, one of the people I got to know from the workshops I did while on my spiritual travels. Many of you will know her from the talks we've given together in Bucharest. She is a special person in my life who has been such an incredible help to me and who is extremely interested in everything that has an influence on our lives – and not just the things going on within us, but external factors, too. One of the things she has encouraged me to do for some time now is to eliminate plastic from my life. Why mention this now? Because at the time I didn't yet have this water filtering system at home and I used to drink water from plastic bottles instead. I was aware that plastic was not good for our health, but I hadn't delved any deeper into the subject than that. At her suggestion, I did some reading and research, I watched a few videos and I learned just how toxic plastic can be to our lives, both from a health point of view and in terms of its effects on the environment. For example, I learned that water changes its pH in contact with plastic. I therefore set about eliminating plastic from my life as much as possible and telling as many people as possible about what I had learned. I came to the conclusion that it's not possible to completely eliminate plastic from our lives, though we are able to gradually reduce its use. Indeed, it's a long process, and the point is not to resort to extreme measures, but that we gradually become aware of the changes we can make on a daily basis.

Last summer, I became involved in the Plastic Free July campaign, an international movement which, in 2016 alone, attracted one million participants from 130 different countries. The idea was to reduce the amount of plastic we use for a certain amount of time, and I took up the challenge. The actual statistics that convinced me to do this were as follows: every year we throw away 300 million tonnes of plastic (just imagine the implications for the planet's oil resources!); it takes up to a thousand years for plastic to degrade; one million birds that live at sea and over one hundred thousand marine mammals die because of the plastic in the oceans; the use of products containing BPA can lead to precocious puberty, infertility, diabetes and insulin resistance, obesity, heart disease, genetic defects, behavioural disorders, as well as breast, ovarian and prostate cancer. Bisphenol A, or BPA, is an organic compound that was discovered in 1981 and is used in the production of certain plastics. It is found in food containers, bottle lids and boxes, plastic plates, glasses and cutlery, plastic water bottles, baby bottles, toys, medical equipment, piping, CDs and DVDs, electronic devices and so on.

While on the subject of water, there used to be this running joke at the Andreea Raicu office. I was so keen on drinking water that I was always telling my colleagues to keep themselves hydrated, and I would repeat this advice so many times that it became a kind of catchphrase. Whenever someone complained about something, we'd all say that the solution was – yes, you've guessed it! – to have a drink of water :). So, if you're unhappy with your weight, you get headaches and you suffer from dry skin and chapped lips, then my advice to you – apart from diet, medical tests, pills, body lotion and different kinds of lip balm – is first to try drinking more water.

The change won't happen overnight, and this is quite normal. If we suddenly give our kidneys four litres of water to filter, when they'd normally only have half a litre a day to deal with, then naturally our bodies will give off signals that something is wrong. So hydration should be performed gradually, allowing our bodies to become accustomed to healthy habits. We should increase gradually the amount of liquids we consume each day, and make sure we spread out our consumption throughout the day, not just drink it all at the same time.

**Note**

**Coffee, black tea, green tea, all of which contain a substance called theine, dehydrate the body and have a powerful diuretic effect.**

## The body needs rest. And so does the mind!

*"Think less, feel more."*

– OSHO

Have you ever wondered why there are so many advertisements for insomnia remedies? I can remember, one year ago, around March, when the ASCID patients association and the

Romanian Pulmonology Society launched a campaign to raise awareness of the issue of sleeping at the wheel. In their press release it said that insomnia, the most frequently encountered form of sleeping disorder, affects between 6% and 12% of the population. That seems like a lot to me! It also cited statistics saying that women are almost twice as likely to develop insomnia as men. Children, too, not just adults, suffer from sleep disorders and unfortunately the number of those affected is on the rise.

If our sleep schedule is interrupted, our entire body – our cognitive functions, metabolism and especially the communication between our brain and our other organs – will suffer as a result and, in trying to survive, produce large amounts of cortisol, the stress hormone, and adrenaline, which are the weapons the body relies on when under stress and drained of energy to cope with fatigue. A lack of sleep also affects the secretion of the hunger hormone (ghrelin) and the satiety hormone (leptin), often resulting in overeating. Consequently, the body retains any supplementary calories and the resulting excess weight will be very difficult to lose, even if we exercise and eat healthily. Drawing on my own experience, in what follows I will try to convince you to place greater importance on resting and to do everything you can to avoid sleepless nights. Our health and – if this is a greater motivator for you – our physical appearance are at stake! Before I do this, however, I ought to begin by telling you that I didn't always think this way.

Ever since I was young, people close to me would say there's nothing you can't achieve if you really set your mind to it. Being a beautiful woman (even if I do say so myself) and given the widespread belief that such women aren't particularly capable in other areas, especially in terms of intellectual pursuits, I have always felt a need to prove to others that I was strong and capable of working really hard. I can remember being so determined that had someone told me I would have to be on set for 30 hours flat then I wouldn't have batted an eyelid. As a result, especially during my 20-year career in television, sleep was never a priority for me; it was more like a hurdle to be overcome. It was something that was meant to happen only when I found time for it.

I still notice today how people are engaged in a competition as to who got the least sleep. I too, some years ago, used to believe it was a matter of pride to sleep as little as possible, leaving you more time to get stuff done. I would feel exhausted and would eventually have to get some sleep, but I didn't have a real schedule, because at this point sleep wasn't a priority in my life. My work schedule came first and I was ashamed to admit to being tired and needing rest. Do you know what the need for sleep was synonymous with in my mind back then? With wasting time. I would later come to understand that the reason I didn't notice my lack of sleep was because I wasn't in touch with my body and, for that matter, I wasn't in touch with myself.

For a long time I was one of the most active people on the planet, a master of multi-tasking, because I always wanted to be productive and to demonstrate that I was capable of doing as many things as possible all at the same time. I had set out to prove to everyone that I was more than just a pretty face or a well-toned body, that I was someone who had gone beyond her limits and overcome the prejudices held by those around her. And while I achieved what I was aiming for, there was a price to pay. The crazy pace of my life made me crack and I was exhausted and unhappy. I thought nothing was enough, that I should never stop, that I still had so much to learn and too little time to do it all in. Everything happens so quickly in today's world, meaning we don't have the time to do anything properly and we're always under pressure to press on. I feel society is always setting us targets, happiness criteria, for us to strive to achieve, with the result that we no longer know who we really are. Are all these things we're chasing our own desires, or are they chosen for us by those around us? I realised that for too long in my life it was other people who had mattered, not me!

You know what I find really sad? That in trying to achieve perfection we sleep less in order to make time to do all the things we set out to do; but without rest we lack the energy to do the things we need to do. It's a vicious circle we must escape from, because our health and happiness are at stake! In my desire to do this, step by step I discovered the philosophy of slow living, which involves being conscious of everything I do, no longer paying attention to multiple things at the same time, no longer doing things robotically, and instead being truly focused and present. I sleep as much as I need to recharge my batteries, which helps me to have positive energy as well as beautiful skin and, above all, I realise that this improves my chances of delaying the appearance of wrinkles. It's certainly no accident that the first range of products from Vichy designed to correct and delay the signs of ageing in your complexion is called Slow Âge. I really like the analogy between the art of living slowly, beautifully and consciously, enjoying every moment, and the concept of beauty that has stood the test of time with a little help from personal care products.

Sleep is a need, a necessity, it is part of our lives. I have now reached the stage at which I have a connection with my body and I no longer want to stay up all night, and if I do my body immediately lets me know about it. In order to function properly, I need to get between seven and eight hours of sleep a night, because at the crazy pace we lead our lives, our brains need time to regenerate. During the day, we gather so much information, but it's never enough. We always want to be up to date with everything that's going on and to learn everything there is to know about anything, to accumulate it all, not to miss out on anything. This immense quantity of information is stored in the brain – with most of it possibly being of no use to us – and in order to be able to begin a new day properly, our body needs time to process all these things and to rest.

While we sleep, the brain goes over the events of the previous day, catalogues and stores them, deleting the ones it considers of no use. During the day, the cells in the brain and the body accumulate toxins. When the rest of the body is resting, the brain begins clearing out these impurities and getting ready for a new day. Even negative emotions are processed, so in the future, when we come across them, the body will know what behaviour to adopt to avoid suffering.

I've heard a lot of people say they don't feel the need to sleep, that they feel fine after just four hours of shut-eye, or even less, every night. Maybe this works for them, but I came to realise that it doesn't apply to me. Back when I also used to skimp on sleep, I wasn't aware of my needs. And because I had forbidden my body from sending me signals – and even if it did, I would only ignore and stifle them – I naturally ended up believing I no longer had any needs.

My friends always poke fun at me because I'm able to sleep anywhere and in any situation, even while standing up, so I guess I'm just the type who quickly succumbs to sleep's embrace. Which reminds me of when I was on a trip to the Seychelles some years ago and, not having found a better way to get to a neighbouring island, we ended up taking quite a small and overcrowded local boat. The ocean had become pretty choppy and my friends got really scared and began to feel sea sick, only I slept through it all as if nothing had happened. Even sickness, in this case brought on by the sea, manifests itself in me in the guise of a relaxing… sleep :). In fact, I've never had problems sleeping and I am able to fall asleep really fast. During really stressful periods, when it feels like none of the things I normally do to relax are working (e.g. meditation or conscious breathing), then I take some melatonin or some other homeopathic remedies to help me get to sleep, but this happens only very rarely.

I like it to be very dark in the place where I sleep, and this is really strange because before my trip to India I always wanted there to be some light in the room. I like my bedroom to be extremely well-aired and I use soft, fine bed linen that gives me a sense of well-being. Before going to sleep, I often read a little or listen to some meditation music, and I light candles to create a warm, pleasant, relaxing atmosphere in the room. I basically try to send my body messages to say that it will be going to sleep soon. I also avoid using my phone and nor do I watch any television, even if I still have a television set in my bedroom I haven't actually switched on for many years now.

I read an interesting book in which it said that the thoughts we take with us when we go to sleep in the evening are very important, because this information enters our subconscious and stays there. For example, if we feel angry, sad or unhappy about something before going to sleep, i.e. we're in a really bad mood, then the next morning we will wake up feeling just the same. A habit I've developed in recent years is that every time I go to bed, I think of three good things that happened to me that day and then thank God for them. Feeling gratitude helps me to be optimistic and focus my attention on the good things in my life and not the things that poison my soul.

In order not to end up hating our alarm clocks, we simply need to tell our bodies that we only need to sleep a set number of hours and to suggest a time at which to wake up. I don't know about you, but whatever tune I set as my alarm sound, I always end up hating it. Or at least I used to! Although I'm actually someone who loves mornings, back when I used to get very tired and stressed, I would associate waking up in the morning with feeling miserable and being unwell.

Coming back to the idea of getting up early without an alarm, I, who had always been something of a doubting Thomas, didn't actually believe this was possible when I first heard the idea while on a course – that is, not until I had tried it for myself and discovered it felt fantastic. The mechanism is really simple: even if I know I'm not going to get much sleep and won't be sufficiently rested the next morning, I try not to go to bed thinking that waking up the next morning is going to be really difficult. Instead, I tell myself I'm going to make the most of the time I have available for sleep, however little that might be, and I think about how I am going to get to see the sun rise or enjoy a special breakfast. I didn't have an alarm clock with me during the workshop I took part in, and so after it was recommended we begin to think in this way and to suggest a time to our bodies at which we wanted to get up, the next morning we all still woke up around the exact same time the alarm, had we set one, would have gone off at. Wow! I was surprised but also excited! Then I remembered how, when we were children and were going on a trip, our parents didn't need to wake us up because we were so excited that we'd wake up at the right time anyway and, what's more, we were only too happy to do it. This is why I think the information we transmit to our subconscious in the evening is really important for how we feel the next morning. We basically transfer the energy, whether positive or negative, we have in the evening to the coming morning. So I've become used to communicating to my subconscious that, although ideally I'd like to sleep for longer, I only have x number of hours available and I'll find the time to make up for these lost hours. I then wake up the next morning not feeling tired or grumpy – and without having set an alarm.

The first things we should do in the morning are the more creative things we have to do, things which fill us with positive energy, because the mind is rested; what we should not do is look at our phones, because this device only fills the mind with the information we cleansed it of during the night. When your mind is clear, you have the capacity and clarity to see things the way they really are, as opposed to the way you would have perceived them if you were still tired, and you also have more imagination and patience.

For me sleep is the best medicine there is; it is a truly fantastic resource, and I've learned that I can't function properly if I don't listen to my body's needs in this respect. I'm pleased that after working on my self-awareness, all the meditation I've done and the many books I've read, I've come to understand that it's necessary – vital, in fact – that we sleep for between seven and nine hours a night. Below I will list some of the symptoms I've felt myself, together with others I've read about, as a result of not getting enough rest. They include the following:

- irascibility – when we don't sleep properly lots of things begin to annoy us that we wouldn't normally notice
- headaches
- inability to concentrate
- inability to learn/remember things
- lack of energy
- excessive appetite (the body needs energy, and if you can't take this from time spent sleeping then you'll take from food instead) and all kinds of hormonal imbalances
- back pain
- dry skin
- loss of libido
- depression
- heightened emotivity

- increased predisposition to disease
- chronic tiredness, which can even lead to death

Lack of sleep may not only lead to the onset of Alzheimer's, it also plays an important role in aggravating existing cases. Sleep deprivation reduces the brain's ability to eliminate toxins, thus accelerating the onset of this ruthless disease. There are many studies showing a link between sleep deprivation and depression, diabetes, heart disease and cancer.

When someone asks me about my beauty routines, I tell them that if I get a good night's sleep and drink plenty of water then my face will look impeccable the next day. It's important to sleep in bed linen made from natural materials, e.g. cotton and silk, which helps us to relax.

We need more sleep today than our ancestors did because we have a lot more information available to us and our brains need more time to process it all. For example, if I don't get enough sleep, I become irritable, my ability to concentrate decreases, I lose patience and I'm more sensitive than usual. When I feel things are getting to me more than they should, I realise that I must be very tired, and so I drop everything and get some rest. One hour later and the problem no longer seems so serious.

If I had to choose between sleep and exercise, then I'd choose sleep because sleep gives me the energy I need to do physical exercise in the first place. However, we shouldn't confuse laziness with tiredness! It's one thing to find it hard to motivate yourself to go out for a run or go to the gym, because it's easier to stay in bed and you're finding it hard to leave your comfort zone; and it's another thing to feel that you're exhausted and you don't have the energy to do anything.

Years ago I would feel guilty when I slept late. Now I'm extremely happy when I'm able to do this, and the results are fantastic: I have more energy, I find it easier to concentrate, my immune system is stronger, my skin is beautiful and I feel wonderful. Did you know it's a good idea to use satin pillow cases because they don't absorb the oil on our skin? I also read that it is recommended that we sleep on our backs, because if we sleep on our bellies, this causes wrinkling, which in turn affects the elasticity of the skin. Similarly, if we sleep on our sides, we risk getting larger bags beneath our eyes.

We have to try not to ignore the signals our body sends us. The body warns us whenever there's a problem, but we're so caught up in our hectic lives that we don't have the time to do anything about it, nor are we accustomed to listening to what the body is telling us. "Beauty sleep" is not just a throw-away expression, and I don't think it was coined by accident. A recent study by Vichy shows that, depending on our lifestyles (which may involve lack of sleep, exhaustion at work, stress, etc.), the tired appearance of our skin will be accentuated, with the result that wrinkles begin to appear, the dark rings beneath our eyes get worse and our skin becomes dry and loses its radiance. The area around our eyes suffers the most from sleep deprivation, and the bags beneath our eyes become more pronounced because our blood circulation has become worse and our blood vessels begin to change colour. What's more, wrinkles are more likely to appear and the general appearance of our skin leaves much to be desired. They're not wrong when they say that when we don't get enough sleep we can see it on our face, because we look older.

So, insufficient or poor quality sleep accelerates the signs of ageing, reduces the ability of the skin to regenerate during the night and leaves us feeling unhappy with the appearance of our complexion. I can completely relate to the findings of this study! Stress and tiredness are responsible for the secretion of cortisol, the stress hormone, as well as a weakening of the immune system.

In the long term, it can increase the risk of our developing psoriasis, acne, herpes, seborrheic dermatitis and other skin conditions.

During the night, the skin not only regenerates, with the skin cells repairing themselves and toxins being eliminated; it also gets itself ready to deal with the challenges of the coming day, such as providing protection against ultraviolet rays, pollution and aggressive environmental factors. Contrary to expectation, genetics is responsible for only a small proportion of cellular ageing – just 20%. The exposome, with its crucial role in cellular ageing, is responsible for the remaining 80%. This term encompasses all non-genetic factors that cause cellular decay: stress, lack of sleep, tiredness, ultraviolet light, tobacco, alcohol and unhealthy diets, to name but a few. As all these factors are responsible for the ageing of our face, and it's impossible to eliminate them from our lives, we need to take action on two levels. Firstly, on an internal level: we should limit as far as possible our exposure to the factors making up the exposome. This, as I advised you at the beginning of the book, means eating healthily and not following extreme diets, doing physical exercise and hydrating ourselves correctly, and, especially, sleeping long enough to replenish our energy reserves and allow our skin to regenerate. (It's also important to give up smoking and to reduce unfiltered exposure to the sun, but I will deal with this subject in more detail in the next chapter.) Similarly, we also need to act on an external level: we should use products that delay and slow down the appearance of the "marks" time leaves on the skin. This is why I never go to sleep without first applying some cream containing special ingredients like Resveratrol, Baicalin (an antioxidant root extract), Bifidus (probiotic-derived), and thermal water, which helps the skin stay young and hydrates it deeply.

If we are to go by what the specialists tell us, then sleeping from ten o' clock at night to six o' clock the next morning is much more restful than sleeping from one in the morning to nine the next morning. However, I believe that perhaps even more important than this is for us to listen to our bodies and to rest when they tell us they need to, although it is still advisable to go to bed before midnight. Between seven and nine hours of sleep per night should be enough for us to rebalance our bodies after a long and challenging day. (Of course, an exception is to be made in the case of sick people or people who have undergone medical procedures or experiences that took a lot of energy out of them.) This doesn't mean, however, that we should go to town when it comes to how long we sleep for. If, in the absence of other factors necessitating supplementary rest, we regularly exceed the recommended seven to nine hours of sleep mentioned above, then this can give rise to a disorder called hypersomnia or excessive somnolence. As you might imagine, the number of people suffering from this condition is relatively low, but it's still no laughing matter, as it can lead to depression, dementia, hormonal imbalances and liver disease, among other things.

**Did you know?**

**Today, we sleep 20% less than people did one hundred years ago.**

While I don't normally have any trouble getting to sleep, there were times when I'd arrive home dead tired after a really long and exhausting day and my only desire was to get myself into bed and to forget it all. However, from too much stress and exhaustion, I would find myself unable to shut my eyes. Sleep seems very far away at these moments and I'm sure there are plenty among you who have also found themselves in this situation. So it may be that we are unable to fall asleep despite being extremely tired. Why does this happen? Because of all the thoughts that never stop flowing. Night time is when everything finally goes quiet; the phone no longer rings and emails stop arriving, our work for the day is done and it's time to be with ourselves, to be aware of the thoughts we were unable to hear during the day due to all the noise around us. Our thoughts, worries and problems are louder at night than our tiredness and they mean to make themselves heard. Regrets about the past, projections onto the future, imaginative ideas and all manner of other scenarios place us in a state in which we are incapable of entering the land of sleep. And when we finally do manage to nod off, the alarm rings and the time set aside for resting is over. A new day beckons and there's no more time for relaxation and rest, our sleep-deprived bodies will have to struggle to keep up. But they won't be able to keep this up for long! Every thought that takes us back into the past or projects us into the future stops us from enjoying the present, and it is the present moment that really matters.

The greatest challenge in all this whirlwind of projections and soul searching is to silence our thoughts, to free ourselves of the burdens that stop us from living in the present and, above all, to get some rest. I'd like to share with you now a few things that have helped me deal with these situations. The first of these is guided meditation, which can help us eliminate stress and find inner peace. You'll find a lot about this on YouTube as well as via all kinds of dedicated apps. It can be helpful to try to concentrate on your breathing, which can also be an effective method. At first this might seem difficult, especially as it has to be done without help, but it's by no means impossible. You need to focus just on your breathing, which should be deep. Last but not least, we need to become conscious of our bodies and aware of their sensations. Lying in bed, we begin by focusing our minds on our bodies and everything we feel, from breathing to the way the body feels in contact with the bed. These are the methods I use to focus my attention on the present and to silence the thoughts that won't allow me to sleep. With a little practice and discipline, this approach always works for me, so perhaps it will be helpful to you too.

—

## Non-invasive therapies I have tried and am happy to recommend

*I believe it's important to do things that are right for you. And the right things will come when you're ready.*

As those of you who have shown the patience and curiosity required to get this far through my book will have noticed – and let me congratulate you on your determination! :) – I believe that our health is one of our greatest responsibilities and therefore should not be taken lightly. A tincture, a plant extract or some tea will not cure a disease, but the studies, experience and professionalism of specialists in the field will. However, what I want to tell you here is about what happens before you end up consulting one of these specialists. Yes, I believe that allopathic medicine is able to provide us with many solutions. But I also believe holistic medicine can help us avoid having to resort to these solutions in the first place. At the risk of sounding clichéd, I will say it again: prevention is better than cure. So before undergoing treatment for a given symptom, we should first ask ourselves what the cause is, which is precisely what I did after suffering a number of health issues that forced me to seek out the most effective solutions.

Although I now feel at home with these alternative forms of diagnosis and treatment, for a long time I was sceptical and preferred to spend my money at pharmacies. I've already told you about the medicine drawer at my parents' house, which I'd resort to whenever I felt the slightest discomfort. Yes, I grew up in a family that firmly believed in the "institution of medication": at home there was always a drawer full of boxes, strips and bottles of pills that the entire family would turn to whenever the first worrying symptom reared its head. Of course, these diagnoses were made either by the patients themselves or by the "house doctors" – i.e. my mother or one of my aunts – and so we used to self-medicate all the time. I certainly can't recommend this to anyone!

"Got a headache? Take this pill!", "Oh, you must have neuralgia/indigestion/a migraine…", "You clearly have an issue with your gall bladder/liver/sinuses/joints…" or "Whatever it is, just take one of these, it'll do you good! Anyway, don't worry, we'll get you to the hospital right away!" – that's how bad things were in our family, but at least I can laugh about it now.

And even after I grew up, I continued taking lots of pills. What was I really doing? I was treating the symptoms, not the cause. Why? Because I hadn't been taught to look for it. Today I treat illnesses in a direct relationship with my state of mind and soul. I believe the human body is very intelligent and that it possesses a really good self-defence mechanism. We only need to learn how to decipher the messages it is sending us. And many of our complaints are essentially psychosomatic, in that what we feel on the inside also has an effect on the outside. I learnt more about psychosomatic effects during my trip to India, which is where I also came to understand how important it is to seek out the cause of our problems and not just treat the symptoms. When I had a herniated disc, for example, my body simply gave up from having been overworked, so preventing the recurrence of painful symptoms didn't only mean avoiding certain movements, but also paying attention to what I eat, keeping myself hydrated, doing as much physical exercise as my body allows and, in particular, taking good care of it and avoiding exhaustion!

I have tried ozone therapy and bioresonance testing (this is how I found out about certain complaints I had which I probably wouldn't have discovered so soon using conventional investigations!). And I've decided to tell you a little bit about the benefits of each. Because, when it comes down to it, this is what it means to take care of your health: the more careful you are, the greater your chances of leading an easy and quiet life for as long as possible. But I wouldn't want you to think I'm encouraging you to stop going to see your doctor and to exchange doing some medical tests for a ticket to India (although a journey towards yourselves, wherever it takes place in the world, may well provide you with many solutions). As I said before, I believe allopathic medicine has an important role to play in our lives. But it is equally important to look for other methods of maintaining the health of your body and, by strengthening it, protecting it from disease!

## Bioresonance therapy

I've always been a rational person who first needs to test and understand things before recommending them, and I've never taken the advice of others seriously except when I believed it was really necessary to change something. Whenever someone told me about an alternative therapy, for me it was just another reason to laugh and poke fun at the person in question. I can remember how I kept on hearing about bioresonance and just how sceptical I was about it.

"So you're saying it will help me detect diseases early, even those caused by negative emotions? Yeah, right! And I suppose it'll cook and go to the gym for me as well?!" – this was the kind of ironic answer I would give to those who suggested I try this kind of therapy :). I'm different now. My experiences have transformed me, and I've become far more open to new things and no longer automatically reject certain theories and procedures without even reading up on them first.

And yet, one day I told myself I'd give bioresonance a go, if only to see what it was like. I walked into the consulting room of Cristina Bogdan without any real expectations and… I was in for a shock because although I was only expecting to have a bit of fun trying out yet another form of therapy that promises lots but fails to deliver, I was amazed by the results. Although I didn't tell her exactly what was bothering me at the time, my friend listed the reasons why my body was not functioning properly with an accuracy that left me lost for words. She basically told me what it was I was suffering from, even though I hadn't actually mentioned any specific ailment to her. As she read out my results, I stared at her as if something unreal was happening to me, because she simply reeled off all the symptoms, all the unpleasant conditions I was experiencing at the time, and these were things only I knew about. She also told me I wasn't spending enough time outdoors, how I slept at night, what symptoms I had at certain times, etc. – I really couldn't believe what was happening to me. It felt like I was on 'Candid Camera' and someone close to me was having a laugh at my expense and soon they'd be telling me it was all just a joke. Unfortunately, however, I left there feeling quite distressed, because the results of the tests didn't look good at all and were in fact an accurate reflection of my condition.

I realised that things are not always the way I thought they were and that, before casting judgment on another alternative therapy, I'd better read up on it first, to see how things stood. Cristina, my friend, although an allopathic doctor, had also specialised in various alternative therapies, such as ozone therapy and bioresonance, and she duly recommended a number of homeopathic products to me. Naturally, I was expecting all my complaints to disappear in the space of a week, only I hadn't taken into account that healing is a slow process and that these products, although highly effective, don't produce results overnight. So, it took a lot longer, but the effects eventually kicked in and I began to feel much better.

Bioresonance is a branch of vibrational medicine.[22] Starting with Einstein, who concluded that matter and energy are two forms of the same thing, studies have shown that matter is a form of "frozen energy", with matter and energy being inseparably linked. Our body functions both mechanically (via the muscles, heart and joints, etc.), based on a form of biochemical communication, and as a system of integrated circuits formed of the cell membranes and the intercellular structures, which communicate via electromagnetic messages. Bioresonance testing picks up the characteristics of the bio-fields of biological structures.

"The human body has an electromagnetic energy pattern that changes as a function of external electromagnetic stimuli and

---

[22] "Vibrational medicine is a science that is both old and new, a synthesis of the most effective ancient healing techniques and the latest scientific discoveries relating to the dual nature (in terms of energy and matter) of the atoms and molecules we are made of." – PhD Associate Professor T. Trandafir and PhD Assistant Professor Mihaela Gheorghiu.

which can result in modified health states, mild imbalances and disease. By testing the specific electromagnetic frequencies of each cell type we obtain a map of the electromagnetic imbalances compared with a normal and healthy pattern" – so reads Cristina Bogdan's by-the-book definition of this alternative therapy. Put simply, in the form of a comparison I came across in my research and which I liked a lot: the bioresonance device scans the body like anti-virus software scans a computer, seeking out every kind of virus, disease, weakness, anomaly or sensitivity. You get the results on the spot, and the feedback you receive paints a picture of the energy state of the entire body. During testing, the clinician analyses any changes that may have appeared and suggests a course of corrective therapy be undertaken before the disease appears (prevention). It is a non-invasive and painless procedure that does not involve any radiation and has no adverse effects and which lasts between 60 and 90 minutes. Testing may be followed by one or more sessions of therapy, depending on what ailments are discovered, as well as various recommendations by the specialist in terms of lifestyle, diet and the use of natural remedies.

I still go for regular bioresonance testing, but this doesn't mean I don't also do my usual medical tests, because I don't believe that only alternative therapies should be used to help treat disease, but that they are often able to provide us with many clues as to the cause of a given health issue.

## Ozone therapy

The first time I tried ozone therapy was at a wellness centre in Spain, as part of a rebalancing programme involving both a macrobiotic diet and exercise, meditation, serotherapy and ozone therapy. I must admit that afterwards I felt like a different person: I had more energy, my skin looked better and I realised, once again, how important it is to give your body the things it needs, as well as the role alternative therapies can play in our lives. Whenever I feel tired and my body signals for help, I do a course of ozone therapy, which gives me a lift.

Ozone is a molecule with three oxygen atoms; more precisely, it is a gas. To keep the three atoms together requires large amounts of energy, and the energy released when it decomposes triggers various beneficial reactions in the body. Ozone therapy has a detoxifying, revitalising, antioxidising, anti-inflammatory, analgesic, antibacterial, antiviral and antifungal effect, being used in the treatment of skin and vaginal infections, as well as hepatitis B and C. It is recommended in cases of joint, muscle and ligament pain, it relaxes the body, it has a beneficial effect in cases of type 2 diabetes, it enhances physical and intellectual performance, it improves blood circulation and it helps in cases of sleep disorder, depression and kidney disease. What's more, it reduces cellular oxidation and boosts the immune system and the resistance of the body to aggressive treatments, it slows the ageing process and reduces fine wrinkles and cellulite. It is used successfully in cases of cervical and lower back pain, herniated discs, rheumatoid arthritis, vascular disease, Parkinson's disease, Alzheimer's disease, acne, psoriasis, ovarian cysts, lesions to the lower limbs and arthrosis. To date no contraindications and side effects have been discovered when undergoing ozone therapy on standard doses.

Ozone therapy can be applied in different ways, depending on the complaint and patient preference, the most frequently encountered forms being injections and insufflation via the rectum or vagina.

# PART 2

# BEAUTY

# 13

# The regrets of youth and some long lists of complexes

*Time is the most precious resource you have. Don't waste it on things that don't matter.*

We enter this world with so many special things and we acquire many others along the way. The body is the first of God's gifts to us, even if we often fail to notice, let alone appreciate, its qualities. We take these things for granted, as if we were entitled to them, without stopping to think for a moment that we should be grateful we have them. We believe everything revolves around us and that we deserve them. And it's the same with our health, we only come to realise the importance of these things when it's much too late and we don't have them anymore. But I don't mean to begin the second part of this book on a pessimistic note, not least because beauty – both physical and spiritual – is a wonderful gift.

There's something beautiful to be found in everyone, even those who only find bad things to say about themselves when they look in the mirror. The ancient Greeks said that everyone is endowed with minute fragments of the perfection of the Universe, meaning we are creatures who aspire to immortality and we carry within us the stuff the gods were made of. What hinders us from becoming aware of our true potential is our tendency to always look down, to see our defects and shortcomings, instead of raising our gaze towards greatness. Maybe this is our particular appeal, as mortals, to be perfectly… imperfect. And of course I'm no different in this regard, as I have sinned when it comes to beauty, identifying so many things about myself I considered to be defects, only rarely being able to enjoy my real qualities – and even then only with reluctance, with hidden fears, with a lack of generosity…

Now I wouldn't want you to think that in the past I would, for example, neglect to take care of my skin, for I was the (un)lucky owner of hundreds of different creams :). While not very often, I would still go to beauty salons and I had more treatments then than I do today; not to mention that, probably like every woman, I simply loved buying lots of personal care products. Throughout my life there have been only a few cosmetic products that have found a permanent place on my shopping list and which I would buy a second time, because, as with the diets I've tried, I've always been curious to try whatever was new on the market. And, yes, it goes without saying that I have experimented with a lot of different face masks, in fact this became a kind of hobby for me!

I have always had a certain attachment to my personal care and beauty products. Perhaps too strong. As I write this, for example, I can remember how in the past I would never stay over at a friend's or my boyfriend's house if I didn't have my creams with me. And I broke this rule only very rarely. I inherited this passion for cosmetics from the other women in my family – especially my mother, but also her sister and my granny – who wouldn't leave home without applying some cream and tending to their physical appearances. For that matter, all the other women in the family were also always well groomed, and so they instilled this habit in me, too. Genetic inheritance played a big role. I often look at my mother, for example, and although she's not getting any younger, the years have treated her kindly and many people praise her for the way she looks after herself. I have to say I'm proud of her, especially as I'm able to be objective and to observe that she has always been a beautiful woman.

When it comes to the sins of my youth, I have many regrets. I remember how when I would take off my makeup, I would be so brutal with my face, it was as if my skin was immune to the harsh way I was removing the makeup. This again showed that I didn't love my body and hadn't realised how important it is to treat it with love and tenderness, as if it were my most important friend. Beauticians and makeup artists who saw me clean my skin were shocked at what they saw and would wonder just how I could still manage to look so good after inflicting such mistreatment on my face every day. I didn't possess the gentle motion required when cleaning your face, when massaging and pampering it, even in the short time we have available in the morning or at night.

The idea of beauty I had as an adolescent and young adult was therefore different from what I believe today. This is only natural: age doesn't just etch fine lines into our faces, it also reflects experience, wisdom, greater knowledge and balance. If someone had told me twenty years ago that I would come to see beauty in this way and think like this, I'm certain I wouldn't have believed them. For starters, I wasn't even aware of how much the things I was doing were affecting my skin. I would always make sure to remove my makeup, but without being aware of the process, without realising how much my skin needed to breathe.

I used to wear tons of makeup, go to the tanning studio, spend a huge amount of time in the sun and wouldn't apply much sunscreen, especially at those hours of the day when the sun's rays are at their most dangerous. All because I so badly wanted to have dark skin. I thought that if I just applied some cream afterwards, after the skin was already burnt, things would sort themselves out on their own. I wasn't aware of – or simply chose to ignore – any information on the consequences of these habits that were so harmful to my skin. I can also remember using a high coverage foundation, because, having a light complexion, I thought my skin was transparent and I had this constant feeling you could see all the blood vessels in my face. Working in television, I was used to spending all day with makeup on and my skin would be covered in this way. It became a routine for me, but my skin was visibly affected after hours and hours spent wearing too much makeup, not allowing it to breathe.

There was also the time I worked as beauty editor for *Viva* magazine and would receive lots of different products for testing that I simply adored trying out. Indeed, the pleasure I take in collecting cosmetics dates from this time. Even today, if anyone were to see my bathroom, they'd have no doubt about my passion for personal care products – I really have an amazing amount and have become quite attached to some of them, even though I don't use them all the time. I like knowing that they're there, that's all. It's another guilty pleasure of mine, though this time it's not about food but relates to my beauty routine. Come to think of it, I actually have far fewer of these products today than in the past! Oily, buttery and coarse scrubs for delicate skin, face and body creams, body oil, various lotions, serums, tonic water, anti-ageing products, face, body and hair masks – at one point it felt like I was suffocating and I was forced to become more selective in what I use. But if I'm honest I must admit that I still have (rather) a lot!

As an adolescent I made sure I took care of my skin, only once or twice did I go to bed with my makeup still on, after which I always felt awful. On that occasion, I was very tired and fell asleep without realising it, and the next day my face felt dirty and my skin all clogged up. What a paradox: although I was using dozens of different creams to care for my skin, I overlooked the fact that the cigarettes I so much enjoyed at the time were affecting it – even if I wasn't a heavy smoker – or that I was developing wrinkles from exposure to the sun. I thought the price of having a tan was not too much to pay. My little pleasures, even if extremely damaging for my health, were more important to me, and I thought I could get away with it by using hydrating cream.

In the following pages I will tell you more about my experiences of beauty and skin care, about my relationship with the sun, my frenemy :), about how I learned to take better care of my skin, as well as what I think about cosmetic surgery and what my daily personal care routine entails. I will provide you with a brief list of what things are never missing from my arsenal of beauty products, as well as the different face and body treatments I've tried out over the years. And, as many of you keep asking me how come I don't look my age, I will describe how I go about trying to delay the appearance of wrinkles without resorting to the scalpel, as well as the importance of identifying what factors can damage the skin and age it prematurely. So, welcome to my world of beauty! :)

# 14

# An artificial standard and my plea for change

*The over-enhancement of images gives rise to frustration.*

Princesses are beautiful, queens are majestic, even the pretty, hard-working and kind-hearted Cinderella of children's tales provides us with a role model for our lives. We grow up full of pre-established ideas about why we need to be beautiful, clever, powerful women, always home early and good housewives, while also being sexy divas to our partners with high moral standards who manage to expose evil and hypocrisy and serve as examples to younger generations. Need I go on? Goodness, the list of things we're expected to be is so long, but there's no way we can live up to it all, as we simply don't have the time or the energy! We're people, not robots – and I don't think even robots would be able to perform so many tasks so flawlessly.

When it comes to beauty, if anything the standards we must strive to achieve seem to be even higher. And no, I'm not perfect, I'm sorry to have to break the news to you, but then there's a silver lining to this confession: I feel good, fantastic even, in my own skin. And I'm telling you this even though I know I don't always have the flattest tummy, the tightest skin, or eyes that don't have bags under them. Oops, I've let the cat out of the bag! But it's really no big deal, there's no harm in a little diversity! :) Ahh, and before I forget, I also don't have any magic powers and nor did Prince Charming fight the dragon for me. Consequently, every step I have taken in the realm of beauty has been accompanied by challenges and I have learned a lot on my own.

In most cases, the beauty industry (self-)manufactures immaculate people who are seen as role models. This has led to the creation of artificial standards – otherwise why would anyone be surprised that Cindy Crawford has stretch marks at the age of 52? And these excessively enhanced images give rise to frustration – how can anybody who sees Cindy in a picture looking impeccable, showing no traces of the passing of time, feel anything other than confused? As someone who knows what it's like to be on the other side of the curtain, I can honestly tell you that the most important thing is for us to accept reality. To seek out the true reality, not an artificial reality. First accept your body as it is and do your best to keep it healthy, and only then should your focus shift to making it beautiful. The beauty of this is that achieving the former comes with the latter thrown into the bargain. However, before I was able to see it this way, I had to go through a lot of different stages – and I have to say it wasn't easy!

As this book recounts important parts of my story and explains how I got to this point in my life, I think it's important to describe here the toxic and quite literally dangerous relationship I've had with the sun over the years. It's not easy for me to talk about these things, which, at the end of the day, were my own decision, but I strongly believe that even if only one person who reads these lines takes my advice about protecting themselves from the sun, then I will have achieved my goal. So: "Hello (again), my name is Andreea, and I used to be addicted to… tanning!" Like a reptile soaking up every last ray of sun, I would spend hours on the beach, motionless, in order to have darker skin; I'd go on exotic holidays, to sunny destinations, above all the seaside, where in theory people go to relax, and I'd set the alarm for seven in the morning so I could get to the beach as early as possible. Now I wouldn't want you to think that at lunchtime I'd take my things and go off for something to eat and a rest… no chance of that! No, I'd stay there till evening, literally frying myself, because I thought it a terrible shame to return home without as strong a tan as possible. I wanted to have darker skin so much, I became (almost) obsessed and was often left with a number of "souvenirs" after a beach holiday, especially in the form of hyperpigmentation and sun burn, which I would then go to great lengths to conceal.

I must have got sunburn dozens of times! My face would get so red, but there was no stopping me. "Come on, Andreea, let's grab something to eat!" the people I was on holiday with would say to me. "No, I'm not leaving the sun, I'll only eat something if I can have it brought to me here on the beach," I would say in reply without a second thought. I wanted all of the sun for myself and I was determined to get a tan in order to hide all the imperfections only I was able to see. I was in love with the idea of being tanned!

I used to believe – incorrectly, as it happens – that if I used sunscreen then I wouldn't get a tan. Wrong! However, unfortunately many people still believe in this myth! The reality is that if we apply sunscreen and avoid the sun around lunchtime, when it's at its strongest, then we both won't get burnt and will avoid the risk of developing skin cancer! Admittedly, it might take us longer to get a tan, but our skin will eventually still darken and it has the great advantage of avoiding the appearance of wrinkles and the various diseases that can appear as a result of overexposure to the sun. It's like with medicines: we know that if we eat a certain thing it's going to make us feel sick, but instead of avoiding eating that thing, we risk it and then take a pill afterwards to help deal with the unpleasant symptoms. As I said earlier, we treat the effects, not the cause. Isn't it better to tan ourselves slowly, in a healthier way, rather than to get so burnt we don't know what to rub into our skin to stop it hurting and to avoid blotches?

So, high and low factor sunscreen for the face, sunscreen for the extremities, sun sticks, low and high factor sun protection oil, which I used to use after spending time in the sun, hydrating lotion… it was all something of a paradox: I thought it important to take care of my skin and so I'd stock up on creams, but at the same time I'd still expose myself to the sun for hours on end. I remember how I'd take a special butter with me on holiday that I'd always pack because I knew I was going to get burnt. Wouldn't it have been better to prevent this from happening in the first place, rather than end up having to treat it afterwards? :) Anyway, long story short, almost half of my travel bag would be just creams!

Now, when I think back, it seems funny, but at the same time I feel frustrated and I can't believe how reckless I was. I remember arriving at a friend's place in America, from where I went on for a holiday in Barbados. When I got back almost black in colour from that superb destination, my friend, who knew how sensitive a subject tanning was for me, made fun of me and teased me, saying: "Do you mean to go back home like that, without a proper tan? Go down to the tanning salon and get yourself some colour!" Her words remained imprinted on my mind, as did her advice, so – yes! – I did indeed go to the tanning salon to top up my tan after a week's sunning myself in Barbados, so desperate was I to have a tan… How irresponsible I was!

Nothing would have stopped me in the past from going to the tanning salon, and I didn't realise quite how dangerous it is. Even if I was able to see how my skin aged quicker after these sessions and I could feel it was no longer so smooth and had a dry texture, I still kept on going. The wrinkles around my eyes, for example, became even more pronounced, and yet nothing would stop me. I remember thinking it was super cool to have a tan during winter: when everyone was wearing boots, I was in sandals and a short skirt, my legs were well toned from the gym and, of course, nicely tanned. I felt it was worth the risk, but the truth is I wasn't fully aware of the implications of my actions. It seems terrifying to me now, and I wouldn't recommend anyone go to the tanning salon today. It should be banned!

You know what intrigues me? I see people who know all of this already, who know how dangerous artificial tanning is, but they choose to go regardless. It breaks my heart because I realise we're voluntarily exposing our bodies to such dangers. Essentially, a few minutes at the tanning salon is equivalent to a whole day spent in the sun, and it goes without saying that it's not natural and not without adverse effects. It is so aggressive on the skin! It's like signing our own death sentence in terms of the appearance of our skin.

Any other regrets? Well, I used to sunbathe topless. Now that I've learned what this can do to you I feel like going up to young women who still do this and saying, "Please cover yourself! You don't realise the risks you're exposing yourself to!" I hope that you, my dear readers, will learn from my mistakes, because it is not cool at all, as I used to believe, to expose yourself to the sun during peak hours, with only some oil, and possibly without even any sunscreen at all, on your skin, and, moreover, without a bra. It's complete madness! When we're 20, we unfortunately don't think about these things, our only desire is to look good; but now, many years later, we realise that our health is paramount. But experience teaches us that things can change at any moment. What do I do now? I lie in the sun only during the first few hours of the morning, depending on the destination, and in locations where the sun's rays are very strong and where there's a risk I might burn I only sunbathe between 8 and 10 in the morning and then again from around 4 or 5 in the afternoon onwards. Otherwise, I don't spend any time in the sun.

The change in the way I choose to expose myself to the sun didn't come overnight; it was a long process that took place together with other important changes in my life. My "awakening" took place right before I left for India. It didn't happen as result of the fact that I was getting older, rather the first thing I began to become aware of was that I was at risk of getting skin cancer. Yes, I realised that it could also happen to me! Especially when we're young, we tend to believe that nothing will ever happen to us, only other people ever suffered from serious illness. But it's not true! I realised that the sun was very aggressive, and after becoming more aware of my own body and of what can happen, I began to realise the possible consequences of my actions. But the change I made not only meant reducing the number of hours I spent on the beach, it involved a whole new lifestyle, from changing what I ate and giving up smoking, to changing my hydration, sleep and physical exercise regime, etc. It was a change that came naturally on all levels, a transformational process that occurred in time, and so I didn't have to force myself to do any of this, I simply no longer felt the need to do things like I used to before. "You must do this or that" doesn't exist for me, I think I've already told you I'm a stubborn person and difficult to convince, so it's only after I myself feel the need to do a given thing that there's any chance of success. Lots of people warned me about the risks associated with sunbathing, and they advised me not to overdo it, but until I became aware of this myself, their words were lost on me.

I remember reading about an experiment that influenced me and motivated me to stop spending so much time in the sun. The experiment involved two twins who lived in different countries throughout their lives: one in Australia, the other in England. A number of people who didn't know they were twins were asked to guess their ages. However, no one guessed that they were sisters, although they shared many common features, and all those asked said that the one living in Australia was much older, by as much as 10-15 years, than the one living in England. As a result of repeated exposure to the sun, the Australian sister's skin was much more wrinkled and older looking. They also had different lifestyles, but according to the experts, exposure to the sun played the biggest role in this process. This gave me food for thought, and I studied the two images closely and with a lump in my throat.

Looking back, I would say that my habit in terms of exposing myself to the sun can be divided into three different stages. During the first stage, which lasted the longest, I would spend many, many hours in the sun and use far too few products with an SPF. This was followed by a second stage, in which I would again lose count of the number of hours spent in the sun, but at least I was now applying sunscreen. The third stage has seen me go to the opposite extreme: I now realise that it is important not to be out in the sun around midday and that I should bring all kinds of special lotions with me in order to avoid sunburns. In recent years I have therefore become much more careful when it comes to tanning myself and I now religiously protect myself from the sun's UV rays. Today, whenever I leave the house, and whatever the season, I apply a bit of sunscreen to my face.

To bring this subchapter to an end, I feel I should tell you about another problem I had after repeatedly exposing myself to the sun: hyperpigmentation. The dreaded hyperpigmentation! :)

While on holiday in Thailand, right on my last day, after having spent a long time in the sun, I looked at myself in the mirror and I got a shock. I couldn't believe it! A number of terrifying large dark patches had appeared on my face. It looked like I had a moustache, so enormous was the patch on that part of my face. My forehead was also covered by a huge brown patch, which at the time and to my dismay – I find it funny today :) – I thought resembled the map of Africa. Last but not least, there were also a number of large dark patches spread across both cheeks. I couldn't believe it and I started to cry! I thought I'd never be rid of them! I imagine lots of you will also have encountered this problem and that you can therefore also identify with my story.

After I got back to Romania, I went straight to the doctor, who told me, as I was expecting, that it was a case of hyperpigmentation resulting from exposure to the sun. This saw me embark on a mad rush to rid myself of these ugly patches. I purchased and experimented with a multitude of different moisturisers, both Romanian and foreign made. And given how people in Asia don't like tanning themselves and are very concerned with protecting themselves from the sun, I even ordered some products from Japan as well.

I was working in television at the time and, as I hadn't been able to hide these patches, I really didn't know what to do next. I tried many different procedures, including lasers, even resorting to a skin whitening treatment – that is, until someone told me to try using vitamin C, internally and externally. To my surprise, it worked; after years of being embarrassed to leave my home without a thick layer of foundation on, the patches were gone, and ever since a vitamin C serum has become a constant feature of my personal care routine. I still get these patches today, but only very rarely and they're much smaller than before, and, what's more, I know exactly what the cause is – either I have forgotten to use my vitamin C serum or I didn't apply enough sunscreen before spending time in the sun – and I am quick to take corrective measures. So, if we want to avoid hyperpigmentation, we first need to identify the type of sunscreen that is best suited to us; we shouldn't necessarily just use the same product as other people, especially as, as you will know well, there are different types of skin and what is suited to one person might not be of much use to us.

In conclusion, I will only say this: we need to take care when it comes to choosing our beauty routines and not to believe everything we read on social media or in magazines. I wanted to have a tan, I thought it would make me look more beautiful, but I overdid it and damaged my skin in trying to live up to the beauty standards I told you about at the beginning of this book. I am grateful that I saw the light early enough and that I haven't been left with any serious marks on my face – a sign, perhaps, that I was lucky, but also proof that the personal care products I use have helped limit any damage. If I hadn't made this change, I would surely find myself having to resort to all manner of invasive procedures in order to wipe the years off my face now and my self-confidence would have taken a serious bashing… or maybe not :). This is my story, for better or for worse, a tale of what things you shouldn't be doing and, by the time you get to the end, what things you should be doing. I hope you learn from my mistakes, love your bodies and try always to be balanced!

# 15

# A manifesto for natural beauty

*Cosmetic surgery won't solve our emotional problems.*

I've always asked myself whether the aim of cosmetic surgery is to "improve" the body or, in fact, to calm the soul. I'd like to say from the outset that I thought long and hard before writing something on this subject. The subject of cosmetic surgery is very sensitive and it would be nice if it didn't become a matter of public debate, especially as I believe that everyone, whether famous or not, has a right to privacy. And yet what I have noticed is that if you say nothing, your lack of words is rarely taken as a sign of discretion. Rather, it is put down as a fear of speaking out. So I no longer wish to sit on the side-lines and will give my opinion on the subject here.

Yes, I agree with cosmetic surgery, but only under certain conditions. I think it should be undertaken only after having exhausted all other means of resolving or accepting our problems. If someone is a few kilos overweight and, instead of adjusting their diet and doing some exercise, they opt to have liposuction, then I have good reason to believe they are making a mistake.

I don't think it's right to slice up our bodies merely because we can afford to do so financially and because we prefer to remain within our comfort zones. In this sense, it's a matter of will, not a physical issue, and this, I think, brings us to the nub of the matter: when someone goes under the knife, it's not always about solving a problem with the body, but the mind. I apologise if I disappointed you, but the truth is that the scalpel can never remove the pain in your soul: the lack of self-confidence, fear, shame that set in when we become preoccupied with a particular aspect of our physical appearance we're not happy with.

Thank God we haven't yet invented an on/off switch for our emotions! We'd probably be hammering the off button the whole time. We can't simply switch our feelings on or off as we please – and for me this is the most beautiful thing about what it means to be human: the impossibility of being 100% in control of your emotions. I strongly believe that we are souls before being bodies, and this is something we should be grateful for in every waking moment. Our emotions are therefore very important and can be read directly on our faces. Sometimes they render even the saddest of gazes beautiful; or, on the contrary, they "intoxicate" our physical appearance. Have you noticed how beautiful we are when we fall in love or when we experience, if only momentarily, a state of pure happiness? Words cannot describe the correspondence between physical beauty and inner beauty! Consequently, I believe that before focusing on what can be seen, on the physical qualities we possess, we should first pay attention to what we feel. Because a woman who loves herself and feels confident in herself is one step ahead of one who, although very beautiful, is unhappy with herself or even depressed.

Whatever we don't like about ourselves can turn out to be a quality, although the opposite is also true. I'll give you an example about myself: throughout my adolescent years I had a complex about my mouth. I thought my lips were too big, I didn't like them at all and they even earned me an annoying nickname. I would dream of how, once I turned 18, I would have an operation to reduce the size of my lips. As I grew up, I began to realise that they weren't so bad after all, in fact they were even a distinctive feature. Ironically, you can still find articles in the press claiming that I injected my lips with hyaluronic acid. I find this amusing and I invite those who accuse me of doing this to look up some pictures of me when I was little and they'll soon see that nothing has changed. The moral of the story: something we once saw as a physical defect can be transformed into a quality. And not by means of cosmetic surgery, but thanks to the passage of time. In fact nothing has changed about me physically, only mentally. The story of my lips was just an example.

As I told you in the previous chapter, I've been through many different stages and have suffered from a multitude of complexes, but the one that haunted me year after year was the one I think earned my appearance the most criticism: the bags beneath my eyes. I've already admitted that when I was younger and less confident, especially after getting hyperpigmentation from overexposure to the sun, I was terrified of going out into the street without any makeup on. I didn't like the way my skin looked, I would find faults and developed what you might call a pathological obsession with Photoshop: after every photoshoot, I wanted all the photos, every single one of them, to be edited. I wanted them touched up, a little here, a little there, until, bit by bit, I was no longer myself. I was perfect, but I wasn't me – although I wasn't aware of this at the time.

The problem, however, was all in my mind. The reality was I was born with bags under my eyes. For years I'd wanted to have them surgically removed, but I was so afraid of the pain I didn't have the courage to go through with it. What's more, I was afraid it would change my face and I wouldn't be happy with the results. I simply couldn't imagine willingly allowing a doctor to stick needles into my face, to cut into me, to inflict pain on me… No, I couldn't do it. Luckily, my fear of the doctor proved stronger than me. But in no way do I regret not having had this cosmetic surgery. I later solved the problem in a way that I'm not sure was much easier, but which was certainly less painful: I worked a lot with myself and came to accept myself as a woman who just happened to have this particular facial structure! I also learned to reduce the bags beneath my eyes by means of a healthy lifestyle – I sleep longer, drink more water, have a balanced diet and I meditate. The results came quickly, and the more I became reconciled with my body, the more care I would take of it; and the more I came to like it, the more those around me came to like me.

So for many years I had a complex about the rings I had, and still have today, under my eyes. I felt hurt by the nasty words said about me, although I never held a grudge against anyone, because I understood that this was a problem I had with myself and that others were merely exacerbating something that was not right in my mind and my soul. After understanding how important it is to be happy with your body, exercise, feel good in your own skin, whether wrinkled or not, after I accepted myself the way I was, I became free of this complex. Not by means of the scalpel, but by showing confidence in myself. It's taken me almost forty years to be able to think in this way!

I've seen many beautiful women who have chosen to have operations because they were afraid of ageing, because they were always finding things they didn't like about themselves and considered themselves ugly, with the result that they almost weren't themselves anymore. I feel incredibly sorry for them when I see the way they end up looking after undergoing too much invasive cosmetic surgery! I believe that a woman who is able to accept her age is far more beautiful than one who has subjected herself to dozens of extremely invasive procedures, always seeking to improve a little something here, a little something there. I hope with all my heart that when I grow older I will be able to accept my age and to live a beautiful life, without being fixated on the past and ideals of beauty that are not real and are not suited to me and my age.

We live in a world in which everyone wants to look perfect; indeed, the pressure to achieve perfection is felt in every aspect of our lives. Only the other day, I noticed how many social media apps there are out there designed to make us look beautiful, i.e. a narrow jawline, no wrinkles and an impeccable smile – tools which in practice only alienate us from who we really are. If we don't have confidence in ourselves and if we don't accept who we are, we lose control and end up subjecting ourselves to all manner of invasive procedures; we enhance every image of ourselves, sometimes so much that we are no longer able to identify with ourselves and no longer recognise ourselves. We're not just processing these images of ourselves, however; on a deeper level we are also processing ourselves.

Beauty is more than just a look; it's an attitude, a state of mind that goes beyond the limits of physical appearance. I know it seems hard to believe, but I only began to see myself as truly beautiful after having achieved balance – that is to say, only recently. However, as I have already pointed out, for a long time I felt tempted by cosmetic surgery, as I saw it as being able to provide a solution to my endless complexes. I was influenced by the press and critical voices, who didn't see me first and foremost as a human being and only then as a public figure – one day they'd be saying I had rings and bags under my eyes, the next day that I wouldn't leave home without any makeup on. I suffered so much I ended up believing I didn't look good at all and that I would have to do something about my face. And, yes, there were moments when I gave in and allowed my weaknesses to take over.

While on the subject of sincerity, as I told you earlier, I too have suffered from a lack of self-confidence and have been through many phases of self-rejection. I remember how one day, many years ago, a friend called me to tell me she was going to have Botox injections and she suggested I try it too. I told her I would go along with her when she did it but that it wasn't something I wanted to do myself. I didn't have a clear idea of what the procedure involved; I was afraid of the pain and I wasn't even aware of the implications of doing such a procedure, because there wasn't much information on the subject available at the time. However, once I found myself there I allowed myself to be convinced and agreed to give it a try. At the time, I only felt the pain, I couldn't see any change. But a few days later it felt as if my face had gone all stiff, which I thought was terrible. I am very expressive and move my face a lot, and, given that I was working in television at the time, I needed to express emotions through facial expressions. It was as if someone had tied me up, paralysing me, and I told myself I would never do this again.

Not having learnt my lesson, there then followed a second experience, one which, however, served to cure me of Botox… at least until now :). I was working in television at the time and was constantly squinting my eyes under the spotlights, I decided to have Botox injected between my eyebrows. It felt extremely unnatural, but I deemed it necessary. I asked the doctor to give me a smaller dose than what he was actually proposing. When he said that anything less would be impossible to administer, I gave up on Botox there and then, and that was my last experience of this kind. I felt it wasn't natural and now I'm very pleased that a lot of time has passed since then in which I haven't done anything like that again. I found it highly amusing how, after I had given up on the idea, one of my best girlfriends kept on asking me what I had done, because I looked so much better!

It's kind of ironic how when I was 30 years old and my skin was much younger and therefore more beautiful, I would find myself tempted to inject myself with Botox, whereas today, at the age of 40, I not only no longer think about resorting to that sort of thing, I don't think I even need it; it's not suited to what I want and how I intend to allow time to pass over me. This is how I feel right now, but who knows, maybe in five, ten or fifteen years things will change, although I hope I will be able to accept the passage of time in as natural a way as possible.

In putting all of this down on paper, I have relived so many intense moments from my past. It's incredible to be able to reach a stage at which you are no longer afraid to open up about such personal things and are happy to talk about them and to express yourself freely. I recommend from time to time trying to write down some of the things you like about yourself from a physical point of view and then to think about what you could do to improve those things you believe still need a bit of airbrushing. But don't undergo treatments at clinics offering invasive procedures; do it in your own home instead. Give yourself the opportunity to get to know yourself better, to listen to your emotions and to look at yourself in the mirror as if you're looking at your best friend, someone you admire and love unconditionally.

This is not just something I read about in a book, and I am also not immune to the desire to achieve perfection – of course, I, too, when I look in the mirror, want to see a relaxed, beautiful, calm and carefree face staring back at me. It's one thing to want these things and another not to be able to stop yourself from obsessively testing out everything that appears on the market. We do this in response to the pressure we feel to achieve the perfection we see in magazines and on television, but also out of a refusal to accept the fact that time is constantly passing.

Invasive beauty treatments, when taken to excess, transform a naturally beautiful face into something devoid of all expression, with unnaturally high cheekbones, overly inflated lips and a waxwork-like complexion. I've said it before and I'll keep on saying it: I am not against having procedures done that allow us to correct minor things we don't like about ourselves or help us to "cheat" time. I don't judge those who do them, because I have tried them myself and I also don't know what the future has in store for me. That being said, I am a firm believer in an idea that should be extremely important in every aspect of our lives: balance.

More than any cosmetic surgery, balance helps us to look good. A balanced lifestyle allows us to feel good about ourselves and this in turn has an extremely powerful influence on how we look. When we are in harmony with ourselves, we look kindly on ourselves and became better able to accept ourselves for what we are. Natural beauty exists; you only need to recognise it and to truly believe that it belongs to you!

# 16

# The impact of the environment on the skin and other harmful effects we should protect ourselves against

*Skin that stays youthful is, without a doubt, the ultimate wish of all women.*

Some three or four years ago, my attention was drawn to an idea that has revolutionised the beauty industry: the exposome. I've read a lot about this subject and I can hardly wait to share a few, hopefully very interesting, things about it with you. As I've mentioned already, this is an umbrella term for all the factors responsible for facial ageing and it can be divided into two main categories: environmental factors – UV rays, pollution, climate (heat, cold, humidity) – and those related to our lifestyle and emotions (smoking, stress, fatigue, diet, mental activity).

Experts working in the cosmetics industry take a keen interest in the exposome, because, as you know, the skin is the body's largest organ and its interface with the external environment.

Consequently, the impact of these factors is first felt on the skin. If the integrity of the skin is affected as a result of the action of the exposome, the entire body suffers as a result. After more than four decades of research, the experts working for Vichy have come to the conclusion that the exposome reflects the body's reaction in general, and that of the skin in particular, to its exposure to different aggressive factors. They also discovered, as part of a study carried out in 2013, that 80% of the symptoms of ageing are caused by exposure to UV rays! The pigmentation, modification of the texture – drying, peeling, irritation, thinning of the epidermis – and wrinkling of the skin are all accelerated by UV rays.

Before setting out to get a tan at any cost, the way I used to do in the past, I urge you to think twice – or even a hundred times for that matter – about it, your health is at stake. Irrespective of whether it's UVA or UVB rays, it's important to know or to remind yourselves that both have a negative action on the skin. UVA rays are always present in the atmosphere, whatever the season, whether it's sunny or cloudy outside. They are so powerful that they can pass through clothing and even sunglasses. Some experts believe UVA rays to be relatively safe (it is these types of rays that are used in tanning booths), while others, including the researchers from Vichy Laboratories, reject this idea. They say that UVA rays play an important role in the process of photoageing, i.e. in the premature ageing of the skin, and the production of free radicals, leading to intolerance to the sun – red skin, itching, rashes, abnormal pigmentation and even some forms of skin cancer.

UVB rays are to blame when we burn our skin. Unlike UVA, UVB rays are not the same strength all year round. They are more intense during the summer months, although they can also be reflected by snow, so it's important we protect ourselves at all times. UVB rays are responsible for the occurrence of most types of skin cancer.

To be sure we're protecting ourselves correctly, we should take care when choosing sunscreen, especially when heading to the beach. UVA/UVB protection should be written somewhere on the bottle. Similarly, we should use sunscreen with an SPF. In order to know how long your sunscreen will last, multiply the SPF by ten and you'll get the time, in minutes, we can safely spend in the sun without burning.

Air pollution, on the other hand, causes inflammation within the body and leads to oxidative stress. The experts at Vichy carried out a study to determine the impact of urban pollution on skin. The study involved 189 volunteers, both men and women, who were aged between 18 and 60 and split into two groups: one living in Cuernavaca, a city 84 km south of Mexico City, the other in Shanghai, in China. The results of the study leave little room for interpretation: those living in a polluted atmosphere were affected by photoageing to a much greater degree. The production of sebum increased and a change occurred in the composition of the substance secreted by the sebaceous glands, with the result that the subjects had drier skin, despite using moisturiser, and were therefore at greater risk of developing eczema and skin irritations. The scientists concluded that the harmful effects of UVA and UVB rays were amplified by pollution, which through photo pollution (cumulative exposure to UV rays and polluting particles), speeds up facial ageing exponentially.

**Did you know?**

**Every time cigarette smoke is inhaled more than 4,000 dangerous substances enter the lungs, accelerating the ageing of the face, teeth and skin.**

Thanks to extensive research by Vichy and other scientists into the negative effects of smoking on the skin, it was discovered that this dangerous habit leads to the appearance of wrinkles. What's more, smoking is also associated with serious skin conditions, such as psoriasis and various types of skin cancer. Cigarette smoke reduces blood circulation in the capillaries, destroying important cells that contribute to the production of collagen and elastin. Consequently, the blood vessels become narrower and the skin is no longer correctly vascularised, which means less oxygen reaches the cells. The skin thus loses its capacity to regenerate and becomes sick, altering its appearance and quality. There is also evidence to show that tobacco smoke is phototoxic, i.e. it becomes even more toxic in the presence of UV rays, leading to the destruction of the cells in the skin.

There are many studies and research projects detailing the negative effect on the skin of each different type of exposome, and I'd have to write an entire book on the subject to cover them all. But it's not my intention to produce an academic work, I merely wish to make you think (more) about this subject. I don't want to alarm you unnecessarily, but I believe it is my duty to warn you that, under the influence of the exposome, the skin loses its elasticity and radiance and the production of collagen slows down. This process is profound and irreversible, a so-called silent ageing, in the sense that it is slow but sure. And because it's not sudden, it can be deceptive, because we are tempted to believe it won't affect us and that it will be a long time before we begin to notice any signs of ageing on our face. We often only realise that our skin is in need of help when it's already too late and wrinkles have already appeared. I advise you to compare different photos of yourself taken over the years, especially more recent ones, and you will see how quickly the wrinkles began to appear on your face, as well as how your skin looks in other regards.

So far I've listed the things "responsible" for beautiful skin: both those that have to do with diet and those related to exercise, rest and hydration. To this we can also add meditation, which I will discuss in the third part of this book. Together, these things represent the positive factors of the exposome, with beneficial effects for the entire body and especially the skin. And if you're wondering what you can do to correct and slow down the process of facial ageing, then try to follow the basic steps that form part of a healthy lifestyle and which have an amazing ability to counteract this phenomenon.

Naturally, a considerable contribution to the process of counteracting the effects of environmental factors and protecting the skin from the effects of the exposome undoubtedly comes via the process of skin care. Vichy was the first company in the world to create a range of products based on scientific research into the exposome. It's called Slow Âge and it helps the skin to age naturally and beautifully – or gracefully, as I like to put it. These products contain a number of active ingredients that play an important role in ensuring the health of the skin and which I mentioned previously when I touched on my night-time skin care routine (Baicalin, Bifidus and mineralising thermal water from Vichy), as well as UVA/UVB filters, which attenuate the effects of the exposome.

Baicalin is one of the 50 plants used in traditional Chinese medicine. It has antioxidant properties, being better in this regard than vitamins C and E. Baicalin root extract limits damage to the skin caused by dangerous sun rays and pollution.

Bifidus is obtained through the fermentation of the Bifidobacterium longum bacterium and strengthens the protective barrier of the skin. By applying this ingredient, the skin becomes less vulnerable to aggressive environmental factors, with the result that both dryness and sensitivity are reduced and the ageing of the skin is delayed.

Vichy Mineralizing Thermal Water, which comes from French volcanoes, is rich in minerals, 15 to be precise, which fortify and regenerate the skin.

Resveratrol is another effective ingredient that prevents wrinkles and which is normally found in black fruit and vegetables, the best known of which being grapes, especially the darker ones. This substance restores the firmness of the skin and protects it against the harmful effects of UV rays and pollution. What's more, recent studies carried out by Vichy Laboratories show that resveratrol encourages the body to produce antioxidants which inhibit the aggressive action of environmental factors.

The skin is our main protective shield against environmental factors and it deserves all our care and attention. You can have excuses or you can have results when it comes to your anti-ageing routine. But I'm sorry to have to tell you this, you can't have both. I place a lot of importance on my skin care routine, which always involves moisturisers with an SPF and anti-ageing ingredients, and I'll tell you more about it in what follows.

# 17

# My daily personal care routine

*No one knows my body better than I do.*

Public figures, celebrities, call them what you will, don't inhabit a perfect, intangible world cut off from reality – not even Hollywood stars do. Apart from when they have to dress up for official events, or when they have to walk down the red carpet and pose for the photographers, with their public image being taken care of by a team of assistants, they're really just normal people who eat (some even cook for themselves), exercise, follow a personal care routine, and so on and so forth. Don't you find it hard to picture them not all dressed up and without any makeup, taking out the rubbish or sweating away at the gym, their hair all in a mess, or maybe just brushing their teeth?

I've noticed that when photos appear in the press of stars who leave the house not looking like their pictures on the front covers of magazines, especially those from the other side of the pond, their fans feel disappointed and, above all, confused. Why? Because the reality appears to be different from what they were used to seeing in the press, because they can see that their role models are not perfect, because we feel the need to see in others what we feel is lacking in ourselves. And we invest them with so many qualities that when they don't live up to them all, we feel let down. But hey, they're people too, it's not fair to treat them like robots!

When I read the messages I receive on Facebook and the comments left below my blog posts, or when people ask me questions about my personal care routine, I realise there's lots of people out there whose opinion of me does not quite fit with reality. I feel people's impression of me – and, for that matter, of all public figures – is that I spend a lot of time with the hairdresser or beautician. Well, I'm sorry to disappoint you, but it's not really like that. Most of the time I take care of my skin myself!

Of course, as I've already told you, I like trying lots of different personal care and beauty treatments, I'm up to date with all the latest developments and I frequent various beauty centres and spas, but my life and interior balance do not depend on them. Nor do they depend on the latest technological innovation that promises to do it all for me. That's why, as you may have noticed, through images and live streams posted on social media, I've recently been showing you what my face looks like in the morning, without any makeup on, without having come straight from the beauty salon, as well as how I cook and how I exercise, what I look like when I'm at the office and so on. At first, some people didn't quite recognise me and pointed out things that didn't seem perfect to them, while others were surprised at my courage and didn't know what to believe. However, the majority of you – and I'm so proud of you for this! – understood that I don't possess the gift of perfection and you learnt to accept me the way I am. What's more, you were able to identify with me, Andreea, with everything that makes me who I am, but also those things that brought me to where I am today; just as I am also often able to identify with your various problems, concerns and joys. In the end, that's what friendship is all about, isn't it? We each give our best and get it back tenfold. And I have so many reasons to be grateful!

I'm digressing a little, I know, but I felt the need to point out again just how much I appreciate all the support I've received from you. Coming back to my personal care routine, I'm very happy with the self-care system I've arrived at, because no one knows my body better than I do, and it's a far more time-efficient way of doing things to boot. There's no waiting for appointments, I don't waste time getting there and back, I decide for myself what products to use and can tell what's good for me and what's not. As part of this odyssey of personal care, I pay a lot of attention to what products I use because I don't want to take risks when it comes to my skin. And you should do the same! Every mistake, every unsuitable product used, can have long-term repercussions, some of them irreversible. Don't apply any product to your face you haven't read about first so you know it's suitable for you. Don't conduct experiments and, as the Americans like to say, keep it simple!

A lot of people ask me what products I've tried, which creams are best and all kinds of things relating to my personal care routine. It's true that I love trying out different creams, as I'm an incurably curious person, but I believe there's no product in this world that will help you if YOU don't help yourself. So the most important things in my life – without which I wouldn't be able to look my best – are as follows: sleep, hydration, physical activity, diet (the time of day you eat at is also incredibly important) and meditation. Without these things I don't believe it's possible to look good, especially over the age of 25.

Someone once told me that when you reach 40 you will have the skin you deserve. There's so much truth in these words! At this age, your skin begins to repay you for all the investment you've made in it. It's like with a handbag or a pair of shoes: if you treat them well and look after them, they will look good and you'll get a lot of use out of them. I no longer spend so much time in the sun and I sunbathe only during the permitted hours, depending on where I am. What's more, I always apply sunscreen, don't eat sweets – did I mention how in the past I used to be a massive fan of candy drops? – and I also try to do, wherever possible, all of the things I've told you about in the previous chapters.

What's the first thing I do as part of my morning care routine? There's no doubt about it, cleansing is a really important stage of my beauty routine and it determines the effectiveness of all subsequent stages. It's like with a house: if the foundation isn't strong, no matter how beautiful the structure itself, it will be at risk of collapse. I really believe that instead of doing an intrusive procedure every now and then, it's much better for me to follow a permanent cleansing routine at home. It's natural and meets the daily needs of our skin. So just as I brush my teeth every day and don't rely only on professional tartar removal, I believe we should adopt the same approach when it comes to our skin. During this first stage of my personal care routine, I regularly use thermal water, which I often keep in the fridge, because as soon as you spray cold water onto your face, you force the face muscles to flex, as if you are exercising them.

I can't imagine my morning routine without the use of thermal water (in fact, I can but I choose not to! :), it's a product I value highly, a kind of "Good morning!" greeting I address to my skin. It's such a pleasant and relaxing feeling to apply this product to my face. After applying the thermal water, I allow it to work for a while and then remove it with a tissue. I sometimes use some makeup remover as well, but not always, it depends how my skin feels after the thermal water.

I also always use a vitamin C serum, or some other type of serum, depending on the time of year – the idea being that I always have these kinds of products in the house. This is followed by the application of a hydrating cream and an eye cream, after which I apply some sunblock. When I don't have any filming or important projects on, I avoid using foundation, and instead use some CC Cream, which hydrates the skin, hides any imperfections, provides protection against sun damage, minimises the look of pores and mattifies, brightens and evens out the tone of the skin.

My evening care routine is slightly different. At the end of the day, especially if I have the time, I like to remove the makeup on my face using a device with a rotating brush and that on my eyes with micellar water or a special oil; I then apply a serum, face cream and some eye cream. Once a week, my beauty routine also includes exfoliation and masks: I'm a big fan of clay face masks and apply all kinds of products with hydrating ingredients. My arsenal of beauty products also includes eye patches for when I want my face to look really good.

When it comes to body care, I love exfoliating my skin and trying out various scrubs. In my bathroom I keep a natural glove made of Aloe Sisal for massages, which leaves my skin feeling silky and helps me to relax. I use it whenever I get the opportunity, and the effect on my skin is fantastic. I like to add Epsom salt or oil to my baths, as well as all kinds of other essences and substances that cleanse and hydrate the skin. When I have the time, I think it's wonderful to just lie there in the bathtub and to enjoy the water. I use a lot of body lotion: I like to keep my skin hydrated, to feel that it's smooth. My favourite products include those containing shea butter, cocoa butter and cocoa oil. And I think I must have a tube of hand cream in every handbag I own. I really don't like having dry skin.

When travelling, changes of temperature, time zone, air pressure and altitude all affect the skin, dehydrating it, irritating it and putting it under stress. I imagine you've already noticed for yourselves how the skin is the first to reflect the changes the body undergoes, which is precisely why we need to take such good care of it. Consequently, my luggage always contains some hydrating cream with an SPF. What I also find really helpful is to double the amount of water I normally consume, so I end up drinking around four litres a day, because the skin tends to become dry, especially when on a flight. I like to call all these things I do to take care of my skin when I'm away "my therapy for tired skin".

# 18

# *Slow Âge* or how to slow down the ageing of the skin

*"The beauty of a woman only grows with passing years."*

– AUDREY HEPBURN

Is this really true? Do we really grow more beautiful, not only wiser, as the years pass? How is this possible? These words by Audrey Hepburn, who you will know from famous films like *Breakfast at Tiffany's* and *My Fair Lady*, made me think. When people ask me who my role models are in terms of femininity and style, the first name that springs to mind is that of this superb woman.

Did you know that some lists rank her as the most beautiful film star of the last 50 years, while others even crown her the most beautiful woman of the last century? However, it wasn't this that impressed me most about Audrey Hepburn, but the way in which she managed to live beautifully, to continue to display her beauty like a visiting card, an expression of her moral virtues, even as she aged. Her personal care routine, so different from those promoted today, bore fruit because she was very careful about her sleeping patterns, she always tried to be optimistic, and loved other people and saw the good in them. "For beautiful eyes, look for the good in others; for beautiful lips, speak only words of kindness," was how Audrey Hepburn replied to journalists who asked her about her beauty and fashion secrets.

Audrey Hepburn is a source of inspiration to us all! So, what did one of the most beautiful women in the world deem most important? Not the scalpel used in cosmetic surgery, but accepting your age and your natural beauty. And, what's more, she believed the way we feel is also reflected in our skin. I would be so happy if more beautiful women like her were to come to the fore today, to prove to us that age is just a number printed on our ID cards. I hope that when the time comes I will be able to resist all temptation and to be one of them! For we can still be beautiful without resorting to invasive procedures. It's all a matter of accepting who we are, balance and focusing on the basics, things which, although not at all complicated, we still forget to do. This all comes under the umbrella of a healthy lifestyle.

Inspired by women such as Audrey Hepburn, who found the resources required to promote the idea of natural beauty, I decided to appear more often in public without any makeup. The result? At first, as expected, people advised me to put on some makeup, as they were surprised to see I had bags under my eyes or that my hair wasn't perfect. They were intrigued as to why I would want to publish images that hadn't been digitally enhanced. To be honest, I wasn't bothered by all these observations. Why? Because I had realised that I didn't have a problem. I am a woman of (almost) 41 years of age. And, yes, there are days when I feel tired and have bags beneath my eyes, my hair is a mess and I don't wear heels or some fancy dress . Yes, I am as normal as can be, not some kind of Barbie doll. I accept myself the way I am, with all the "defects" a section of the public ascribe to me. I prefer to honour reality rather than to erect sandcastles built from foundation and powder.

That perfect person the public had become accustomed to seeing when I was a model or working in television was not me, but an idealised projection. I've already told you about the time in my life when I tried so hard to prove to the world my life was perfect that I felt I couldn't breathe. I wouldn't allow myself to be my real self, someone who had bad days as well as good, someone who from time to time felt tired, someone who wanted to leave the house dressed wearing just jeans and a T-shirt. Out of the question! I had to be perfect – because that's how I had taught those around me to see me and now they were forcing me to keep up the act. I was the victim of a vicious circle that I myself – "aided", which of course, the entire showbiz industry had created. When I felt I was at the point of losing touch with my authentic self, I fled this so-called perfect life. I broke free from the chains I myself had wrapped my life in. My departure for India was therefore really a form of liberation: I spent a month living without any makeup, without any face masks, without any expensive clothes. But, perhaps most importantly, I was no longer an artificial character playing the role of the perfect woman.

My relaxed approach today, my acceptance of my weaknesses and the smile on my face when people ask me things that in the past would have hurt me – all these things I paid for in years of anxiety and pain. I chose the difficult path because none of the people around me seemed real, unenhanced... they all seemed fresh out of the box, so how could I be expected to stand out, to be different? But now I don't have to play a role, because in this book I have removed (almost) all my masks. And it feels so good!

I feel good and, as a consequence, I look good. Precisely in that order! Because I've brought some order to my life. Do you know what I learned to do on my own and I sincerely recommend you to do, too? To stop striving to have all the features of a perfect body because this won't help you to have a perfect soul. And the soul is the most important thing we have – it is immortal, it is the essence of our existence.

Last year I accepted a challenge and said yes to a project that took me out of my comfort zone. I decided to appear naked on the cover of *Marie Claire* magazine without the pictures being enhanced in any way, in order to sound an alarm: we are cosmeticising our lives too much! We apply too many filters to our photographs to make ourselves more beautiful, brighter, wrinkle-free, to appear carefree, flawless and closer to perfection. A perfection that doesn't exist. It's just a mirage, which I too, unfortunately, promoted for many years until becoming aware of its toxic effect. In those pictures I had makeup on and my hair was done up, but my wrinkles weren't removed and the shape of my body wasn't corrected, with those taking the pictures neither "adding" nor "removing" anything from me. I'm still the same today, one year after this experience: I have bags under my eyes and expression wrinkles and I show signs of the (soon to be) 41 years I have been alive for and which have made me who I am today.

"A woman can keep one secret – the secret of her age," said Voltaire, but I tend to believe that these words are open to a different interpretation today. Over the years we've learned to keep secrets, sometimes we're even better at it than men, but we're becoming increasingly specialised in an art form that speaks not to our relationships with others, but our relationship with time: the art of concealing the imperfections in our faces and treating age as if it were just a number. What helped me to be happy with the way I am, with all my imperfections, was learning to accept the passage of time.

There are two main paths of action we can take when it comes to the battle against ageing: lifestyle and cosmetics, and in terms of the latter this is an opportune moment to mention Slow Âge, the first skin care range, launched by Vichy that corrects and delays the appearance of signs of ageing on the face, which are aggravated and even triggered by the exposome. Their daily fluid moisturiser has an SPF of 25 and their daily moisturising cream an SPF of 30, while the eye cream combats signs of ageing even before they appear.

I think it's incredible that a company as big as Vichy is getting behind the idea that the skin be allowed to age slowly, naturally and beautifully, provided we maintain a strict care routine and make informed choices. Because, beyond focusing on the products that protect us from the exposome, the goal of those studying this subject is far more wide reaching: it's about education, explaining to the general public that the end goal is not to remain forever young – that's impossible – but to age beautifully and to manage how the process occurs. The first time I heard about the exposome it made me feel sad, because I hadn't realised just how much lifestyle and environmental factors were affecting my skin, but I was at least happy that people were at last showing more interest in the subject and that a campaign like this was promoting ideas I believed in. So I thought it would be wonderful to partner with them and for me to help pass on the message of the people from Vichy. And, above all, to encourage my readers to take it on board!

I also thought it would be interesting to call this subchapter "Slow Âge", because, viewed in the cold light of day, while we can't stop time, we can slow it down a little and delay the ageing process, especially when it comes to our skin. But how? By adopting a lifestyle based around the concept of balance, by not resorting to cosmetic surgery and by using products that protect us from environmental factors and help us to ditch our bad habits and to feel good in our own skin.

One of the books that changed my life and helped me understand the slow movement was written by Carl Honoré, a promoter of the philosophy of slow living, called *In Praise of Slow*. The author recalls how his life used to be so busy before making a change, always racing against the clock, that the version of Snow White he would read to his son ended up having only... three dwarves. He also observed that we, humans, especially those of us struggling to meet our deadlines, have stopped enjoying the time we spend with loved ones and rush through life instead of living it. His solution? Living slowly doesn't mean doing everything at a snail's pace, but dealing with everything at the right speed, i.e. slowing things down so we are able to feel and enjoy them. We should also try to include moments of peace and quiet, not just to rush about and feel stressed the whole time, to be calm, to meditate and to discover the miracle that is mindfulness.

The author recommends we try to stop living according to our to-do lists, and once in a while to disconnect ourselves from technology and the never-ending list of things we have to do at work. Only then will we be healthier and have more energy. And this also applies to how we get used to the idea that time is passing. If we become frightened and end up doing a load of pointless things just to stave off this process, we will only be lying to ourselves and won't see the desired results either. Instead we should be enjoying every stage of our lives, getting to know our bodies and accepting our age. No to mention, loving ourselves the way we are!

Perla Servan Schreiber, who launched the first magazine based on the slow philosophy called *Clés*, says that there often exists a confusion between "growing old properly" and "staying young". We should be guiding ourselves according to the former, a goal anchored in reality that won't send us off on a wild goose chase. We can't stay young forever, however much we'd like to, but, yes, I agree that we can grow old beautifully, in a proper manner, enjoying each new stage of our lives as it comes. The concept of slow living therefore means to live in the now, to consciously experience every moment and, above all, to prioritise quality over quantity. "Age is not a disease. So whether nature is more forgiving of us or not, let us become accustomed to our own age. Let us look kindly on it, on this body that is changing, on this perspective on life that is constantly shifting. Only by accepting and recognising our age will we have the capacity to remain who we are by giving it the right amount of care," says Perla Servan Schreiber.

## Ways to protect our skin against the passage of time

- Try to have a balanced lifestyle
- Enjoy spending time with loved ones, don't work during your free time, don't become slaves to technology
- Give up smoking and moderate your alcohol consumption
- Apply sunscreen every time you leave the house
- Cleansing your skin, even if you didn't use any makeup during the day, is an essential part of your evening ritual
- Choose face and eye creams containing vitamins and antioxidising ingredients, which fortify the skin from the inside, such as resveratrol, baicalin (aids the appearance and multiplication of P53 cells which hinder the ageing of tissue and the body), Bifidus, mineralising thermal water (which

aids cellular regeneration)

- Use serums containing vitamin C and nourishing compounds
- Exfoliate your skin at least once a week and apply intense hydrating masks, especially in winter
- Make sure you eat foods with antioxidant properties (grapes, cranberries, cloves, carrots, blueberries, cinnamon, avocados, pumpkin, broccoli, sweet potatoes, tomatoes, cabbage, cantaloupes, peaches, apricots, apples, plums and walnuts)
- Make sure you do some physical exercise every day and get at least seven hours of sleep a night
- Drink plenty of water
- Meditate, breathe correctly and learn to love your body

# 19

# Beauty treatments and therapies I have tried and am happy to recommend

*"Feeling real" beats "being perfect".*

"Of course her skin looks great, she must spend hours at the beauty salon!" Or, worse: "I'm sure she's had lots of cosmetic surgery, she just won't admit it." Maybe you, too, have thought the same, or maybe you heard similar things said by people around you but you chose not to trust everything you heard from questionable sources. I'd be very happy if the latter were true. I would like, once and for all, to place all my cards on the table, to eliminate all doubts. I know many people must think I spend a lot of time in beauty salons and in the consultation rooms of medical aestheticians, but I'm afraid I'm going to disappoint them. In fact, I only do so when absolutely necessary and, even then, it feels as if I'm using up time that could be spent on more important things.

I'm not consistent when it comes to cosmetic procedures. As

already mentioned, I've never been a great fan of these procedures, preferring instead to keep a selection of different creams at home. And, what's more, I don't really have the patience! There are other reasons, too, which I've already told you about. Perhaps the most important reason is that I'm afraid of needles and – like everyone else for that matter – of pain.

Many years ago, my friend, Dana Sota, told me that after 35 there are no beauty procedures that don't involve at least some pain. Although she's a specialist in beauty strategies, I stubbornly refused to believe her. I wanted to have impeccable complexion, so I told myself I'd prove her wrong, and this is how I discovered all kinds of minimally invasive procedures meant to help me keep my skin hydrated and radiant. I'm convinced many of you are in the same boat as me, so let me tell you about the various things I've tested in this area. But there's something I should mention first: I wanted to retain my natural beauty, I didn't want to spoil it with all kinds of extravagant procedures that would distort my face. This led me to discover Intraceuticals and Sublime, which are non-invasive facial rejuvenation treatments with a lot of benefits for the skin. But I also felt I should try other things, such as homeomesotherapy, mesotherapy and lymphatic drainage. I will describe all of these in detail in the following pages.

Homeomesotherapy is a procedure I can warmly recommend, although I myself found it too painful, despite my skin looking really great afterwards. In fact, I only managed to do one or two courses. Admittedly, I first tried this procedure many years ago, when my resistance to pain was much lower. As to mesotherapy, I can remember feeling really stressed out at a certain point in my life, I wasn't getting enough sleep and so I thought I try mesotherapy, which the doctors from the beauty salon I was using at the time were often recommending to me. After refusing a number of times, when I finally said I'd give it a go, they didn't know whether I was joking or serious. The results were good and, although it's also a painful procedure, I still do the odd course of mesotherapy, albeit only rarely.

Did I already tell you that I would not to be able to stand it when anyone touched my face? Not, that is, until I discovered facial massage. Wow! It has an immediate effect on my skin and simply makes it look a lot more radiant. That said, I still only rarely get around to doing it. I'll now tell you a little bit about each kind of therapy in turn, with the proviso that this is only my experience of them, not a medical treatise, so I'll limit myself to the most important information.

## Intraceuticals

As I've frequently said when asked about my secrets for a radiant complexion, I only do cosmetic treatments when I feel I need a massage to help tone the muscles in my face, and I only do more sophisticated procedures occasionally. There is, however, one procedure I try to do regularly and which is never off my list: Intraceuticals. I adore this particular treatment because it helps me to instantly obtain a beautiful, radiant and hydrated complexion, pain-free.

Intraceuticals, a rejuvenation and intense hydration treatment based on hyperbaric oxygen, is a non-invasive way of introducing hyaluronic acid, vitamins and antioxidants into the skin. It has the same effect as Botox, but is not the same thing. I go for this treatment at the Elōs Skin & Laser Center, where I've also done all kinds of other non-invasive procedures. The Intraceuticals treatment has an intense effect on fine wrinkles and dark rings under the eyes, while also increasing the radiance of your skin.

The treatment can be customised to meet your particular needs and is effective in the treatment of hyperpigmentation and acne. In order to obtain long-term effects, a course of six sessions, once a week, is recommended.

## Sublime

I resort to this particular treatment during busier periods and when I have a lot of events to attend. The results are seen quickly and last for a number of days. I really like this procedure because it is simple and extremely relaxing, and after each session my skin feels healthier and cleaner. One of its greatest benefits is that I can do it before any event, as it doesn't leave any red marks on my skin. Quite the opposite: my complexion becomes more radiant.

This procedure helps reduce fine wrinkles, it affords the skin greater radiance and reshapes your facial contour. Sublime procedures are meant for use on the face, neck and cleavage area, and are based on elōs technology, which combines bi-polar radio frequencies with infrared, acting within the dermis on the collagen and elastin fibres. The energy distributed using a special applicator over the entire surface of the skin heats the dermis to a temperature of 42 degrees, having the role of tightening the collagen and elastin fibres, as well as stimulating the production of new fibres. The procedure takes up to one hour, a time I like to spend relaxing.

While undergoing this treatment, a special gel is applied which protects the skin and acts as a conductor for the radio frequencies, and you can feel the tiny heat impulses being distributed over the entire surface of the face. I think it's important to mention that this beauty treatment needs to be done every four weeks, with a recommended four such sessions every three to six months. It is used to treat fine wrinkles, ameliorating deep wrinkles and restoring tightness to the skin.

There are no major contraindications and it can be used at any time of the year.

## Homeomesotherapy

While all my girlfriends kept telling me about the benefits of Botox, I chose to avoid this particular procedure, although I did instead try out a different method of caring for my skin – homeomesotherapy. This involves targeted injections of homeopathic preparations into the parts of the skin we wish to treat. In my case, I tried it on my face. After a session of homeomesotherapy, my face appeared more rested and more radiant, because the cocktail of ingredients used contains small concentrations of nutritive substances, which work quickly and efficiently. These include amino acids, vitamins, minerals, organotherapeutic substances, nosodes (biological remedies) and classic homeopathic drainage and phase remedies.

According to Dr Cristina Bogdan, "these are injected only into acupuncture areas" so that the results can be seen as soon as possible. These ingredients are in a dynamised form and act as mediators in the physiological metabolic reactions in our bodies such that they are quickly recognised by the human biological system. As already mentioned earlier, I found this to be a painful procedure, but it depends on each individual's resistance to pain, skin type and so on. It also involves the use of a topical anaesthetic, which does its job fine as long as we show some patience – something which has never been my strong point! :(

It's recommended you do one session every seven days over the course of five to eight weeks, and then once a month after that, to maintain the effects. The exact frequency and duration of this procedure is decided based on age, health condition and any prior treatments undertaken. Homeomesotherapy improves skin tone, reduces wrinkling on the face, neck and cleavage, revitalises and tightens skin tissue and… the list goes on and on. What's more, it can also be applied to the rest of the body, where it has beneficial effects on stretch marks and cellulite.

## Mesotherapy

Besides Sublime and Intraceuticals, while at the Elōs Skin & Laser Center I also tried NCTF 135 HA Mesotherapy. The name sounds really complicated, but essentially it's just a type of anti-ageing treatment that stimulates the skin from the inside, without altering its form or natural expression. The procedure consists of a series of micro-injections of hyaluronic acid and is considered an innovative technique in the field of cosmetics because it uses a unique product on the market containing a complex of 53 different ingredients (hyaluronic acid, vitamins, minerals and antioxidants).

The purpose of this treatment is to re-establish the hydration level of the skin and to stimulate the production of collagen. This process results in an improvement in the volume of tegument, thus preventing cutaneous ageing and reducing the appearance of wrinkles. Areas that can be treated include the face, neck, cleavage and hands. This procedure guarantees visible results following a course of five fortnightly sessions: the skin becomes more radiant, supple and elastic, fine wrinkles disappear, and the treated areas are visibly transformed.

## Cellenis PRP

This treatment is also called the "vampire therapy", which I find amusing, as, to be honest, it bears no relation to the realm of magic or the occult. And the analogy to vampires doesn't seem that good to me either, but then if it helps people to understand the procedure better, then what can I say? :)

According to Filis Demirgean, a dermatologist at the Elōs Skin & Laser Center, "Çellenis PRP is a treatment that involves the injection of platelet rich plasma for the purpose of healing and rejuvenating your skin. It is based on a simple idea: the utilisation of the body's own resources in the process of halting the ageing of the skin." One of the most important factors involved in the complex process of healing and rejuvenating the skin is the role played by platelets, the cells found in the blood that are immediately activated when damage occurs. These are like tiny reservoirs containing over 40 growth factors involved in the regeneration of epithelial tissue, increasing collagen production and the formation of new blood vessels.

"The treatment involves the harvesting of a small quantity of blood from the patient that is then centrifuged for 10 minutes in order to separate the platelets from the rest of the substance. The resulting product is introduced into the dermis using microscopic needles to obtain a skin rejuvenation effect in the treated area: the face, the neck, the cleavage, the hands, and so on. Where necessary, an anaesthetic cream is applied. To obtain the best results on fine wrinkles and post-acne scarring, a course of three sessions, once every four weeks, is recommended," explains Filis Demirgean, the dermatologist who gives me this treatment.

## Lymphatic drainage

If you ever find yourself at the practice of Cristina Bogdan, which by the way is called Naturopathya Med, then the first thing she'll tell you is that "lymphatic drainage is the best gift we can give to our skin". It was from her that I learned that "the lymphatic system is both the body's drainage system, eliminating metabolic by-products (residues, cellular debris, proteins and pore water), as well as an important part of the body's immune system because it contains lymphocytes and leukocytes. A sedentary lifestyle, consumption of processed and preserved foods, stress, internal pollution (excessive coffee consumption, regular and high alcohol and tobacco consumption, pesticides, etc.), as well as external pollution (cosmetic products containing parabens, preservatives, water containing chlorine, perfumes, deodorants containing metals, various cosmetic powders, etc.) lead to an overloading of the lymphatic system, which then becomes a source of inflammation in the body and a trigger for disease and allergies."

Lymphatic drainage treatment, performed gently but efficiently (manually, between 45 and 90 minutes per session), at least twice a year, in courses of six to 10 sessions once or twice a week, depending on individual need, is a good method of detoxification, combats cellulitis, helps with weight loss and reduces intolerances and allergies. It also enhances cellular regeneration (the skin looks better, wrinkles are reduced), lowers water retention in the body and reduces the effects of chronic fatigue and stress. Last but not least, it helps us to sleep better.

# PART 3

# PERSONAL DEVELOPMENT

# 20

# Mindfulness or how I was able to bring order into the disorder of my life

*Problems are inexhaustible. Our health isn't!*

Go back almost two decades, and not only did these ideas not resonate with me, but I would react sarcastically whenever someone mentioned things like mindfulness (which I didn't have the slightest clue about at the time), meditation, rebalancing energies and so on. It was the same story with alternative therapies: while I'd often get a kick out of making fun of them, I never went to the actual trouble of finding out what each of them entailed. I was a highly sceptical kind of person who lived by the simple rule that "what I can't see doesn't exist". I found it hard to accept any theory or principle that relied on things that had no physical form and were intangible. But there are certain things we are only able to understand when we are ready to understand them. This willingness to understand things generally only comes into play when we have a problem and are in need of solutions. Exceptions to this rule are few and far between!

Although outwardly I appeared to be enjoying a great life full of all those things that are meant to make you happy, this was only true on the outside. In reality, my life had become awash with clouds of anxiety and fragility, born on the winds of celebrity, and the idea of perfection; and even when I tried my best to let the sun in, other, seemingly darker, more oppressive, more unforgiving clouds would only follow in its wake. Everything I did made me unhappy. The negative thoughts and aggressive treatments I was subjecting my body to at the time gave rise to anxiety and depression. I ended up being only the storm and almost never the clear sky. I was trapped in a never-ending cycle of painful experiences that had become my everyday reality. Naturally, I ended up asking myself why the sturdy-looking castle seen by others – that is to say, my life – was in fact built on sand and thus lacking strong foundations.

I went through various phases – sadness, anger, fear, and an incapacity to adapt to what was happening around me, to name just a few from what was a very long list. What helped me get through this painful time? Besides using sarcasm to conceal my weaknesses, I also had a tendency for introspection and would try to find out what was behind the things that were happening to me and that I was feeling. In that sense, it was my curiosity that saved me, as curiosity is one of the main qualities found in people who are looking to grow.

So it was out of a desire to find out why I felt the way I did that I began analysing why I was unhappy, even if on the face of it I had all the things needed to lead a fulfilling life. These questions helped me connect more with myself, to have the patience to listen to myself, to find myself amid troubled waters, navigating between my thoughts and fears, and to understand myself better. So I began to look for explanations for my contradictory feelings, to seek solutions, and to become less stressed at the thought of others placing different labels on me. I judged myself, I reproached myself and I sought out the root causes. And while I did find some answers, I'm still searching for others, which can also be said of the solutions, for the process is ongoing and I'm always discovering new things about myself and trying to push my limits. I didn't do all this in order to save my image, but because I realised this was something I needed to do for myself.

Being mindful is one of the most important things in life. Unfortunately, so many things happen because we fail to live in the present moment. We are no longer conscious of what we eat, we leave home and before we're half way down the road we ask ourselves where we're going, whether we locked the door and turned off the lights in the house – this often happens to me when I'm not firmly anchored in the present! All of this proves that we are not truly in the present when we do things. When having our lunch, for example, we often chat on the phone at the same time, browse the internet or continue working on something, with the result that we no longer really taste the food we're eating. And this is such a shame, as it is only when we are mindful that we notice the smells caressing our senses, that we are able to truly enjoy the food we are eating and that information is able to reach the brain in a different way.

Mindfulness is the art of living in the present, and to achieve this it is first and foremost important to be honest with ourselves, to shed our prejudices, to stop judging ourselves and to try to see the things around us in full color rather than just black and white. Even if we lead fast-paced lives, with social pressures and deadlines weighing us down and our to-do lists growing ever longer, it is vital that we always remain in the present, that we focus our attention on every action we perform, however mundane.

Ever since we were little we've been told what to do, what

to feel, how to react – essentially how we're supposed to live our lives. "It's not nice to be sad!", "You look a lot nicer when you smile", "You look ugly when you cry!" are commonly heard expressions, and for a man to cry is considered a sign of weakness. So we become a ball of emotions, of frustrations that never see the light of day and continue to grow, only heaping more pressure onto us in the process. In order to become conscious of these emotions we need to embrace mindfulness. The present. To be present in our lives.

We are people, warts and all; we have our good days and bad days; every emotion we feel allows us to take a step forward, to discover ourselves and to grow. Difficult situations are part and parcel of our lives, we must accept them and not hide them for fear of insulting or angering others. Emotions should not be classified as being either right or wrong; they are all feelings that shape us as individuals, they help us mature, they make us accept ourselves the way we are and they set us free at the same time. In the end, mindfulness is a meditation technique, a moment in which we are able to be alone with ourselves, even while in an active state.

When I went to India, my view of life changed. Although I'd spent my whole life striving to have the perfect body, to look impeccable and to live up to the expectations of others, I came to understand that none of this would help me look good if things weren't right on the inside, that is, if I wasn't balanced. Balance occurs the moment we come to know ourselves, the moment we accept ourselves and love ourselves the way we are.

This journey to my soul, which I just so happened to undertake in India, helped me to achieve balance, with all that implies, and to find inner peace. And there was no shortage of confirmation that things had changed for the better after having begun to accept myself the way I was! Take, for example, a photographer friend, someone I'd worked with and done many photoshoots with in the past and who has known me since I was 20. One day he came up to me and asked me if I had something special done to my face, by which he meant a cosmetic procedure. Well, no, I hadn't had anything special done, I was just a lot more relaxed in myself. I had managed to eradicate all the emotions I had been storing up for decades – like anger, sadness and frustration – and my face was radiant as a result. I was reflecting a state of harmony and joy that came from within. Everything I learned there helped me to have confidence in myself and to be at ease with myself regardless of what was going on around me (of course, I'm not talking here about exceptional and truly traumatic events). Calm, happiness, joy, balance – these are not determined by things that occur on the outside, but what exists on the inside.

For a long time I had been telling myself I needed to be in a relationship to be happy, that I needed a job, a house – I still consider these important things in anyone's life, but they are not the only things in our lives that bring us happiness. The time we spend with ourselves is very important because otherwise we don't know who we really are. I remember how, at one of the mindfulness workshops I have given, I asked the participants to write down what I wanted them to do as homework – namely, to provide an answer to the question "Who am I?" They could hardly believe it. They thought it was a strangely simple question, banal even, but I told them to go home and think about it and to give me their answers the next time we met. The following week they told me it had been the hardest assignment they had been given yet. It's hard to come up with an answer that doesn't mention our families, homes, cars, jobs, friends, clothes and all the other things we have.

When I first came back from India (where I learned how important it is to be an observer of yourself and your life, of all the experiences and situations that happen in your life and to know which lessons you need to remember), after three months of learning to be able to analyse myself objectively, one morning, as I was leaving home, I noticed how I was carrying loads of different things around with me: gym bags, a thermos, a lunch box, some books and laptop, etc. At some point, I don't know how I did it, but I managed to spill the contents of the thermos all over me and then to drop my lunchbox as well – I'm sure you've also had days when you felt all the stars were aligned against you. Well, my first reaction – something I'd become used to doing in similar situations before – was to get annoyed and to feel I had a headache coming on. However, my reaction then suddenly transformed into something completely different: I began to laugh. I put myself in the place of an observer and I was able to see just how many things I had been planning to do within a short span of time. It would have been much simpler to have broken it all down into separate trips. And the result of all my rushing around and trying to do hundreds of different jobs in record time was to waste time: following my little accident I had to go home and change, grab some other things, wipe off what was dirty, and so on.

Right now, as I write these words, another telling example springs to mind. Before going to India, while I was still working in television, I came home from work one day in a terrible rush and immediately began getting ready to go out to an event. I went into the bathroom, put on some foundation, blusher, mascara, etc. – all at Formula 1 speed. Because I was in such a rush, I managed to cover myself in mascara, which had begun to run, and instead of leaving the house and getting there on time, I was forced to remove my makeup and start all over again. This time a lot more carefully. Digressing for a moment, can you imagine what I would have looked like if I'd gone out looking like that?

I was aware even then that I needed to take much more care when doing things, which doesn't necessarily mean doing them slowly, but at a pace that allows me to do them well. Why do you think there are so many sad, angry, disappointed and aggressive people out there? Because they don't live in the present, that's why. Because to lead a calm, peaceful life, to avoid becoming suffocated by our thoughts, requires us to be conscious of the reality we inhabit, as well as not to rush things beyond what we are capable of.

Mindfulness has helped me to regain control of my own mind and my life, to differentiate between the things I truly want for myself and those things others expect of me or think I should be achieving or aspiring to. I want to be able to enjoy each day, however stressful and busy it may be, and to have the strength to say "stop" when I feel I am starting to speed up again and feel myself adopting the values of those around me which don't resemble my own. By learning to live in the present I have become aware of the reality I inhabit, not the one my mind usually creates for me. My life is now as calm as it can be, I no longer allow myself to be bombarded with thoughts that would leave me feeling incredibly tired and disheartened before and would see me become lost in the mad rush of today's world. I take each moment as it comes: I don't ask myself "why?" but rather "why not?" And, most importantly, I live in the present moment, accepting the past which I have no way of changing and leaving all projections of the future to one side – something which not only took up a lot of my time, but also left me feeling afraid of what might happen next.

The concept of mindfulness changed my life. But I don't want you to think of it as being something really complicated, where you have to stand in a corner, isolated from the world, cut off from everything you've experienced up to now. It also has nothing to do with religion or philosophy; it's not a sect, a fad or anything to do with metaphysics. It's all about the control we have over our own minds, about how we can identify our real needs and how to differentiate between our expectations and desires.

It often happens that what is the generally accepted idea of happiness becomes our own idea of happiness. As a result, when we finally obtain the things we've been chasing after so actively we find we're not in the slightest bit satisfied. Why? Is this not what we really wanted? We are bombarded from all directions – on the television, on the street, on the radio, on the internet or via other means of communication – with all kinds of advertisements, holiday ideas, unique travel and investment opportunities, cars, houses, one more appealing than the next, all of which are accompanied by the promise that they will bring us that much sought-after happiness. And this is where the rush to accumulate the money with which to buy all these happiness-inducing products begins. Unfortunately, at some point during this process people start believing they are the things they possess: houses, luxury cars, investments, expensive handbags, large bank accounts. They end up identifying with them, and if life deprives them of these things they are left feeling completely worthless. But it is not these things that make us happy and they don't define us as people either.

In India, I learned something really important that has helped me a lot since: "Find out who you are because only then will you know what it is you want." We often believe we know ourselves simply because that's what's considered normal. Often, the conditioning of childhood and society suffocates our true selves. We also often refuse to see who we really are. Who are we when we're not being a parent, a child, a brother, a sister, a manager, a simple employee, an actor, a doctor, a president, a leader? We keep ourselves so busy in our lives that we lose the connection with ourselves, and that's why we feel a strong feeling of futility, maladjustment and dissatisfaction every time we come face to face with ourselves.

I would like to suggest an exercise that I have done myself and which may help you a lot, too. Over the space of a week, take half an hour each day in which to be with yourselves, with no phone, internet or television to distract you, and spend it thinking with your heart, not your mind. Ask yourselves what things you like and what not, what things are really important for you and what your most hidden desires are. I know it can be difficult the first day, maybe the next day, too, but you'll get there. I'm sure of it! Breathe deeply and relax. Only then will you manage to discover what's really in your soul.

# 21

# Meditation, the "gymnastics" of my soul

*Thoughts are a projection of our reality.*

Have you ever tried to stop what you were doing to just stand still? Without doing a thing? Without reaching for your phone, calling your best friend, drinking a coffee or a cup of tea, or being afraid of becoming aware of your thoughts? Well, I hadn't either until life taught me a lesson I'll never forget. It's an experience I hope you'll learn from and which will help you to avoid the ill-advised path I embarked upon many years ago.

Have you noticed how whenever we have some free time we're always tempted to fill it with something? The explanation for this is simple: when we set aside some time just for ourselves, a million thoughts and emotions appear that make us feel uncomfortable. So if we just do something, anything, we can block them all out and can avoid coming into contact with them. We are frightened of being alone with our thoughts and especially our emotions because, inevitably, this causes us pain. Many people are afraid of being left on their own with their thoughts precisely because that's when all their demons rise to the surface: it's when we realise that we'd rather be doing something else with our lives, but we don't have the courage to do it, that we have forgotten our dreams, that we don't know where we're heading, that we no longer know how to love those dear to us, that we are profoundly unhappy. So what do we do? We avoid being alone and listening to all the thoughts that dart across our minds at incredible speed. Because if we had the courage to do so it would only make us suffer. And who wants to suffer? The truth is we're really afraid to feel things. And when we just stand still and do nothing all the feelings and all the emotions we've become accustomed to repressing ever since childhood start to rear their heads.

It's about all those feelings and emotions we've learned to hide deep down inside of us, because, as I said earlier, we've been told ever since we were little that it's shameful to be sad, to be angry, melancholy or even too cheerful. We've learned to keep all these feelings really well hidden deep down in the depths of our soul, because it's shameful to externalise them. It's how we were brought up. Our parents and our families taught us as they knew best, so there's no point in being angry with them. We need to understand that they were only trying to do right by us, for they too were once raised and taught in this way. They only wanted to give us the best.

After years spent repressing all kinds of different feelings and moods, as soon as we interrupt our busy daily routines, even if only for a moment, all these things are released and rise to the surface. That's why it's painful to be on our own and to feel all that sadness and why, because we feel wretched, we end up targeting all our bitterness at those around us. As a result we feel even sadder and it seems we'll never find the light at the end of the tunnel.

What else did I notice? That if we show the courage to be alone with just our own thoughts and to meditate, then others will consider us a bit strange. For example, at work, if we take 10 minutes off and go and sit on a bench, just us together with ourselves, other people will throw us some bizarre looks. They ask what's wrong, even if we only want to rid ourselves of all the stress around us and to clear our minds. This is because people are not used to just sitting there. What's more, many people believe that if we're not doing anything then we're wasting time, we're deemed useless, we're always supposed to be doing something, always supposed to be of use… only slouches and layabouts sit around doing nothing.

Even for me, after so many years of meditation, there are moments – admittedly now only rarely, but particularly in times of crisis – when I still find it hard to be alone with myself.

I find it hard to battle my own thoughts, because once the first thoughts appear, others soon follow in their wake. The thoughts that overwhelm us in these moments are thoughts we store up every day, thoughts about things we do or things we don't do, about people and about absolutely everything we come into contact with in the space of a single day. When you are no longer present in your life you start to think about all the problems you've had, all the situations you've found yourself in before; you start dissecting it all, thinking how you might have acted differently; you turn everything over in your mind and fall prey to different scenarios; you regret your actions and project all kinds of situations onto the future; and all of this produces a state of anxiety. The really sad thing is that in most cases our thoughts are negative. Did you know that according to research we have between ten and twenty thousand thoughts an hour and around seventy thousand thoughts a day, and of these ninety percent are recurring thoughts?

There comes a time in life when we can no longer keep going straight ahead, because if we did we would hit a wall, and so we have to decide whether to take a left or a right turn. I used to be very stubborn and when I found myself faced with this kind of decision, I simply wouldn't accept it, because I didn't believe there was anything I couldn't do and that I wouldn't be able to scale the wall. And yet, one day I became stuck on a path in my life, and, whether I liked it or not, I had to make a decision and to accept that not everything had to be the way others wanted it to be or how I'd told myself was right. All the conditioning that had brought me to this point, telling me that I should do X or Y, was stopping me from seeing other options; I simply believed I had to do it, whatever the consequences. It took me a long time to realise I was living in a world in which most things are only about what is visible on the surface, a world disconnected from the truly important things in life, a world in which just by breathing and eating you become sick with frustration and anxiety. It's a world in which totalitarianism and conformism are in the driving seat and only very rarely do you find any authenticity. But not everything is gloomy and desperate: we need only achieve a state of balance and learn to accept ourselves and to put a stop to our negative thoughts. The change is in us – I think you might have heard that expression before!

Coming back to my past, after I had acquired almost everything I wanted, I grew tired of fighting against things that got in my way, with a wall that was blocking my access to happiness, and I gave up. It was an internal conflict, that unpleasant state that arises when what you're doing is not leading you towards what you really want. I no longer recognised myself in the things I was doing – in other words, I was going through a crisis. The conflict was so great that I fell into a depression, into a "life-paralysis". I could no longer go on in this state, it was unbearable, so I had to stop and listen to what was going on inside of me. Depression spreads like a contagious disease, and excess – which appears everywhere, as a result of all the frustration that builds up throughout the different chapters of our lives – leaves us increasingly disconnected from ourselves.

Meditation helps us to be present in our bodies and not to fall prey to our thoughts, to allow our brains to rest, to connect with ourselves without feeling tired and dominated by everything going on around us, and to know exactly what is happening to us on the inside. It helps us identify our emotions and needs. If we fail to do this we end up feeling frustrated, which can be a trigger for, or even aggravate, depression. I know this from experience: I've been through many difficult moments myself, something which today helps me understand those suffering from depression. I've been there and I know what it's like. Especially as it usually comes after a peak: in most cases, just after we've reached the top of the mountain, where we are told by those around us that we are going to find a box full of wonders, a magic lamp containing the solutions to all our problems, we fall abruptly into the abyss of depression. Because we fought hard to achieve various things, things we never truly desired but which we adopted wholesale, borrowing them for ourselves from those around us as if they were absolutes. Because we became caught up in a competition: who's the most beautiful, the richest, the cleverest, who takes the best selfies, who has the most likes, who eats the least, who has the slimmest legs, who has worn the most wedding dresses, who… everything is a competition. And we become carried away on a wave that tears us away from our own course and forces us into orbit around artificial standards. We forget who we are, we repress our emotions and we don't allow ourselves to achieve a balance. And the more we ignore it, the deeper the emptiness within us. This is the shortest route to depression. Don't be afraid to cry, to free yourselves from stress, to talk to those around you about your problems and the thoughts gnawing away at you. Experience every mood, allow yourself to have sad days, to eschew the competition generated by the expectations of others. The more you accept all the different emotions you feel, the less you will conceal and the more you will live. The more help you seek when you need it, the more beautiful your life will be.

Sometimes we're like one giant herd of sheep, all being led in the same direction; a herd we are afraid to leave because it's risky not to conform to the majority. If we don't behave in the same way as those around us then something is deemed to be amiss, we're placed in the "defect" category and we stop scaling walls. But I decided to stop running away from what I feel and no longer remain stuck. Instead I would weigh up how much of what others tell me I should do is really the right thing for me and what I should give up on in order to be able to move forward and find balance.

Tired of so many questions and so much frustration, I remember being at home when I decided I could no longer go on like this. It was then, following some experiences that had a great impact on me, that I realised that life is the most beautiful gift and that I should enjoy it, whatever happens. I allowed myself to be guided by this idea and found the strength to view things differently, to be more aware of other people. I began to be more open, to stop complaining about situations and things I didn't understand, and to let things happen of their own accord.

Then, no longer feeling crushed by the pressure of "must do this, must do that" and so many preconceived ideas, it just so happened that someone would give me a book that would help take a different view of the things that were bothering me or someone would recommend to me a self-awareness course or a talk that gave rise to many questions and contradictory feelings. The change began to take place before I actually realised it was happening to me. I can remember a conversation I had with someone during this time who asked me if I'd heard of Osho.

I replied that I knew who he was, but that I didn't know that much about his life and teachings. "Did you know that Osho invented his own forms of meditation? Let's meditate together," the person in question urged me. Unfortunately, I never made it to that course, but it was probably blatantly obvious how much I needed to meditate, otherwise there'd be no explaining the text message I got from that same person containing all kinds of explanations as to how I should proceed. There were lots of details and suggestions about how to relax. I was amazed and pleasantly surprised by the gesture. If only for the sake of this person, who took the trouble to send me all this information, I decided to give it a go. I performed the meditation as suggested and it felt incredible. I experienced various states that are hard to express in words.

Meditation gives me the space I need to cut myself off from all the things existing on the outside, to be present in the moment, to rest my mind. When we're in the present, we are only aware of the present moment and we cease thinking about anything else. Only when we cast off our everyday burdens do we realise that we live in an incredibly hectic world, a world in which we are unable to find the time for anything, in which we constantly feel tired and are eternally dissatisfied. We often want nothing more at the end of the day than a bit of peace and quiet. However, the moment we stop, the moment we say to ourselves "that's it, I'm going to relax now", the mind sets to work. What's more, it becomes increasingly "noisy". It is in these moments of "peace and quiet" that we begin to remember all the things we haven't done, all the phone calls we have to make, even the long list of things we need to buy.

If we want to relax our minds, we must first relax our bodies. People who lead busy lives can't simply click their fingers and suddenly begin meditating. Like I used to, they probably see meditation as a waste of time. Taking all of these things into account, Osho developed various forms of meditation, each of which lasts one hour, is divided into different parts and begins with a physical exercise, a series of movements, a form of dynamism. More precisely, in order to reach ourselves we need to cut ourselves off from all the thoughts haunting our minds. How do we do this? Through movement. Movement helps us to shift our focus away from the mind and towards what is happening in the body. We start by dancing, running or anything else involving movement, then gradually reduce it. We spend a lot of time in our heads, but what we really need to be doing is spending time in our bodies, allowing us to relax and come into contact with what we are feeling.

Active meditation is a technique that helps us to connect with ourselves. This is why, for example, we feel great when we go to the gym. Apart from the fact that we are secreting hormones that induce in us a feeling of well-being, physical exercise helps us to become aware of our bodies and free ourselves of thoughts. When we use gym equipment, for example, or when we do yoga or another form of movement, we need to be careful, otherwise we might lose control and hurt ourselves. So whether we want it or not, we need to be present, to perform our exercises correctly, to have a goal in mind and to follow only that, not to let our thoughts draw us into too many different moods and deny us the joy of the present moment. I recall how once, while I was at the gym, I had the feeling that my instructor had not explained properly how I should be doing my exercises – I told you I was stubborn! :) As a result I began to doubt myself, I lost my balance, put my foot down wrong and ended up breaking my leg. This was an important lesson for me and one that unfortunately left me in quite a lot of pain and with a feeling of powerlessness I hadn't experienced before. Since then I try not to let myself become beset by doubts and not to have too many thoughts when I go for a run, rather to focus on my goal and to enjoy the activity itself. Being so absorbed by my thoughts, I was not aware of the movements I was making, I wasn't in the present, and this ended up being to the detriment of my physical health. Exercising is one of the best ways for us to relax, to enjoy the present moment and to feel good.

When I'm feeling stressed, I have to concentrate harder and because my mind is full of thoughts and it's hard to stay still and meditate peacefully, I choose either active meditation (and here I recommend those developed by Osho) or exercise. Still on the subject of meditation, I have a bit of news to share with you. I hope you will like it, because it's good news. More precisely, it has to do with a project I'm really excited about: I've been working on a programme of guided meditation because I feel the need to help other people, too, and because I get a lot of questions concerning the best forms of guided meditation. So I can hardly wait for you to see what it's all about and for you to tell me what you think.

Exercise and meditation help us to calm our minds and prepare us for those moments in which we are alone with ourselves, in the present. I meditate every day, it's one of the first things I do in the morning. I don't look at my phone, or surf the net, rather I try to prioritise things that are most important for me and for my state of well-being, and I spend 10-15 minutes just with myself. Meditation is not the same every day; there are days on which my mind feels rested and it's easy for me to be present in the moment, but there are also days when my mind is more unsettled, because we, too, are also not the same every day, with the result that our actions will also be different.

Meditation helps us remain in the present moment and witness what happens without reacting, only responding to things. In practice, during an active meditation session, our attention will shift from the mind to the body, allowing both our mind and body to relax.

I must admit to feeling pretty exasperated by all the thoughts I had the first time I tried to meditate. It felt as if I would never manage to silence them, to empty my mind of everything. But as time passed, despite all my anxieties and insecurities, I was able to learn to befriend my own thoughts. I was able to stop paying them so much attention and as a result they "departed" of their own accord. And when they refuse to give up easily, I now understand that I need only to accept their existence. They are my thoughts and are a part of me. I have stopped judging myself for not be able to dispel them. In recent years, and after I began meditating, I have learned that it is important to allow the emotions within me to rise to the surface, to process them, to feel them, to experience them. This is how we can free ourselves and live our lives without any unwanted baggage, without this suitcase full of emotions which have the power to influence our behaviour and even the decisions we make in our lives.

# 22

# A diary of (un)spoken thoughts and gifts wrapped up as resources

*Sometimes silence and writing can heal.*

We are used to channelling all our energy into what's going on outside of us, without focusing our attention inwards, without thinking about who we are, what we want and what we feel. The way we live our lives depends on the people and the events taking place around us, without being conscious of our inner selves. It is for this reason that most, if not all of us, need to learn to build a relationship with ourselves, to get to know, accept and to love ourselves. It took me some time to realise that the most important relationship in my life is the one I have with myself. It took me many anxious years to get to know myself, to respect myself, to love myself the way I am and to accept myself.

When we were little, nearly all of us kept a diary, I'm sure you did too, and for various reasons: we were afraid of the way we felt, wouldn't talk openly about our feelings and we didn't trust others. But we'd put our feelings down on paper and our diary was our best friend. I've hung on to all of my diaries and it makes me smile every time I go back to them. I remember having the same type of diary every year, only the colour varied: black, burgundy or green. The lengths I used to go to hide them! :-)

After I became an adult and my life got really busy, keeping a diary ceased to be a priority for me. In fact, I stopped entirely, it seemed childish somehow and I didn't think it would be of any use to me anymore. But a few years ago, I rediscovered this pleasure, which is why I published my *Trăiește frumos* ("Live Beautifully") diary, notebook, agenda and 90-day daily planner, and I was pleasantly surprised to see that many of you really enjoyed using them, because they provided you with that space all of your own where you could say whatever you wanted without fear of anything – neither of being judged nor of being reproached by anyone. I strongly believe that if we are to have an encounter with ourselves then it's important to give ourselves some time and write down what we are feeling.

I prefer writing in a notebook/diary/agenda with a pen or a pencil, not an electronic notepad – it's a different, much more pleasant sensation. I don't write in my diary every day, only when I feel I need to make a decision, or when I feel stressed, overjoyed or very sad. It helps me to disconnect from my problems, vent, stop me bottling them up inside of me and to view them from a different angle. Come to think of it, I think keeping a diary has saved me in many situations where there didn't appear to be any solutions. It has helped me to understand myself better and to do exactly what I wanted to do.

A diary helps us to reflect on ourselves, to be much more aware of the way we are living our lives and to become conscious of everything we didn't know about ourselves before. It is a place where we allow ourselves to ask questions about our lives and about what we feel; a place where we can note down things that make us smile and things that make us sad. It doesn't matter how trivial you consider all the ideas you note down, what's important is that you're honest with yourself and in what you write. It's wonderful to be able to express ourselves in a place where no one judges us, no one questions us and no one makes fun of us.

There are no rules, no right or wrong ways to keep a diary. If we are honest about our thoughts, a diary will act like a mirror allowing us to view the different parts we are made of (some of these we will recognise, others we will be discovering for the first time). We will thus learn to appreciate our qualities, to analyse our souls, to get to know ourselves, to discover ourselves.

It's very important to ask ourselves questions, because we are often unhappy with our lives but lack the courage to identify the underlying problems. The answers we get may not be the ones we wanted, but they will help us to arrive at a place where we feel content. You can't get to know someone without asking them some questions. For example, when we love, we show an interest in what the person we have feelings for does, how he or she feels, we're interested in everything he or she thinks and so on. As we are the most important person in our lives, we need to (re)discover ourselves and to find out as much about ourselves as possible. When we discover our needs and find out who we are, we also discover the best ways to show our love for ourselves. I see so many people who say they're bored, they're lost, that their lives don't have any meaning – I believe this is a form of a lack of love for oneself and it needs to be rectified.

It's important to be realistic, I've never believed in the kind of happiness you find in books or fairy tales. The glass is always half full, only we often find it hard to see this. We're so fond of playing the victim that we become addicted to the role. Maybe some people don't think I'm in a position to talk about these things. I don't mean to contradict anyone, but merely wish to remind you that we are all human and we all have our problems, regardless of age, race, religion or social standing. Try to see the good side of things, because there always is a good side. Do you think there weren't things I wanted to do and that I wasn't really upset when they never happened? But I realised that life has other plans for me, perhaps much better ones. Our existence on earth is too short to spend dwelling on the bad things in life! It's important to enjoy everything life has to offer us.

We can't change overnight from "everything is terrible" to "everything is perfect", but we can, as I've already said, try to discover methods that resonate with us and that help us to gradually make this change. One way to start is by becoming conscious of our negative thoughts and to put a stop to them. If, for example, I go into my office and see it's in a mess – which, believe me, can happen :-) – then I try not to focus on this. Instead I think about how I can become better organised or am grateful that it meant I came across a book I'd forgotten about or that it's very peaceful or that I have a plant that seems to last forever, etc. We can all make small changes in our lives, but we must start by taking small steps. Let's say, we meet someone whose hair has been messed up by the wind. Instead of focusing on her hair, we could tell her we like her makeup or find other things to like about her. It's impossible not to be able to find something good in other people, and I really do believe in the saying that beauty is in the eye of the beholder. We choose what we see and the way in which we relate to others, so why not turn this into a pleasant experience?!

## Let's do an exercise

Try to spend a whole day being conscious of all the thoughts you have, to identify the negative ones and to stop them. Then spend the next week trying to change them and concentrating on things you like. At the same time, write down in your diary the things you like about yourself and then read them out loud whenever you find yourself feeling a bit down.

By answering the questions I suggest below you will begin to see things much more clearly and will realise where you're doing things right and where you need to make improvements. Of course, this is only a starting point, and you might also want to try asking yourself different questions to help you in this endeavour.

- What makes you happy?
- What is it you need?
- What relaxes you?
- Who is the most important person in your life?
- What things are most important to you?
- What makes you angry?
- What's your greatest fear?
- What makes you cry?
- What gives you energy?
- What's stopping you from doing the things you'd like to do?
- Do you like what you do?
- When was the last time you told someone you love them?
- When was the last time you took a risk?
- What makes you feel fulfilled?
- Who are the five most important people in your life?
- What would you give up because of fear?
- In what ways do you put yourself under pressure?

Another step towards getting to know ourselves better and living a balanced life comes when we begin to become aware of our resources. We live in a society in which we overexert ourselves, we work until we're exhausted, like robots (I speak from experience when I say this, and, yes, I must admit to often breaking down). We wake up feeling stressed and go to bed feeling just as bad, and then we do it all over again without realising that it takes resources to do all these things. The first time I was asked what my resources were, I didn't know how to answer. I felt stumped by the question. I, who could only see my body's flaws and limitations, was supposed to talk about my resources? Well, it seemed to me I didn't have any at all. In fact, it hadn't even crossed my mind just how many resources we have. But, of course, I couldn't have been more wrong!

It was only afterwards that I understood that our resources are those things that give us energy, that make us happy and make us keep going. It's like not putting any petrol in your car but still expecting it to run. And, of course, our body needs constant refuelling.

I realised that my resources are the time I spend with myself, as well as with people who love me unconditionally and with whom I feel safe, the time I spend in nature, meditation, massage, exercise and sleep. The time I spend in the bath tub relaxing is also an important resource for me, while time spent at the seaside also provides me with lots of energy.

**Exercise**

**Take a sheet of paper and write down what your resources are, what things give you energy. Yes, write them down, because when we feel overwhelmed we tend to forget everything. It's very important to become aware of our resources so that we are then able to access them when we feel exhausted.**

# 23

# Breathing techniques with healing effects

*"Life is aspiration, respiration and expiration."*

– SALVADOR DALI

"A workshop on breathing?? What could it teach me that I don't know and do already: to inhale and exhale? It's not rocket science! No to mention, it lasts for 21 days, from morning till night." These are just some of the thoughts that passed through my mind when I first heard about these kinds of events. The truth is I didn't have a clue just how important it is to breathe correctly. Without realising it, we often breathe only superficially, which means we also live superficially. Only by learning to breathe deeply will we be able to live deeply as well.

Sometimes, during really busy periods, I find myself beginning the day already feeling really stressed out. I'm sure you've experienced the same thing. As soon as I wake up, my mind starts reeling and I think about all the things I have to do that day and all the things I didn't manage to get done the day before. Even during a yoga class, my mind is sometimes all over the place, because there's no controlling it, thoughts come and go as they please. In moments like these, I like to focus on my breathing, because this helps us to be in the present, to create a connection with ourselves and the moment we are experiencing.

Breathing brings us back to the now, and so when we want to relax or enjoy the present moment, it becomes an essential tool. Breathing begins now and finishes now, it is an action we do in the present – not the past, not the future. It is a fantastic thing we can use to experience things authentically, in all their complexity. There are times when I find it hard to concentrate on my exercises, but as soon as I start breathing, as soon as I concentrate on what's happening within me and the present moment, everything seems to get easier; my mind relaxes and my thoughts slow down.

It took me many years to realise just how important breathing is in our lives. Unfortunately, most of us are not conscious of the way we breathe. If I were to ask you about your breathing right now, whether you're conscious of the way you are breathing, what would your reply be? Rapid, deep, frantic? How would you describe it? Well, I can tell you that most people, myself included, often breathe only superficially. And this happens because we're not used to breathing deeply and consciously.

Ever since we were children, we have been brought up to repress our emotions. From all the things we're told we're not allowed to do, our stomach has contracted. Out of fear, our breathing has been transformed from abdominal into shallow breathing. If you observe a child, you'll notice their abdomen is very relaxed, full of air, and when they breathe they do so abdominally. Unlike adults, children have fewer fears and concerns. Instead they have more confidence in themselves and are very relaxed, which is why they are able to breathe correctly.

As time passes, we contract, more precisely, our stomach contracts and the way we breathe changes as a result.

> **I'd like you to do an exercise** that I use regularly in my courses. Take an apple in your hand and, with your eyes closed, spend five minutes just touching it. Afterwards, start to smell it but still without looking at it. Then take a bite out of the apple, chew it and experience the sensation you get from this action. Now write half a page, or as much as you like, about what goes through your mind while doing this exercise.

Interestingly, most people say that this experience reminds them of their childhood, and they also remember other things connected with this fruit, but only very few actually do what they were asked to do, i.e. to describe the texture of the apple, its smell, how they thought it looked, etc. Very few people write these things down because we're not used to being in the present. It's interesting how, with the help of an apple, our thoughts take us to so many places other than the present moment. The past is one of the factors that stops us from being happy. When we're sad and going through a difficult time, we cling to happier times from the past. We yearn for them, we compare an unhappy present with the past and, as a result, our current obstacle seems impossible to overcome. We dream up all kinds of wonderful scenarios instead of focusing on the creation of new memories. We study the apple only in order to remember the past, not so as to be able to enjoy it in the present.

Another factor that stands in the way of fulfilling our dreams and which stops us from enjoying the present is the future, which we project in all kinds of different ways. We create an idealised image of it, which in most cases never comes to fruition, and so we spend our days waiting for it to happen. There are three categories of people: those you live in the past, those who feed on an imagined future and those who are anchored in the present. The last category are the happiest, they are the only ones who take full advantage of the most precious gift we have: life.

During the busiest time of the day, set aside 10 minutes just for yourself, during which you should focus all your energy on your breathing, on what you feel when you inhale and exhale, on how your body reacts. Place one hand on your chest and the other on your abdomen and breathe deeply through your nose until you feel your lungs filling up with air. Hold your breath for a few seconds and then gradually allow the air to escape through your mouth. The idea is to breathe through your abdomen, not your chest, and to feel only the hand on your abdomen moving as you breathe. The exhalation of air should last slightly longer than the inhalation. Try doing this exercise for 10 minutes. Your pulse and blood pressure will gradually reduce, and your blood oxygen level will improve.

When we meditate we become aware of our emotional and our physical states, and the best way to eliminate the stress we feel on a daily basis is to observe our breathing. Even if it seems hard to believe, breathing helps the body and the mind to relax. You can use breathing exercises to alleviate discomfort and to oxygenate the brain when you have a headache.

Breathing helps us to create space, to bring order to those thoughts that won't leave us in peace, especially in the evening, when we find it hard to get to sleep or to rid ourselves of the tension that builds up during the day, when stress takes control of our bodies. With the help of breathing exercises, we can exchange our everyday feelings of stress for a state of relaxation. When we are aware of our bodies, it becomes easy to observe when we are anxious and tense, even while breathing. It really ought to be the other way around, the body should find relaxation through breathing, exhaling negative thoughts and inhaling peace and quiet.

**Did you know?**

**One of the reasons we feel tired and stressed is because our breathing is too short and rapid.**

## Exercises for how to breathe in threes

Whenever you feel stressed and your mind is flooded with all kinds of different thoughts, take a pause and try this simple breathing exercise: breathe in for three seconds, hold your breath for three seconds, then exhale for a further three seconds. Repeat this exercise ten times. You may find it complicated at first and start to feel a little dizzy, but this is only because you're not yet used to it. As the body relaxes it will start to feel better and better. However, everything should be done with patience and determination.

# 24

# The unexpected power of gratitude

*Gratitude should be the lens through which we view the world.*

Ever since I was a child, I was taught to be grateful, except that, as time passed, I forgot how to enjoy what I have and I began to focus on the things I didn't have. I think this is something that happens to us all. We are somehow so preoccupied with identifying the things we don't like, the things that are missing from our lives, things that aren't going well, that we forget to enjoy the really great and beautiful things we take for granted. Yes, many of us take things for granted, believing we deserve them. Perhaps it's not true. I constantly hear people saying that it's normal to have the things they have. Really? How's that? It's sad that we don't realise how many things we've got until we begin to lose them. It would be better if we were to consider ourselves lucky for having so many things to enjoy before it's too late.

My trip to India, where I had so many amazing experiences, really changed my perspective on life. Among the many extraordinary things that happened to me there, I remember a conversation with a taxi driver, whom I ended up talking to about all kinds of things, and I was amazed by the way he viewed life. We got talking and I asked him about various traditions, where he lives, what he thinks of Europeans and so on. I found out that he lived really far away from his place of work, and to get there he needed to take about three different types of transport, a total of five hours there and back, on top of working a 10-hour shift each day. Can you imagine how little time he got to spend with his family and how hard he had to work to make ends meet? He told me that he lived in a single room together with his wife, child and parents, earned around 100 dollars a month, tips included, but he wasn't unhappy. On the contrary, there was a special energy about him, a joy in his eyes that took me by surprise. I asked him how this was possible, and he gave me an answer which, for all its simplicity, was incredibly powerful and transformational for me. He told me he always focuses on what he has, not what he doesn't have. And he said he has so many amazing things: a healthy family he gets to see every day, a good job in his own country, he doesn't need to leave India to work abroad, as many others from his country do, he has wonderful parents and, most importantly, he is happy that they are all together. He couldn't understand why he wouldn't be happy. "I'm ready to receive more when Existence deems me worthy of more" – I can still remember his words today.

It was my final day in India and this experience was like a breath of fresh air to me. It made me realise how I viewed life, how many wonderful things I was losing sight of just because something might not work out the way I wanted. This experience motivated me to focus on the beautiful things in life, because regardless of how angry and sad we are or how gloomy life may seem, there are always at least three nice things in our lives we're not aware of. The fact that our loved ones are near to us, that we have the power to do many things, that we are healthy, that we have a job, even the fact that we are alive – it's up to each of us to realise what things we should be grateful for.

How often do you think about people who were good to you? How often do you say thank you to them? Some years ago I might have said the odd thank you to the people around me and to God, but I'd never have thought to do it regularly. The hardest part came when I got to the lesson in which I was supposed to learn to be grateful to myself. I thought it really weird to be thanking myself for all the things I do for myself. I really couldn't get my head around it. After listening to a lot of explanations – because that's just the way I am, I'm a logical person – I understood that it is important to thank the most important person in my life, the one I love the most – because that's who we are in our lives. That is, me! It was difficult at first, but in time this exercise became easier. So I've learned to be grateful to myself, for what I do, and for all the things I have and receive every day.

I'm so happy that I was able to change the way I view life after a long period in which I would only complain about the things I didn't have. I'd express my unhappiness all the time, expending enormous amounts of energy on things that would only bring me even more unhappiness and dissatisfaction. I was upset that things didn't work out as I had planned and I wasn't paying attention to what life was giving me in return. Not to mention feeling any joy.

However, I have come to understand that if I don't enjoy the things I have, I won't receive anything better. How can I receive more, if I don't enjoy the things I have now? God gives us everything we need, when we need it, and he gives us the space to enjoy and appreciate it. Think about it: when you give someone a present and that person is not pleased, or they're never pleased whenever you give them something and always make a negative comment, are you still going to enjoy giving them things in the future? You either keep on giving them things out of habit, but without feeling any pleasure, or you stop doing it altogether. To not forget the wonderful gifts we have been endowed with, it's a good idea to draw up a list of the things that bring joy to our hearts.

For example, I currently feel grateful because…

- God has given me another day to enjoy
- We are all healthy – me, my mother, my family and my friends
- I decided to give up those things that no longer bring me any joy and now only do things out of passion, although I must admit there are still times when I get carried away, but Existence rebukes me and I return to my path
- I meet extremely interesting people every day and from whom I learn so many things
- I am surrounded by wonderful people
- I have the most loving dog on earth
- I love to dance
- When I feel tired and stressed, I go out into the park and look at the lake and this calms me and fills me with energy
- I am able to travel
- I have learned to leave my comfort zone and regularly do things that help me to grow
- My life provides me with many different opportunities from which I can choose what's best for me
- God helps me to be open to all things new
- I have witnessed wonderful sunsets and sunrises
- I have wonderful conversations with the people around me
- I have an incredible relationship with my mother
- When something doesn't work out for me, I don't get upset and I look forward to seeing what God has in store for me instead

...and the list goes on and on. Every day I think of at least three things I feel thankful for and, when I feel sad this helps me to feel better again. Even at the most difficult of times, I try to think of the good things, and not those things that aren't going well in my life.

By listening too much to reason and not focusing on what we feel, we are unable to hear our heart when it sends us signals to say it is happy the way things are and that this is its natural state. Exercises involving reflection and showing gratitude increase the chances of us experiencing positive emotions and reduce the intensity of negative emotions. They also encourage a healthy lifestyle and prevent disease.

### Let's do another exercise:

Each night, before going to sleep, think of three nice things that happened during the day – whether it's a beautiful sunrise, someone who gave you a compliment or smiled at you – and for which you are grateful. This is my favourite exercise from my *Trăiește Frumos* yearly planner. It's important you go to sleep thinking of the joy these things brought you, because they will remain in your subconscious and will be processed by your brain during the night. You will then see that you have a fantastic amount of energy the next morning.

# 25

# The bonds of friendship and the influence of the people we spend time with

*"Tell me who your friends are and I shall tell you who you are."*

– YOGASWAMI

"True friends are like stars in the sky. Although you can't always see them, you can be sure they're always there." This is something that was said to me many years ago by a good friend of mine who was moving abroad. Nothing could be more true. Maybe that's why I liked it and it has remained imprinted on my mind. Owing to some issues at work, I have for some time now neither had the energy nor the necessary state of mind to be with my friends the whole time. But some of them, those who really matter, have stayed with me, they have been there for me, providing me with fantastic support and unconditional love, and for this I am deeply grateful.

I have often been asked whether I have a lot of friends. I'm surrounded by stars that are always shining, whether it's cloudy or not, and I'm very happy for this. They say it's hard to make friends and that it's even harder to make your relationships last, especially at the fast pace we live our lives at, but I find myself very lucky. Many friendships and acquaintances are formed quickly and fall apart just as quickly. True friendships are built in time – something we unfortunately don't have much of at our disposal. When we're little and we're being told that we should always strive to come first, that we're only as good as the sum of our achievements, the idea is implanted into our minds that we should expect to receive praise for our achievements and for all the things we do. And so we always seek the approval of others, we surround ourselves with friends who encourage us and believe in us. If they're not on our side and, however hard we try, they are always criticising us, we end up feeling rejected and abandoned. We give up striving for what we want, we make too many compromises and end up acting out scenarios projected onto us by those around us. This is why it's important to truly get to know ourselves and why we should place great value on those we choose to be our friends.

"We are the average of the five people we spend the most time with" – a statement that ought to make us look at our lives more carefully. At least that's what I did when I heard, many years ago, this statement by the motivational speaker Jim Rohn. Whether we like it or not, our environment and the people around us have an enormous influence on the way we live our lives, think and make decisions, our self-confidence and behaviour. Of course, everyone's personality is different, but studies show that we are influenced by our environment more than we imagine. Negative people, those who find fault with everything, can have a powerful influence even on people whose behaviour is the complete opposite. Ideally we should surround ourselves with positive people, people with good energy, empathetic, balanced people,

people who give us unconditional love and support. People from whom we can learn and who give us their honest opinion, even if it's not what we want to hear.

I have learned that the only way we can grow and develop is when we are criticised constructively by the people we trust. I have spent time with people who find fault in any situation, who complain about many things, or people who are not very confident in themselves, who don't have the courage to try new things, who don't leave their comfort zones and who reject every new idea. However much I try to change their outlook, to offer them an alternative, they rarely truly want to extract themselves from the state they've got themselves into. It pains me to say it, but they often prefer to complain than to seek solutions – but then I also understand that everyone chooses for themselves the moment to make a change, if indeed they want to change, so all I can do is to observe from the outside and not to try to fix things that don't want to be fixed. But then there's a lot more to be said on this subject.

The energy we get from those around us, I believe I can provide you with a convincing example in terms of something I experienced myself. Whenever I would come back from America, I would always be pleasantly surprised by the energy with which I returned. I met some incredible people there, people from whom I learned lots of things that inspired me enormously. Back home, after a week of exposure to the "local vibe", I'd find that my enthusiasm would drop to half what it was before and I too would begin to doubt my ability to do certain things. Why? Because of how my ideas were received here by others. Their lack of confidence would also affect me without my noticing it. Their lack of energy and courage to try new things would sap my enthusiasm and sow seeds of doubt in me. Which again just goes to show how much we are influenced by the people around us.

When I went to India, I wanted to take a friend with me, but the person who helped me organise this trip told me that it was a journey to my soul and that I should go alone. And so I did, and he was completely right. I feel the need to say it again: it wasn't my trip to that country that helped me to achieve balance, but what I learned while I was there. My determination and willingness to try different things are what helped me to begin doing things differently. So, the location is less important, what really matters is that we truly want to change and that we channel all our energies to this cause. Many people believe that once they get to India the things they were lacking on an emotional level will just appear out of nowhere. Wrong! Where we go, the culture, religion and people we encounter all facilitate this process, but it will still always be down to us to make the change.

It's true that I was a different person after I came back from India. I stopped prioritising the needs of others and was paying greater attention to myself, and this led to a change in my behaviour. For the better, I believe, although not everyone agrees! Without becoming a selfish person, I realised that if I don't know how to love myself, then there's no way I'll be able to love those around me, so I set about identifying what was important to me. The idea of loving those around you is so beautifully and profoundly expressed in the New Testament: "Love your neighbour as you love yourself." But if I didn't love myself, then I couldn't have the strength or know how to offer my love to someone else. Indeed I had ended up treating those close to me and my friends just as harshly and coldly as I treated myself. So the first thing I needed to do was fix the issues I had with myself. I wouldn't want you to think that this all happened overnight – in fact, it was a drawn out and painful process, because many of my friends didn't understand what was happening with me and chose to leave me. Despite this, I can't deny that it was also liberating, because I know that those who stuck with me love me unconditionally and didn't stay with me because of what I had to offer them, but because of what I was and still am today.

When you decide you want to undergo personal growth and make changes in your life, you should be aware that people will split into two camps: some will criticise you and will decide that you no longer have anything in common, while others will try to accept you or even to grow with you. It was really hard for me to let go of certain people, both in terms of romantic relationships and friendships, as well as on a professional level, especially as I was brought up with a strong sense of attachment. But I realised that in life we are accompanied by certain people only for a certain period of time, whether long or short, for as long as the relationship is beneficial to both parties.

I can remember something I heard on a course and which at first I thought was very selfish: that we should leave behind those people, things and experiences that are no longer of use to us. But then I came to realise that there is in fact a lot of truth in this piece of advice. It's very difficult for us to leave the past behind, I know this from my own experience, but it's the only way for us to grow. It's important we surround ourselves with people who accept us with all our vulnerabilities, who won't judge without good reason, who offer us unconditional support and accept our past, who love us and value us, who respect us and want to be part of our lives for who we are as people and not because of our status or financial situation.

When I chose to become honest with myself and to get to know myself better, at the risk of upsetting certain people in my life, I found it hard to accept that I was going to lose some of my friends. And there were moments when I was tempted to go back, to compromise, to fight for those relationships, until I realised that there was in fact no going back. I prefer to think of the beautiful things I experienced with those people, to be grateful to them for what they brought to my life and to accept that we are on different paths. By way of a conclusion, I will leave you with this quotation, which I'm very fond of and which I hope will give you food for thought: "Every true love and friendship is a story of unexpected transformation. If we are the same person before and after we loved, that means we haven't loved enough."[23]

**Exercise**

**Try to think of the five people or five activities (because more recently people have been replaced by TV series, computer games and social media) you spend the most time with/doing. As I was saying, they have a big influence on you. In doing this you will realise whether you spend your time learning, discovering new things, relaxing or simply letting it pass by. I'm not saying one is better than the other; I only encourage you to think about the people and activities you spend your precious time with/on.**

---

[23] Quote taken from the book by Elif Shafak, *The Forty Rules of Love.*

# 26

# Self-love... is sustained by good words and thoughts

*Happiness eludes those who stubbornly seek negative things.*

I used to live my whole life for others, less so for myself. If I were to have made a list of the really important people in my life, it would have been this: my mother, grandmother, father, aunts and uncles, cousins, friends, teachers, neighbours and colleagues, and by the time I got to myself… the page was full :-). I was so tired and overwhelmed by all the things I was doing for others, there was no time and energy left to spend on my own needs. Later, I would come to understand and reluctantly accept that when we help others we do so out of a desire to receive something in return: appreciation, gratitude, love, etc.; because we all need confirmation, we have a need to be loved and accepted. What I have realised is that it was okay to help those around us as long as what we are giving them doesn't do us any harm. Of course, there are extreme cases where this does not apply, such as when someone has a serious problem or is in a crisis.

But what does it really mean to love ourselves? I've had a lot of therapy over the years and so I knew what it meant to love myself. Yet, I kept on doing things that told the opposite story. Imagine the following situation: when people come to stay with us, we try to make our guests feel at home and like any good host we go to great lengths to be ready to receive them. We get up early and buy delicious things with which to spoil our guests, etc. We create a nice atmosphere at breakfast, for example, so our guests feel at home. But when it comes to us, our mornings are one big rush. We jump in the shower, get dressed in a hurry and if we eat something, perhaps just a handful of almonds on the way to work, then that's already quite a lot – we don't have the time to enjoy breakfast or to relax from so early in the day. When we want to make others happy, we will find the time, so why then don't we do the same for ourselves? Whenever I forget to do things just for myself, I remember this example and try to be kinder to myself.

I can remember a talk given by Arianna Huffington (whom I think I've mentioned already because I really like her), in which she spoke about our relationship with our phones. We're all wary not to run out of battery and we make sure there are chargers everywhere – at home, at the office, in the car, etc. Or we always carry a portable battery around with us in our bag. If our battery starts to run low and we have no means of charging it, or if the phone switches off altogether, then we begin to panic. It's interesting how much care we take of the battery in this device, which is a very important device for that matter, and yet it is still just a device. But when it comes to us, we don't pay ourselves even 10% of the attention we give to our phones.

In order never to forget to put myself first, and to be grateful for what I have and to keep track of things, I use a so-called vision board, on which I write down all the things I want to happen. With all these plans always on display and by always referring back to them, the brain programmes itself to make them happen.

Sometimes we need a change of perspective, so a board on which to note down our future projects – not just professional, but personal projects, too – will be of great help to us. Mental imagery has a great impact on the cognitive processes in the brain, and the mind reacts strongly to visual stimuli. If we focus our thoughts, emotions and energy on certain things, the law of attraction will kick in and there will be increased chances of our goals becoming reality. Writing things down on a board reminds us why we choose to do certain things, what steps we need to take and what resources we should use.

This vision board should contain impactful words, motivational quotations, drawings or schematic diagrams we make ourselves, various pictures, souvenirs, words that reflect our aims and dreams, etc. Ideally we should make ourselves a new vision board every year but still hang on to those from previous years, so we can study our progress, learn from mistakes and become aware of all the things we've achieved throughout our lives.

At home I have a chic little blackboard on which important people in my life have left me various messages. One of these messages is in English: "Talk to yourself like you would to someone you love." Indeed, we often say nasty things to ourselves and treat ourselves badly. So, when I feel I'm not following this advice, I try to imagine how I would treat someone I really love and begin to be kinder to myself. For example, if I want to tell an employee of mine that I'm not happy with something, I try to think of how I would want to be spoken to in an analogous situation. I think this marks the difference between someone who is conscious of what they are doing and someone who isn't, between someone who meditates and someone who doesn't.

I'd like to know how many people manage to live according to how they feel, listening to their hearts, forgetting the rules, the things said by those around them and the restrictions placed on them, those who ignore prejudice and follow their instincts. How often did you, perhaps like me, give up trying to do what you wanted to do after running up against imaginary barriers, the barriers erected by the society we live in? A forbidden love, unrequited sentiments, powerful desires... have you ever regretted not having lived certain experiences? If the price paid was too high, then perhaps it's time for a change, a change you should make gradually, so you end up treating yourself as you would someone you love.

Authentic self-love has for too long been viewed as an act of selfishness or rebellion. Even today, when there's a lot of talk of how we should know ourselves and accept ourselves, when we say that someone loves themselves, it always seems to have a negative connotation. Yet, love for ourselves acts like an antidote for all that is bad, because it is truly healing. People who are aware of their own qualities live in the present and are sure of themselves, and consequently they don't feel the need to praise themselves or to be praised, they don't focus on destroying other people's images, but instead focus on what they themselves have to offer. A good and honest relationship with oneself, one still grounded in reality, opens the door to happiness, it allows us to have balanced relationships with those close to us, it helps us to step outside of our comfort zones and to persevere when things don't work out for us the first time we try. Reading these lines you might think that I have erected a shrine to myself at home :). Jokes aside, I don't want you to think this takes a lot of effort. In fact, it's about small, but very important things: how you speak to yourself, tend to your body's needs, try to stem negative thoughts about yourself.

You know what I do when I feel I'm straying from what I learned in India? I go out into nature, look at beautiful things, meditate and fill myself with energy. Air, landscape, physical exercise, the company of my dog Efi – all these things intertwine and remind me that, in the end, the purpose of life is to discover what is truly important to us, allowing us to live in perfect harmony. If the world around is harmonious and envelops me in such calm, peace and joy, then why shouldn't I also be able to find within me the resources I need to love myself and to pass on some of my energy and well-being? So, always try to be in touch with nature – it is a cure for the ailments of the body and the soul.

"Only stupid people are optimistic," someone once told me, many years ago, and it left me with a bitter taste in my mouth. I don't believe this statement, although there are people who have developed an unhealthy attachment to feeling sad, who always think that nothing is going to turn out well for them, that things will never be good, that they will never be happy. Pessimistic people don't want to be happy. They want to commiserate themselves, to paint themselves as victims, because victims always get the attention of those around them and this makes them feel important. We can find energy, beautiful things, happiness and love in everything, we only need to show the willingness and desire to accept this.

In fact, experts say that the way we think determines the way our life unfolds. If we are always prisoners of our negative thoughts and do nothing to stop them, we will have a tendency to believe that bad things will always happen. What's more, these thoughts will become deeds. The rationale for this is simple. If we allow ourselves to be consumed by envy of someone, or we seek revenge for something, then our thoughts will lead us to take action against those who are the target of our thoughts. But this won't make us happy. On the contrary! In order to change the thoughts we have, we need to be aware of them. In most cases, however, we're not used to analysing our thoughts.

One of my favourite exercises in my workshops is to ask those present to take a sheet of paper and to write down whatever crosses their mind for around three to five minutes. I recommend you do this, too. You will learn a lot about yourselves and about how quickly thoughts cross our minds. Set an alarm then begin to write down on whatever you have on hand – for example, a diary, your phone or a laptop – what it is you're thinking of. Let your thoughts flow, regardless of how childish or personal they may seem: "I'm having a good or a really stressful day", "How much more should I write?", "It's too hot", "My head hurts", "I'm hungry", etc. – and after the three to five minutes are up, read back what you have written. How does it sound? Total chaos, isn't it? :-) I know, that's the word I hear most often from those who do this exercise with me.

There is no such thing as good or bad thoughts. There are just thoughts which you should be aware of. Therefore, there is no need to fear being judged or that someone will have access to things that are too personal.

The mind is so quick that it establishes connections between things that appear to be unconnected. Have you heard the expression "My mind is like a Ferrari"? I, for one, say this about my own mind, because sometimes it really does travel at incredible speed. Indeed our thoughts are very quick and we clearly won't be able to change something if we're not aware of the problem we have, so we need to listen to our thoughts and to be aware of what we are saying to ourselves. We often notice how we say bad things to ourselves and that all thoughts are nothing but a list of frustrations, fears and anxieties, many of which are dragging us down.

"I can't", "I don't know", "I'm afraid" – in the past these thoughts would constantly be on my mind and would influence my actions. I would find defects, speaking badly of and to myself, and hated my body. When you have these kinds of thoughts – because I know you have them, too – the first thing to do is to make them stop. Of course, we won't be able to tell ourselves right away and to believe that we are the most beautiful, the cleverest, etc. But at least try not to let yourselves be invaded by negative thoughts. Whenever you feel like complaining about something or someone, blaming others for your problems, take a deep breath and then try to block out these negative thoughts.

When I was a teenager, I used to take the bus to school. I liked watching the people next to me and would study them, analyse their expressions and observe their gestures and smiles. Unfortunately, most of them had sad, joyless faces. I do the same thing today, only from my car. I look around me and I see other people but with the same sad faces drained of enthusiasm. It's a shame because in most cases an ability to see the good things helps us to overcome our difficulties more easily, to view situations differently, to attract people with positive energy. Although I'm normally a positive person, I must admit that for a while I even forgot to smile myself. There are moments and periods in which I, too, feel overwhelmed by problems and forget to enjoy what I have. But then I remember what's really important, and this makes me feel better again, allowing me to take pleasure in the smaller things in life and to laugh. It's wonderful to reach a point where we are able to transform all unpleasant moments and things into something that is to our advantage. I recommend you come up with your own set of rules that help you to be balanced and then stick to them, even if they are criticised by the other people in your life. Only then will you learn to take responsibility for your own actions, only then will you learn what it means to fight for a goal and the satisfaction of achieving it.

> *"Who looks outside, dreams; who looks inside, awakes"*
>
> – CARL GUSTAV JUNG

# 27

# Excessive use of social media seriously damages your health or how I turned my phone from an enemy into a friend

*Live this moment, leave the phone!*

From granddaughters to grandmothers, everyone has a technological device today. More recently, women have begun exchanging recipes over Facebook and liking each other's photos. Our hands have become holders for gadgets. We all want to live consciously, to enjoy peace and balance in our lives. We have all the information we need to do this, it's just a click away, the internet is bursting with it. Yet strangely, we fail to live our lives the way we should, the way we want to live them. We're always stressed, always in a rush, always running around with a phone in our hands.

In our fast-paced lives, we forget everything we ever knew or everything that could help us to live peacefully. Over time, I came to understand that we need to repeat information so we don't forget it, or we need someone to remind us of it constantly, and only then will we be able to assimilate it. I, for one, felt a need to perform this exercise on myself. And because I sometimes forget how important the present moment is, I decided to have a tattoo to remind me of it. It says: "This moment matters". Whenever I get into a panic, especially when things don't go the way I want them to, I remind myself that Existence doesn't make mistakes and I read another one of my tattoos: "Trust. Let go." So simple, so real, so helpful.

Could anyone ever have imagined during communism that the telephone would one day turn into a source of stress? I don't think so! Without realising it, this device has ended up taking up so much of our time. Too much! Used excessively, a phone can be the greatest source of stress. We've become used to our phones being an extension of our arms, and I'm the first to recognise this. For many years I was addicted to my phone. I still use it a lot today, but things have changed, because I've learned to manage my relationship with my phone. Have you ever tried spending any time without reaching for your phone? I have, and I felt lost, as if I were missing something really important. Our phones have become our refuge and the information we find on the internet seems to be filling an emptiness inside. The more stressed we are, the more time we spend on the phone, finding out what's happening in other people's lives, doing some shopping and opening as many internet pages as possible. In fact, we need something to distract our attention away from what's going on inside of us, and so the more we use our phones, the further away from ourselves we move.

I've recently noticed that we increasingly seem to want to spend more time with our phones than with those around us.

This scares me. I really don't like it when I'm sitting at the table with other people and they're interacting with their phones rather than talking to each other.

I've also been addicted to technology, but I managed to cure it when I found myself becoming more and more annoyed by the lack of attention shown by the people I would meet up with. Even when it was with my friends, it was like in the joke, we'd get together just "to look at our phones". However, I realised that I was becoming annoyed by something that I was also guilty of doing myself. It wasn't easy, but I managed to "cure" myself of this disease of being permanently connected to a device. Unfortunately, I can't change the past! But I'm happy that I have learned from my mistakes and now when I go out with someone who only looks at their phone, then I stop talking and stare at them until they stop. If we've decided to meet up, then we might at least make the most of this time, to find out what's going on in our lives, and not take refuge in the lives of others far away from us.

People end up living their lives entirely online, in a virtual reality, no longer wishing to communicate with those around them. They become cut off while life passes them by. And because our phone is something we never forget, wherever we are, always there with us and always visible, some time ago I decided to launch a collection of cases inscribed with messages meant to help us reconnect to ourselves and those around us. Many people thought it a fun idea, and they used the cases not just to protect their phones, but also to remind themselves of the things that truly matter to them.

People who spend too much time with their phones in their hands have more negative thoughts, with long-term consequences. Addiction to our phones and social media predisposes us to depression, although we may suffer physical discomfort, too. From the uncomfortable position of our necks when typing, to the tensing of the hands – I know it's hard to believe, but all these things can appear as a result of excessive internet use. If you can't go even half an hour without your phone, then according to a number of studies you are suffering from what is known as smartphone addiction. These devices have us rushing to reply to every message, react to every notification, always be alert, and this stops us from relaxing, even when we're exhausted and want to sleep.

The smartphone is our gateway to social media, the ideal means of escaping our own reality. Social networks give us a false impression of being connected, because they make us think we know what's going on in other people's lives, but really we don't know anything. We only know what they allow us to see, the information those people choose to reveal about themselves. Take Facebook, for example, it's like a competition for who's got the best family, the most perfect job, the most spectacular outfits, the most friends, the best dream holidays, etc. – all of this in a society suffering from the century's number one affliction: depression.

Addiction to social networks and loneliness go hand in hand, even if, logically speaking, our feeling of isolation ought to be lower when we have so many virtual friends. People are born to socialise; however, technology causes us to stop appreciating those around us in favour of devices. Time spent on social networks can result in depression, as we compare our lives with those of others and our lives don't seem half as great. We believe we are friends with these people, but they only show us fragments of their lives, we don't know what's in their hearts, their desires and fears. I believe that being friends with someone means more than this. Our real relationships, offline, face-to-face relationships, suffer because of our constant exposure to the models of perfection promoted on social media.

Many years ago, I attended a lecture by an American professor who said something I really liked. He said that we're living in an era of FOMO (fear of missing out), which is turning into JOMO (joy of missing out). The former is a feeling of disquiet that sets in out of the fear that others do, know and experience more and better things than we do. We are so desperate not to lose out on anything that we don't want to miss a single opportunity. We are permanently tired because we're always running around after too many things and we no longer have the time to look at the beautiful things we already have. We can't do it all, which is what gives rise to the sense of dissatisfaction and frustration. It's one of the many reasons why depression is so widespread, because people don't know how to extract themselves from this mad chase. I can identify with this scenario, because in the past, before making changes to my life, I felt the need to have it all and to rush about from morning till night trying to be everywhere, but I never felt fulfilled and truly happy. I was tired, frustrated and exhausted, because I never had any time for myself, because I was always spending my time on unimportant things that I thought I would get a lot out of. My greatest achievement was learning to say "no" to things that weren't a priority and to decide what was important and what not. That is, I gradually began to enter the JOMO stage, which means I can enjoy being disconnected from technology and no longer feel the pressure to always be up to date with what's going on. Being alone with my thoughts and to have some peace and quiet is just as important as physical exercise, sleep and exercise. In fact, it's a necessity!

I'm often asked the question, "How do you manage to run a business, keep in shape, travel, do physical exercise, eat healthily and so on?" To this I reply with a different question: "What can we do to continue enjoying the benefits of technology and social networks without becoming overwhelmed by a feeling that we're not good enough, that we don't know enough and that our lives are not good the way they are?" Well, the formula I use involves discipline, willpower and a clear picture of my priorities. I make lists of urgent things and things that can wait, and then organise my time so I can get them done, while also leaving myself at least an hour for things that I enjoy doing and which relax me. I still go on social media, I speak on the phone, but there are also moments when I put all my devices to one side and I try to connect with myself and my loved ones. Switching off our phones from time to time can make us feel anxious at first, but I can guarantee you it's worth it! Try it when you get the opportunity and you'll be amazed by the results!

# 28

# Restoring Mind & Body Balance: Alternative therapies I have tried and am happy to recommend

*Every day we have reasons to be happy, we only need to be aware of them.*

## Craniosacral therapy

At first sight, the name of this therapy sounds pretty complicated, as for that matter do some of the explanations used to describe it. I was sceptical too when I first heard of it, but I had promised myself to stop rejecting things before doing a bit of research into them first. So, after reading up on the subject, I gave it a try and was pleasantly surprised by what it entailed and, by the results. I remember doing a craniosacral therapy session and being really impressed at how relaxed I felt afterwards. Especially in India, where I did this procedure far more often, it seemed incredible to me how a person could tell so many things about me just by touching me. Alongside hypnosis and regression therapy, craniosacral therapy helps me solve many problems and to find balance. It's of great help to me during difficult times, especially because it's an extraordinary way of bringing some order to my mind in terms of my emotions.

This technique was invented by John E. Upledger, a professor of biomechanics and a clinical researcher. He concluded that the emotional wounds we acquire as a result of traumatic events are felt both on a physical level – for example, in the form of cysts – and a psychological level, where the symptoms vary: sadness – depression, lack of concentration, insomnia and so on. Consequently, according to experts in craniosacral therapy, the causes of each disease need to be identified first before adjusting the corresponding hormones responsible for our emotional state.

By applying gentle pressure to key points, the therapist eliminates certain tensions built up in the body. A session can last up to one hour and a half and not only helps to relieve pain, but also to treat many different ailments and conditions of the body: powerful headaches, neck and back pain, fatigue, brain disease and spinal marrow disease, depression, anxiety, emotional issues and more.

The first thing you'll notice when you begin a session of craniosacral therapy is a feeling of deep relaxation which lasts until the end of the session. Depending on the type of imbalance in your body, the effects will be felt either immediately or sometime later. This procedure is suitable for all age groups and for both those with health problems and those who simply wish to improve their lifestyle, boost their immune systems and alleviate stress.

## Bach flower remedies

For those of you who think this has something to do with the famous composer, I'm going to have to disappoint you!

Bach flower remedies provide a system of treating emotional imbalances and help us to get rid of all the negative energy suffocating us. And not by the power of musical notes – although they also have many benefits – but with the help of flowers. Sceptics will laugh but the truth is that we can't achieve well-being if we don't pay attention to our emotions. Restoring emotional balance with the aid of these flower remedies involves the elimination of negative emotions and bad habits. When I first heard about these remedies and their benefits, like any doubting Thomas, I was pretty scathing, but then thought I might as well give them a try, as they couldn't do any harm and, to my surprise, they worked.

This method was invented by the doctor and bacteriologist Edward Bach. He believed in the connection between the mind, emotions, the immune system and healing, and he claimed that certain plants aid the process of healing our emotions. He discovered 38 different flower remedies for use in treating the 38 different emotional states that lie at the origin of our ailments – including fear, loneliness, uncertainty, hypersensitivity, disappointment, excessive concern and lack of interest in the present – based on the idea that long-term negative feelings will manifest as physical pain.

Bach flower remedies enhance the emotional intelligence of the patient. Apart from learning a lot about myself during my consultation, the flower remedies helped me to combat depression and no longer be afraid of the things I can't control. Depending on your psychological and emotional profile, you will be recommended different remedies. Working with a therapist is important because it can help us discover our emotions and to realise why it is we're not happy. Bach flower remedies don't come with any contraindications and have no side-effects whatsoever, so in the worst case scenario, the substance in question simply won't have any effect. At the end of the consultation, which lasts about an hour, the therapist will hand you a little bottle containing a single flower or a combination of different remedies.

You may feel the results right away, or it make take a while, it depends on the emotions we are dealing with and how deep they are. Flower remedies help us to express the positive side of our being – the vibration of the flowers counteracts the negative emotion. Our being becomes enveloped in this positive vibration, and the negative part is balanced out and gradually eliminated.

# 29

# A brief introduction to homeopathy and its benefits

*"One's mind, once stretched by a new idea, never regains its original dimensions."*

– OLIVER WENDELL HOLMES

I've told you in this book about the infamous medicines drawer that was a constant feature of my childhood. Over the years, I've made some changes and have been phasing out allopathic treatments, making room for products that are much gentler on the body, including homeopathic remedies, which help me in many situations. A lot of voices have spoken out against homeopathy on various grounds. I didn't believe in them either, until I felt the effects on my own body and now I no longer want to live without keeping a stock of such remedies at home.

It was a particular experience that made me become more open in this respect and to want to experiment further. The moment I began to believe in homeopathy and realised the efficacy of these remedies was when I had reached a turning point in my life, right before my trip to India. I was at a party, where I met a psychologist who specialised in homeopathy. She – for it was the sister of a good friend of mine – looked at me and asked me a couple of questions, to which I – visibly taken aback – replied that it wasn't true: I wasn't in mourning. And this person, who was very self-assured, but with a warmth to her voice, said to me: "Yes, you are, you're in mourning!". After speaking to her for a while, I realised she was right, I really was in mourning – but not in the literal sense of the word, it was a kind of emotional mourning. She recommended I take some homeopathic remedies, and I said I'd give it a go, as in the end what harm could it do, and not only was I not disappointed by the results, I was amazed! It was then that I became convinced of their healing powers.

**Did you know?**

**Approximately 400 million people globally have used homeopathic medicines. Over 400,000 doctors recommend homeopathic remedies in their practices every day. In France, one person in two uses these products regularly and over 83% of people have tried a homeopathic treatment at least once.**

**Information**

**"Homeopathy" is a combination of two Greek words:** *homoios* **("similar") and** *pathos* **("disease"). Substances which, in their natural state would trigger serious symptoms in a healthy person, can, when administered in infinitesimal doses, heal diseases with similar symptomologies. The substances work by stimulating the body's natural mechanisms.**

I'm no scientist, I can't claim it wasn't merely the placebo effect or that they really do have amazing health benefits, but they had a positive effect on me. Whenever I'm feeling stressed, I take some homeopathic remedies recommended by a specialist, i.e. a doctor who has complemented their professional training by learning how to prescribe homeopathic medicine and therefore has gained additional expertise in the field of homeopathy. Lots of people use and recommend homeopathic products: GPs and specialists, dentists and vets.

I strongly believe that homeopathic remedies, like allopathic treatments, should not be taken willy-nilly, just because they worked for someone else, but only on the recommendation of a specialist doctor, because we are all different and so diagnoses and medication should be tailored to each individual. For these remedies to work, we need to identify the causes of our ailments and diseases, and only then, alongside the use of conventional treatments, should we take advantage of the healing powers of homeopathic treatments. However, this doesn't mean downplaying the importance of allopathic medicine. On the contrary, I believe that homeopathic remedies can be used to complement conventional treatments. Which, as it happens, is also what the specialist doctors recommend.

And there's something else: there is no universally valid solution that works for everyone. Just as some people feel better and see results from prayer, others see a benefit in meditation or in spending time doing… nothing at all. Everyone reacts to different stimuli, so for this reason I can't say that what worked for me will be good for you, too. This has simply been my experience, and I don't believe my method of finding balance is the best. What I can say for sure is that it is the method I have arrived at after the many different experiences I've had over the years. However, you must decide what's best for you, depending on your needs, desires, aspirations and beliefs.

Homeopathic remedies, which come in the form of pellets or single-dose vials, as well as in the form of drops, pills, creams and gels, only contain substances derived from plants, minerals or the animal kingdom. There are approximately 3,000 basic substances known as strains used in the manufacture of these remedies. They are gentle, having no toxic effects on the body. At the same time they are sufficiently powerful to have healing properties, undergoing rigorous testing, especially in terms of anti-radiation. Homeopathic medicines are used in a variety of different fields, such as traumatology, anxiety disorders, ENT, gynaecology, paediatrics and dermatology. Used for a long time in hospital obstetrics departments, they have also begun to be used to help patients diagnosed with cancer cope better with the side-effects of their treatment.

There are a number of reasons why I like the homeopathic remedies made by Boiron: on one hand, they are high quality products which I have tested out for myself and which are produced using a unique manufacturing process, i.e. mechanical dynamisation, triple impregnation, with granules and globules produced on site; while on the other hand, in 2015, this company also opened a branch in India, the place where I found the cure for many of my problems. Boiron is a family-run independent pharmaceuticals company, and the history of Boiron Laboratories dates back to as early as 1932, when two brothers established a company that would become famous the world over. A company which went on to help many people, including me, to have a healthy and balanced lifestyle.

Dear readers,

Thank you for having chosen to come on this journey with me. These have been my experiences over many years – in which you have accompanied me as I struggled, denied myself food, blamed and judged myself. They were some difficult, very intense years, but without them I wouldn't have come to understand what it means to be balanced, what it means to be at peace with ourselves and the things we have in our lives.

It is a struggle we are constantly engaged in with ourselves and which no one else is able to do for us. In what were difficult times for me, when my energy and motivation were all but non-existent, I managed to gather my strength and stepped outside my comfort zone, I tried things I'd never have thought of before and I read a lot. All these things helped me to *discover* myself and to become the person I am today.

And because I believe books have been a very important factor in my personal growth, I would like to leave you with the following list of titles that influenced me throughout my journey:

- *The Gifts of Imperfection* – Brené Brown
- *I Thought It Was Just Me (but it isn't)* – Brené Brown
- *Being in Love* – Osho
- *Eat, Pray, Love* – Elizabeth Gilbert
- *The Untethered Soul* – Michael A. Singer
- *A New Earth* – Eckhart Tolle
- *Man's Search for Meaning* – Viktor Frankl

- *The Mastery of Love* – Don Miguel Ruiz
- *The Rebellious Spirit* – Osho
- *The Seven Spiritual Laws of Success* – Deepak Chopra
- *The Saint, the Surfer and the CEO* – Robin Sharma
- *What I Know for Sure* – Oprah Winfrey
- *Miracle Morning* – Hal Elrod
- *The Food Revolution* – John Robbins
- *The Power of Now* – Eckhart Tolle
- *The Four Agreements* – Don Miguel Ruiz
- *The 7 Habits of Highly Effective People* – Stephen Covey
- *The Myths of Happiness* – Sonja Lyubomirsky
- *In Praise of Slow* – Carl Honoré
- *Thrive* – Arianna Huffington
- *Emotional Intelligence* – Daniel Goleman
- *15 Things You Should Give Up to Be Happy* – Luminița D. Saviuc
- *Spiritual Bypassing* – Robert Augustus Masters
- *Emotional Intelligence* – Travis Bradberry
- *Wellth* – Jason Wachob
- *Deep Work: Rules for Focused Success* – Cal Newport

I hope these works inspire you, bring you joy and help you to *discover* yourselves as you really are, because you are wonderful!

With love,

Andreea Raicu

# Bibliography

## Books


**Darren R., Weissman, Dr.**, *Puterea iubirii și a recunoștinței infinite*, For You, 2017

**Diaz, Cameron, Bark, Sandra**, *Legea înfometării, știința forței fizice și alte moduri de a-ți iubi corpul minunat*, Life Style, 2017

**Greaves, Jean, Bradberry, Travis**, *Inteligența Emoțională 2.0*, Litera, 2016

**Gunaratana, Bhante, Henepola**, *Mindfulness pe înțelesul tuturor*, Herald, 2015

**Hudson, Kate**, *Pretty Happy: Healthy Ways to Love Your Body*, HarperCollins, 2016

**Kabat-Zinn, Jon**, *Mindfulness pentru începători*, Trei, 2016

**Kushi, Michio**, *Ghid complet pentru macrobiotică*, For You, 2008

**Lomazzi, Giuliana**, *Rețete vegetariene din toată lumea. Mâncăruri sănătoase și gustoase*, Grupul Editorial All, 2016

**Moore, Jimmy, Emmerich, Maria**, *Carte de bucate Ketogenice*, Litera, 2017

**Paltrow, Gwyneth, Turshen, Julia**, *Tot ce-i bun. Rețete ușoare, delicioase, care te vor face să te simți și să arăți grozav*, Curtea Veche, 2016

**Perlmutter, David**, *Alimente care ucid creierul. Cerealele, zahărul și alți carbohidrați*, Litera, 2016

**Reinhard, Tonia**, *Superfoods: cele mai sănătoase alimente*, Litera, 2013

## Online sources:

https://www.huffingtonpost.co.uk/2014/10/03/alkaline-diet-is-it-healthy-food_n_5925928.html

https://www.webmd.com/diet/a-z/alkaline-diets

https://www.healthline.com/nutrition/the-alkaline-diet-myth

https://www.avocadoninja.co.uk/pages/list-of-alkaline-foods

http://www.marieclaire.co.uk/life/health-fitness/alkaline-diet-what-is-it-and-does-it-work-117075

https://greenopedia.com/alkaline-acid-food-chart/

http://www.acidalkalinediet.net/alkaline-foods.php

https://www.marieclaire.com.au/alkaline-diet-real-person-review

https://www.bodyandsoul.com.au/health/celebrity-profiles/why-elle-macpherson-loves-the-alkaline-diet/news-story/5c871530840c96469494d498be38c01c

https://www.ncbi.nlm.nih.gov/pmc/articles/PMC3195546/

http://www.doctoroz.com/article/25-alkaline-promoting-foods

https://www.telegraph.co.uk/health-fitness/nutrition/alkaline-diet-secret-good-health-just-another-food-plan-taking/

http://www.goodhousekeeping.com/health/diet-nutrition/g4488/alkaline-diet/

https://www.news-medical.net/health/Alkaline-Diet-Pros-and-Cons.aspx

https://www.bbcgoodfood.com/howto/guide/what-alkaline-diet

https://www.today.com/health/i-tried-alkaline-diet-what-its-summers-hottest-cleanse-trend-t37516

https://www.scribd.com/document/150724657/Dieta-Alcalina-2

http://www.napofarm.ro/blog-napofarm/dieta-alcalina-tot-ce-trebuie-sa-stii.html

https://themerrymakersisters.com/10-signs-you-finally-love-your-body/

https://www.sheknows.com/food-and-recipes/articles/1000949/go-fully-raw-with-kristina-carrillo-bucaram/

https://www.livescience.com/26278-risks-raw-vegan-diet.html

https://www.thespruce.com/what- is-the-raw-vegan-diet-3378514

https://draxe.com/raw-food-diet/

https://www.ruled.me/guide-keto-diet/

https://ketodietapp.com/Blog/post/2015/01/03/Keto-Diet-Food-List-What-to-Eat-and-Avoid

https://www.dietdoctor.com/low-carb/keto

https://www.healthline.com/nutrition/ketogenic-diet-101

https://www.menshealth.com/nutrition/ketogenic-ketosis-diet-for-beginners

https://vitals.lifehacker.com/what-you-should-know-before-trying-a-ketogenic-diet-1820361430

http://www.bodyandsoul.com.au/diet/diets/this-is-your-7-day-ketogenic-diet-eating-plan/news-story/69afc07ce5e376f33a052a44386e7fcb

https://www.kushiinstitute.org/what-is-macrobiotics/

https://gourmandelle.com/ro/dieta-macrobiotica/

https://www.webmd.com/diet/a-z/macrobiotic-diet

https://draxe.com/macrobiotic-diet/

https://ohsawamacrobiotics.com/gomf-home/what-is-macrobiotics

https://www.thespruce.com/what-is-the-macrobiotic-diet-3376815

https://www.livestrong.com/article/461267-macrobiotic-diet-meal-plan/

https://legionathletics.com/what-to-eat-on-the-macrobiotic-diet/

https://www.bodyandsoul.com.au/diet/slim-down-with-a-macrobiotic-diet/news-story/79f224494a71ef78e7f519b37614413c

https://www.everydayhealth.com/diet-nutrition/macrobiotic-diet.aspx
https://www.mnn.com/food/healthy-eating/stories/beginners-guide-macrobiotic-diet
http://hipchicksmacrobiotics.com/faq.php
http://www.macrobiotics.org.uk/
https://www.scribd.com/doc/64801243/Dieta-Macrobiotic-A-a-Lui-George-Ohsawa
https://indianexpress.com/article/lifestyle/health/macrobiotic-diet-nutrition-healthy-eating-6182466/
https://www.medicinenet.com/macrobiotic_diet/views.htm
https://www.lightwellhealth.com/recipe/blueberry-bliss-smoothie-bowl-2/
https://thehealthytart.com/fig-chia-pudding/
https://plantbasedlife.com.au/services/food-recipes/89-raw-vegan-lasagna-with-sunflower-seed-pesto-sun-dried-tomato-marinara-cashew-cheese-and-walnut-sausage
https://thefitchen.com/easy-veggie-spring-rolls-with-spicy-coconut-curry-sauce/
https://www.yummly.com/#recipe/Lettuce-Leaf-Tacos-2001302
https://www.marthastewart.com/318401/mango-and-avocado-salsa
https://www.onegreenplanet.org/vegan-recipe/raw-sprouted-hummus-veggie-burger-with-sunflower-bread/
https://gourmandelle.com/ciocolata-raw-cu-caju-raw-vegan-cashew-chocolate/
https://www.onegreenplanet.org/vegan-recipe/recipe-raw-orange-and-blueberry-cheesecake/
https://nouveauraw.com/raw-recipes/crackers/almond-thins/
http://www.macrobiotics.org.uk/our-recipes-baked-vegetables/
http://www.macrobiotics.org.uk/our-recipes-nut-seed-cheese/

https://vanillaandbean.com/grilled-bbq-tofu-vegetable-kebabs/

https://damndelicious.net/2019/05/08/garlic-butter-shrimp-zucchini-noodles/

https://valentinascorner.com/buttered-cod-skillet/

https://www.skinnytaste.com/cauliflower-fried-rice/

https://cafedelites.com/chunky-shrimp-guacamole/

https://www.ruled.me/salmon-benny-breakfast-bombs/

https://www.dietdoctor.com/recipes/keto-mexican-scrambled-eggs

https://cookieandkate.com/2017/overnight-oats-recipe/

https://pinchofyum.com/simple-poached-egg-avocado-toast

https://cookieandkate.com/2017/vegetable-fried-rice-recipe/

https://www.mysweetcalifornialife.com/cinnamon-raisin-brown-rice-hot-breakfast-porridge/

https://www.yogajournal.com/recipes/recipe-savory-quinoa-risotto

http://www.goodhousekeeping.com/food-recipes/a43225/beet-mushroom-avocado-salad-recipe/